Major
Donors

Major Donors

Finding Big Gifts in Your Database and Online

TED HART,
JAMES M. GREENFIELD,
PAMELA M. GIGNAC,
and CHRISTOPHER CARNIE

WILEY

John Wiley & Sons, Inc.

For general information on our other products and services, or technical support, please contact our Customer Care Department within the United States at 800-762-2974, outside the United States at 317-572-3993 or fax 317-572-4002.

Wiley also publishes its books in a variety of electronic formats. Some content that appears in print may not be available in electronic books.

For more information about Wiley products, visit our Web site at http://www.wiley.com.

Library of Congress Cataloging-in-Publication Data:
Major donors : finding big gifts in your database and online / [edited by] Ted Hart . . . [et al.].
       p.   cm.
  Includes index.
  ISBN-13: 978-0-471-76810-4 (cloth)
  ISBN-10: 0-471-76810-3 (cloth)
  1. Fund raising. 2. Fund raising—Computer network resources. I. Hart, Ted, 1964– II. Title.
 HV41.2.M34 2006
 658.15'2240285—dc22
2006004846

Printed in the United States of America

10 9 8 7 6 5 4 3 2 1

About the Editors

Chris Carnie, Founder (1993) and Chairman, The Factary, and Founder and Managing Director, Factary Europe, both leading prospect research agencies. He is a fundraiser and a researcher and the first researcher elected as Fellow of the Institute of Fundraising (IOF) as well as the first Fellow of the Royal Society of Arts (RSA). He was Founder Chair of the IOF's Researchers in Fundraising, and is a member of Association of Professional Researchers for Advancement (APRA), the Association for Research on Nonprofit Organizations and Voluntary Action (ARNOVA), the International Society for Third-Sector Research (ISTR), and a Board Member of the Asociación Profesional de Fundraising (Spain). Chris founded the *Philanthropy in Europe* magazine and is an international speaker including APRA and the International Fundraising Congress. An author, his books include *Find the Funds–a New Approach to Fundraising Research* and *Fundraising from Europe*. Chris lives in Barcelona, Spain and speaks English, Spanish, Catalan, and French and reads Italian, German, and Portuguese. Contact: *chris@factary.com.*

Pamela Gignac, Vice President JMG Solutions Inc., started in Vancouver in 1985 volunteering for Rick Hansen. Inspired, she moved to London, England, and then back to Canada. Experiences in national and international projects in fundraising and prospect research, based on American techniques put into practice elsewhere, have included major gifts from individuals, companies, and foundations to support capital and annual campaigns such as the Prince's Trusts, Canadian and British Red Cross, St Michael's Hospital, and University of Toronto. An AFP, APRA, and Institute of Fundraising member, she's also an international speaker and author of books including *Nonprofit Internet Strategies—Integrating Online and Offline Databases* and teaches at Toronto's Humber College's Fundraising and Volunteer Management program in Donor Relations. Pamela keeps informed of best practices and challenges and knows the importance of research firsthand. Pamela is proud of our profession as well as being the mother of her two young sons, Jeffrey and Patrick, with husband Jeff. Contact: *pamela@jmgsolutions.com.*

James M. Greenfield retired in February 2001, after completing 40 years as a fundraising professional at five hospitals and three universities. He continues speaking, teaching, and writing plus aiding nonprofit organizations in fundraising management consulting services. He and his wife, Karen, continue to live in Newport Beach, California. Jim has written and edited eight books on fundraising management including *Fund Raising: Evaluating and Managing the Fund Development Process* (2nd ed., 1999); *Fund Raising Fundamentals: A Guide to Annual Giving for Professionals and Volunteers* (2nd ed., 2002); *Fund-Raising Cost Effectiveness: A Self-Assessment Workbook* (1996). He is editor of *The Nonprofit Handbook: Fund Raising, Third Edition* (2001) and co-editor with Ted Hart and Michael Johnston of *Nonprofit Internet Strategies: Best Practices for Marketing, Communications and Fundraising* (2005). Contact: *fundrazer@cox.net* or *www.fundrazer.com.*

Ted Hart, ACFRE, ePMT, is Founder and President of the international ePhilanthropy Foundation (*www.ephilanthropy.org*), headquartered in Washington, DC, the global leader in providing training to charities for the ethical and efficient use of the Internet for philanthropic purposes through education and advocacy. Hart served as CEO of the University of Maryland Medical System Foundation, and as Chief Development Officer for Johns Hopkins Bayview Medical Center. Hart is author of several published articles, an editor and author of the book *Nonprofit Internet Strategies* and *Fundraising On The Internet: The ePhilanthropyFoundation .Org's Guide to Success Online*, and a contributing author of the book *Achieving Excellence in Fund Raising, Second Edition*. He is currently an adjunct faculty member of the Fund Raising Management Program at Goucher College in Maryland. He resides in Columbia, MD, with his daughter, Sarah Grace, and son, Alexander Michael. Contact: *tedhart@ ephilanthropy.org.*

Ken Burnett is an author, lecturer, and consultant on fundraising and communications for nonprofit organizations worldwide. He works with UK communications and marketing group Cascaid and the Australian agency Pareto Fundraising. He is a founding board member and former chairman of ActionAid International, a trustee of BookAid International, former vice chair of The UK's Institute of Fundraising, and former trustee of the International Fund Raising Group (now The Resource Alliance). Ken is a fellow of the Institute of Fundraising and an Honorary Fellow of the Institute of Direct Marketing. He's author of the worldwide best seller *Relationship Fundraising,* and its sequel *Friends for Life* and *How to Produce Inspiring Annual Reports.* Two new books are scheduled for early 2006: *Tiny Essentials of an Effective Volunteer Board* (*www.whitelionpress.com*) and *The Zen of Fundraising* (*www.josseybass.com).* Contact: *ken@kenburnett.com.*

Kristina Carlson, CFRE, ePMT, has spent virtually her entire life helping nonprofit organizations raise money. She is an entrepreneur, an author, a frequent speaker at nonprofit industry conferences and workshops, and a student pilot. Kristina serves as President of FundraisingINFO.com, the most trusted, on-demand fundraising support service. In this role, Kristina has helped thousands of nonprofit professionals solve the seemingly impossible. She has created Internet-based fundraising training and consulting programs, including Ask BEE™, and led the development of prospect research services including the DoNET, ProspectINFO, and Philanthropists Next Door.

Prior to joining FundraisingINFO.com, Kristina directed successful capital campaigns, with goals ranging from $1 million to $200 million, for international organizations as well as smaller grass-roots groups. In 2005, Jossey-Bass released *Essential Principles for Fundraising Success: An Answer Manual for the Everyday Challenges of Raising Money,* authored by Kristina Carlson and her husband, G. Douglass Alexander. Contact: *kristina@fundraisinginfo.com.*

Jeff Gignac, CFRE, ePMT, is Founder and President, JMG Solutions Inc., and has worked with over 400 local and national nonprofits since 1992 providing information and technology services, including online fundraising, e-receipts, system evaluations, and training. Jeff's overall knowledge of IT and the Internet, together with his unique fundraising and prospect research insight, truly is unique. He enjoys sharing his experiences, tips, and best practices with others. Jeff is a member of the AFP and APRA, is a frequent local, national, and international speaker, and is an author of books including *Nonprofit Internet Strategies—Integrating Online and Offline Databases*. Jeff teaches at Toronto's Humber College's Fundraising and Volunteer Management and Arts Administration programs. He is an AFP and AHP supporter through conference sponsorships and volunteering, including the AFP International Conference 2003 and Education committees. Jeff lives in Mississauga, Ontario, with his wife, Pamela, and young sons, Jeffrey and Patrick. Contact: *jeff@jmgsolutions.com*.

Kay Sprinkel Grace, CFRE, is an internationally acclaimed independent consultant, speaker, facilitator, and writer. After successful careers in journalism and education, she became a development professional in 1979, working in several organizations before starting her own consulting firm in 1987. Since then, she has worked as trainer or consultant to thousands of nonprofit volunteers and professionals in the areas of board and staff leadership, planning, and capital and annual fundraising. She is the author of *Beyond Fund-Raising* and the coauthor of *High-Impact Philanthropy* (both published by Wiley), as well as the author of *The Ultimate Board Member's Book, Over Goal: What You Must Know to Excel at Fundraising Today,* and *Fundraising Mistakes that Bedevil All Boards (and Staff Too)* (published by Emerson & Church, Medfield, MA).

Nancy Johnson, ePMT is President of Target America, Inc., a leading wealth screening service, headquartered in Fairfax, VA. Nancy has worked with nonprofits for over 15 years in both the research and software arena. She was a consultant for Thomson Financial Wealth Identification. She sold DOS FundMaster for Master Software and the Windows Raiser's Edge for Blackbaud. Nancy experienced the client server environment at People Soft, in the Higher Education division. As the nonprofit community embraced the Internet, Nancy helped promote eTapestry, an ASP application. Nancy is a graduate of Indiana University, holding a BS with a Business Concentration and a minor in Women's Studies. She is a member of AFP and AHP. Nancy is a Master Trainer and serves as a trustee on the ePhilanthropy.org Foundation Board. Nancy resides in Indianapolis, where she raised five sons and is a doting Nana to her first granddaughter. Contact: *nancy@tgtam.com*.

Howard Lake is the publisher of UK Fundraising (*www.fundraising.co.uk*), the online news and information resource for fundraisers and the fundraising industry. Published since 1994, it is one of the leading online tools for fundraisers and has covered developments in online fundraising from the outset. Howard is the author of the first book on Internet fundraising, published in 1996, a product of his 1992–95 pioneering research into the use of the Internet by nonprofit fundraisers. A fundraiser since 1988, he has worked for Oxfam GB, Afghanaid, and Amnesty International UK. He set up Fundraising UK Ltd. in 1996 to provide consultancy to nonprofits in how to use the Internet as a fundraising tool. Contact: *hlake@fundraising.co.uk*.

David Lawson, ePMT, is Senior Vice President of Major Gifts, Sales and Marketing for Kintera. In 1997, he founded Prospect Information Network (P!N) to create a service that would enable fundraisers to more efficiently identify and profile their share of today's new wealth. In early 1998, David introduced P!N ProfileBuilder™, the product of 24 years of fundraising and information experience. P!N was acquired by Kintera, Inc., in March 2004. David began his fundraising career as editor of six editions of *The Foundation 500*. Since the mid-70s, David has been an innovator in the art of finding, profiling, and keeping an eye on America's wealthy. From creating products to developing customized strategies, he has helped hundreds of fundraisers turn the challenges of new prospect identification into mega-gift opportunities.

Professor Stephen Lee is a member of the School of Reputation and Relationships at Henley Management College, where he is also Director of the Centre for Voluntary Sector Management. Having undertaken research and later taught at Lancaster University, Professor Lee entered the voluntary sector in 1982 as Deputy Chief Executive at the Charities Advisory Trust and Directory of Social Change. Following further senior appointments in the not-for-profit sector, he held the post of Director of the Institute of Fundraising (IOF) for a period of 11 years. During this period he established himself as a leading authority on marketing, governance, and business ethics issues. A Fellow of the RSA and one of only four Honorary Fellows of the IOF, he is the recipient of the inaugural Professional Fundraising Lifetime Achievement Award. Current research interests include Trust and Confidence in nonprofit and public sector institutions; Reputation Management; Ethical, Governance, and Data Protection issues.

Susan Mullin brings 20 years of professional fundraising experience to her role as Director of Development at Toronto's York University Foundation, at Canada's third largest university. Susan provides strategic leadership to the campaign and major gift programs working with a team of dedicated staff and senior volunteers. Susan's career began at multilevel health organizations, followed by executive director positions, first at Casey House Foundation, one of the world's first AIDS hospices, followed by a specialty hospital and a social service organization. A Certified Fund Raising Executive (CFRE), Susan is actively involved with the Association of Fundraising Professionals (AFP). Past president of the AFP Greater Toronto Chapter, the largest chapter in the world, Susan chairs the Canadian Government Relations Committee and led AFP's Privacy Task Force. She works closely with elected and other officials to raise awareness and understanding of the impact of privacy and other regulations on charities.

Anthony J. Powell, CFRE, Vice President of Consulting Services, is responsible for the company's 250-employee global professional services division. He joined Blackbaud in 1998 as a fundraising system consultant and has helped Consulting Services grow into one of the company's largest and fastest-growing divisions. Before joining Blackbaud, Mr. Powell spent 10 years in the nonprofit sector in development management and major and planned gift solicitations. He has worked as a major gifts officer at the Smithsonian Institution, assistant vice president for the Greater Baltimore Medical Center Foundation, and vice president and chief operating officer for The Wesbury Foundation. Mr. Powell is a graduate of Allegheny College, where he began his fundraising career as assistant director of the annual fund. A six-time CASE Faculty All Star, Mr. Powell is a frequent speaker at national and international industry conferences.

Sarah Tenney is a Certified Fund Raising Executive and ePhilanthropy systems integrator from Hawaii. Tenney is an experienced international business executive and is skilled in executing scalable business operations while motivating the career aspirations and the technical aptitude of professionals in information technology fields. Currently the Vice President of Operations for BlackBird, a Honolulu-based Citrix and Microsoft network management company, Sarah also is a board advisory member for the ePhilanthropy Foundation, an active Rotarian, a volunteer for the Nonprofit Business Management Certificate Program at Kapi'olani Community College, an AFP Aloha Chapter Board Member & Asia Task Force committee member, and active in Hawaii's National Philanthropy Day Conference development. Sarah is often invited into private, government, and philanthropic initiatives, presents for international and mainland symposiums, and educational venues. As a self-defined electrical engineering dropout, Sarah holds an Executive M.B.A. degree in International Entrepreneurship from the University of Hawaii as well as a B.A. in

Japanese and Chinese Asian Studies. Sarah is married to Dan Tenney and they live in Honolulu.

Andrew Thomas, Chief Executive and Founder, Charity Consultants Ltd., with 23 years' experience in major gifts from companies, individuals, and foundations for capital and annual campaigns for local, national, and international organizations including Save the Children, Oxfam, UNICEF, and the International Institute for the Environment and Development (IIED), coordinating between Washington, DC and London, England. He was also the dynamic Director of the Prince's Youth Business Trust campaign, raising over £40 million in two years from 300 donors. Andrew is a Fellow of the Institute of Fundraising (IOF) and served as board member or trustee for the Executive Committee of the IOF, the International Year of the Disabled, the International Year of Shelter, the Globe Theatre, Friends of the Earth, the International Council for the World Congress on Philanthropy 1991, and the Association of Fundraising Consultants (ARC). Andrew is dedicated to the professionalism of fundraising and is a tremendous mentor and friend to many successful fundraisers around the world.

Peter Wylie, Consultant, P!N/ Kintera, in marketing to higher education and other nonprofits. Peter has a doctorate in industrial psychology from Columbia and established himself as a specialist in helping business partners who had come into conflict. Peter then searched for something else in which to apply his strong background in statistics. He came across a publication for public affairs officers at colleges and universities that mentioned the fact that most institutions of higher education had enormous databases but were ignoring what could be learned from them. Peter took his cue and set off to help university development departments to analyze data on their alumni and donors. Peter's specialty is in training development professionals to develop skills so that they can perform this sophisticated analysis in house. He is now a P!N/ Kintera consultant who is particularly interested in focusing on donor online behaviors as predictors of type and amount of giving.

Ken Wyman, Coordinator of the postgraduate Fundraising and Volunteer Management program, Humber College Institute of Technology & Advanced Learning, has 30 years' experience in fundraising across Canada and internationally. The author of seven books, Ken is a Certified Fund Raising Executive, and was chosen as the first Fund Raiser of the Year by the Toronto Chapter of the Association of Fundraising Professionals. He is an active consultant, volunteer, and board member, and a former journalist/broadcaster. Ken is also a frequent speaker at local, national, and international events including the International Fundraising Conference in Amsterdam. Ken has been a mentor and friend to many successful fundraisers and board members working with small and large organizations. The Humber College program is widely respected and highly regarded by the grads, their employers, fellow professional fundraisers, and the nonprofit community.

Contents

Foreword   xxi

Introduction   xxv

Chapter 1

Prospecting for Major Gifts   *Pamela Gignac and Ken Wyman*   1

Introduction	1
Prospect Research: Background and Key Elements	2
History of Prospect Research	2
Definitions	2
The Role of Prospect Research	3
Case Study: The Campaign for the University of Toronto	4
Small Shop or Large Campaign: Anyone Can Do Research	5
Prospect Researchers and Fundraisers Together	6
What Makes a Good Researcher?	6
Fundraisers Are Researchers and Researchers Are Fundraisers	6
Researchers and Fundraisers Together Creating	
Strategic Partnerships	6
Big Gifts and Major Gifts	8
How Big Is a "Big" Gift?	8
Annual versus Major Donor	8
Integrating Major Gifts Fundraising	8
Prospecting	10
What Is a Prospect?	10
10 Steps that Lead to Prospecting Success	10
Research Techniques and Information Sources	11
Key Words Can Help You Focus	11
Seeking Answers to Questions	12
Information Sources	13
Six Degrees of Donor Development (Relationship	
Management and Spheres of Influence)	14
Calling to Find Out More	15
Prospecting Lists	17
Prospect Qualification	17
Where Do We Go from Here?	18
Conclusion	18

Chapter 2

Knowledge Management, Data Mining, and Prospect Screening
Jeff Gignac and Chris Carnie   **20**

Introduction   20
Definitions   21
Knowledge Management   21
    The Holistic Approach   21
    The Model   22
    Building a Prospect Pipeline   26
    Becoming a Knowledge Manager   27
Introduction to Data Mining and Prospect Screening   28
    What Is Data Mining?   28
    Data Mining Results   28
    Data Mining or Prospect Screening?   29
Tracking Prospects   30
    Really Simple Syndication   30
    What Is XML?   30
    How to Get Started with RSS   31
    How Can Nonprofits Benefit from This?   32
Conclusion   34

Chapter 3

Why Bill Gates May Not Be Your Best Prospect
Peter B. Wylie and David M. Lawson   **37**

Three Important Concepts: Ability, Attachment,
    and Affinity   38
    Ability   38
    Volatility: The When of Asking   38
    The Prospect's Sense of Wealth   39
    Type of Wealth   39
    Attachment   40
    Affinity   41
How to Generate a List of High-Quality Prospects for
    Your Campaign   46
    Isolating High-Ability Prospects   47
    Isolating Prospects with High Attachment   47
    Isolating Prospects with High Affinity   47
    Isolating a Group of Prospects Who Belong to All Three Groups   47

Chapter 4

Prospect Research Policy, Privacy, and Ethics   *Stephen Lee and*
Susan Mullin   **51**

Policy, Ethics, and Prospect Research   51
    The Role of Prospect Research   51
    The Standing of Prospect Research in the Contemporary Context   52

Ethical and Professional Practice Considerations   52
  An Imbalance of Power   52
  Key Components of a Prospect Research Code of Practice   53
  Major Donor Fundraising Code of Practice Including
    Prospect Research   54
  Poor Compliance Equals Lost Donors   56
  The Challenge of Data Protection Legislation   56
Data Protection Regulation: The European Approach   57
  Implementation of the EC Data Protection Directive   57
  European Data Protection Legislation: Key Requirements
    Impacting upon Prospect Research   57
Notification and Registration   58
Conformity with Data Protection Principles   58
Consent   60
  The Practical Achievement of Consent   61
  Personal Information Acquired from Third Parties   62
  Retaining Personal Data and Archiving Personal Information   63
  Personal Information Acquired via the Internet   63
  Publishing (Posting) Major Donor Personal Information
    on the Internet   64
  Personal Data Capture Undertaken within the EC
    by Organizations Located Outside the EC   64
Data Protection Regulation: The North American Approach   65
  The View in the United States   65
  The View in Canada   66
  The CSA Model Code: Privacy Principles   67
Applying Privacy Principles to Prospect Research   67
  Information in the Public Domain   68
  Assuring Compliance with Regulation and Best Practice   69
The Role of Professional Associations and Intermediary Bodies   69

Chapter 5
U.S. and Canadian Strategies   *Pamela Gignac and Kristina Carlson*   **71**

A Tale of Perspectives   71
  It's a Small World   71
Strategies for Research and Approach   72
Prospect Research Strategies   72
  Using Research to Develop Approach Strategies   73
  The Approach Strategy   74
Sources   77
  When to Use International Sources   77
Case Study: Researching a Major Donor   80
  From Florida   80
  From Canada   81
  The British Angle   83
Privacy   84
Trends   84

Chapter 6
International Strategies—Europe and Asia
Chris Carnie and Sarah Boodleman Tenney   **85**

Introduction   85
Europe   85
    History   85
    Getting the Basics Right   87
    Companies: Types   89
    Foundations: Types   90
Finding European Prospects   91
    Foundations   91
    People   92
    Corporate Information   92
Getting Over the Barriers   93
Europe: A Valued Friend   94
As For Asia   94
    Defining Asia   94
    Global Trends Impact Major Donor Prospecting   95
Getting the Basics Right   96
    Philanthropic Culture   97
    Getting into Depth with Prospects   99
Specific Things to Know   99
    Know a Method to Initiate   99
    Know the Traditional Industries   100
    Know the Families: It's Business   100
    Know the Women   100
Getting Over Barriers   101
Other Places to Look for Information   101
Conclusion   102

Chapter 7
Your Web Site—What Does It Say to Major Donors? *Howard Lake*   **103**

Introduction   103
The Trend Continues   103
The Personal Approach   104
    Giving in the United Kingdom   105
    Few Major Gifts Made Online   106
Needs and Concerns of Major Donors   107
Attracting Donors   107
Key Elements of Major Gift Fundraising Online   109

Chapter 8
An Internet Strategy for Major Donor Fundraising *Anthony Powell* **111**

Introduction   111
    The Rise of ePhilanthropy   111
Understanding the Fundamentals of Major Giving   113
    What Is a Major Gift?   114

Collecting Information and Learning More about Prospects   114
    Overflow of Information   115
    Three Major Gift Indicators   116
    Following the Footprints in the Sand   118
Sharing Information and Building Relationships   120
    How to Leverage Information to Drive Fundraising Results   121
    An Integrated Strategy   122
    Interactions and Web Activities   122
    Reports and Analysis   123
    Strategic Business Decisions   123
    Coordinated Constituent-Centric Communication™   124
    Automating Manual Processes   124
Conclusion   126

Chapter 9
Using Gathered Information Effectively within Your Staff and
Volunteer Teams   *Nancy Johnson and Pamela Gignac*   **128**

Introduction   128
Fundraising and Prospect Research Cycle   128
Personal Intelligence Gathering (PIG)   130
Prospect Screening and Review   131
    Prospect Session Agenda   132
    Prospect Lists   133
    Contact Reports   134
The Importance of Information Relevant to Campaign Goals   135
    Overall Benefits of Research   136
    Tools That Can Do the Trick   136
    A Word about the Internet   137
    Can Using an Intranet Be an Effective and Efficient Tool?   137
Capturing Information   138
Other Ways to Keep Team Members Updated   138
Lessons Learned Using Screening Companies in the United States   139
    Geographic Matches   140
    What's in a Name?   140
    Share Your Findings with Others   140
    What to Watch Out For   141
Overall Pitfalls of Research   141
Conclusion   142

Chapter 10
Moving from Prospect Identification to Making Friends for Life
Andrew Thomas and Ken Burnett   **143**

Panning for Gold   143
Moving from Desk Research to Solicitation   146
Prospecting   147
Enlistment   150
Making New Friends   152

Cultivation   154
Are You Ready to Ask?   156
Stewardship: Turning Donors into Friends for Life   157

Chapter 11
Results Analysis and Performance Measurements   *James M. Greenfield*   **159**

Fundraising Is an Investment Strategy   159
  Setting Objectives and Goals   160
Evaluating Prospect Research   161
Criteria for Results   162
  Research Staff Qualifications and Skills Set   163
  Areas of Responsibility in Data Management   165
  Creating and Utilizing Research Data   166
  Research Management   167
Evaluating Research Used in Major Gifts and Campaigns   169
  Prospect Review Meetings   169
  Rating and Evaluation Sessions   170
  Tracking   172
Evaluating Donor Stewardship and Recognition   173
  Stewardship of Donor Funds   174
Conclusion   175
Additional Resources   175

Chapter 12
Challenges for Tomorrow   *Chris Carnie*   **177**

Introduction   177
Major Donors: Major Change   177
  Money, and More of It   177
  New Causes   179
  New Donor Concerns   181
  New Donor Societies   181
  New Techniques   182
Prospect Research: The Next Revolution   183
  The Old Days   183
  Profiling, Fast   184
  Profiling, Outsourced   184
  Modeling   184
  Knowledge   185
  Prospect Luddites?   186

APPENDIX A The CSA Model Code for the Protection of Personal Information   187

APPENDIX B Data Mining and Prospect Screening Checklist   189

APPENDIX C Checklist for a Development Strategy   191

APPENDIX D Sample Contact Forms   193

APPENDIX E ePhilanthropy Code of Ethical Online Philanthropic Practices 197

APPENDIX F Potential Planning Measurements for Results   200

APPENDIX G Sample Job Description Text   203

APPENDIX H Data Grid for Estimating Giving Capacity   205

APPENDIX I Activity Reports   206

APPENDIX J Sample Contact Report   207

APPENDIX K Performance Criteria for Major Gift Staff   208

APPENDIX L Nine-Point Performance Index Analysis of Major Gift Solicitation 209

APPENDIX M Checklist for Major Gift Acknowledgment   210

APPENDIX N Prospect Research Online   211

**APPENDIX O Donor Development and Prospect Research Recommended
                 Additional Readings**   221

Index   225

Foreword

Kay Sprinkel Grace

As I read the final manuscript of this book, I was inspired, educated, occasionally amused, and very intrigued about the way so many voices had come together with such singular cohesion. This is the first truly global compilation of e-research techniques. If the book had stopped there, it would have made a key contribution to the literature of our sector, but that is only where it begins.

Using research as the framework, the authors have approached the identification, cultivation, and solicitation of big gifts from all sides, with the purpose of helping professionals and volunteers wherever they are in the world understand the great treasures they can discover when they use the barely tapped resources of e-research as the first step in a highly personal program to attract big gifts.

Major giving is a complex process that requires a reliable combination of skills and intuition, experience and curiosity, discipline and spontaneity, research and conversation. There are hints of all those in this book. The book is both philosophical and strategic, and filled with an interesting array of directly related and contextual material including European history, Canadian privacy laws, U.S. philanthropic tradition, and just plain practical information.

It is not a "how to" book; it is more "why not?" Truly international in its examples, research, advice, and knowledge, the book's singular message is this: Major giving may begin with research (and should) but that is the launch platform. The best research in the world is only a second-order inference about the person or organization being researched. To gain a first-order inference, you have to talk to the people themselves. This book is rich with avenues and ideas about approaching those people—and generous with cross-cultural tips about conducting cultivation and solicitation in various countries. A prevailing message is "yes." Wherever you are, whether professional or volunteer, in Asia or Europe or Latin America or the United States, you can do it. You can raise big gifts. Really big. Huge. Transformational. *Why not?* The tools and attitudes are here.

Research was a primitive science when I began big gift work, and as a volunteer and then professional in philanthropy, its absence made our personal research (through cultivation) all the more important. How carefully (and manually) we recorded each conversation. How diligently we pored over the daily newspapers and business journals and clipped articles that then were put into the donor's file. A paper file, mind you. And some were very fat. This was not so long ago, but it was "B.C." (before computers).

This book does not ask you to give up personal contact for web-based research. In fact, it stresses quite the opposite: Start with the research but then test it through getting to know the prospect. Then do more research. And then extend the conversation. A continual process of validation ensures the highest possible success. In this book, the discipline of integrating personally garnered information with that provided by the many e-sources now available is a strong current. The book urges us to be observant—to note what the person's office features (you'll love the story of the oil magnate with the passion for geology), what pictures are on their walls, as well as what the infinite research sources tell us about their lives, their wins, and their losses. It also encourages us to rely on observation and intuition to shift our approach to a donor, even when the research has been thorough.

It is up to us to discover the dreams that will lead people into the golden arena of philanthropic fulfillment. The glimmer seldom ignites on the basis of research alone—it takes desire to draw out the donor's dreams and connect them to the work we know will make them come true.

We are in a period of wealth generation never before known on this planet. Recovered from the early twenty-first-century economic dip, individuals are once again self-actualizing through philanthropy. The leadership of people like Bill and Melinda Gates or George Soros, who not only give but make sure the impact of their giving is as great as possible, will be imitated by others. We see it already in the work being done on every continent. Big gifts will continue to grow in number and importance globally as a principal source of philanthropic support. While education and the arts have typically drawn the dramatic big gifts about which stories are written, we have just this century witnessed a new phenomenon. Outpourings of individual giving for natural disasters and the aftermath of war or terrorism have startled even the optimists with their size and impact.

My observations about this burgeoning phenomenon—big gifts—are many. Donor profiles are shifting. Not only are people giving because they seek impact, involvement, and investment, but increasingly the donor searches for you because the highest value is an *issue* about which one cares deeply and on which you are working. Increasing numbers of web sites (e.g., Global Giving) with a global focus carefully profile vetted organizations that match the donor-investor's interest in issues, populations, and/or geography.

There is no standard profile of the big gift giver. That has been the gift—and the challenge—of this century. Big gifts are coming from those who have given smaller gifts to you or others previously, and from those who have not. They may begin with research you initiate on a current or prospective donor, or they may begin with that individual or organization researching you. The web is open to everyone. Stories of people using our same research techniques to find organizations in whose issues and impact they may want to invest are increasing. Some potential major donors are hiring consultants to conduct research on organizations addressing the issues they care about so they can make significant community (local, national, or global) investments.

Ultimately, the authors remind us, research is a critical part not only of prospect development, cultivation, and solicitation but also of the ongoing stewardship with the donor that will maintain an investor relationship. Big gifts are often referred to as one-time-only gifts either by the donor or the recipient, but I don't believe that. My experience—and that of several of the authors—is that major donors who feel they are receiving authentic ongoing outreach, communication, and invitations for engagement from the organization will keep giving at some level. Sometimes their last "big gift" is a legacy gift. Research supports this by keeping us current on the donor's profile so that our personal stewardship can be appropriate.

Philanthropy is in a renewed golden age. People want to help, make a difference, ensure that the things they value will flourish. We have to look to new tools, new strategies, new donors. Just when I thought I had read everything new on big gifts, Ted Hart sent me this manuscript. It is innovative, comprehensive, powerful, informative, strong in its message and information, and an important contribution to the literature of this growing and important part of global philanthropy.

Kay Sprinkel Grace works with clients globally to increase their confidence and capacity to raise major gifts and fulfill their roles as staff and volunteers in managing the entire fundraising process. She lives and works in San Francisco, and has published numerous articles and five books: *Beyond Fundraising* (1997 and 2005) and *High Impact Philanthropy* (with Alan Wendroff) (2000), both from John Wiley & Sons; and *Over Goal!*, *The Ultimate Board Member's Book*, and *Fundraising Mistakes that Bedevil All Boards* from Emerson & Church, Medfield, MA. Her web site bears her company's name: *www.transforming-philanthropy.org*.

Introduction

Ted Hart

MAJOR DONORS IN THE AGE OF ePHILANTHROPY

Successful fundraising involves hard work. As you prepare a major donor strategy you will grow to understand that research is only one of the many steps of the fundraising process, and in many cases a very time consuming one. Although doing research does not immediately guarantee you successful solicitation of a gift, it is an important investment of time and resources. Equally important is to learn when enough research has been done and the human interaction with the prospect needs to take center stage. All too often charity leadership, paid and volunteer, hides behind the need for research, unduly stalling the education and cultivation process.

No matter what research you do, no matter how valuable the information you find, nothing can substitute for direct contact with the prospect, listening and learning from them what their hopes, wishes, and dreams for philanthropic support might be.

Prospect research is best used to identify prospects and then to help guide the most appropriate level of ask. Even with accurate data and research, a high number of funding requests are declined. Usually this is attributed to inadequate assessment of interest, errors in assessment of ability, poorly prepared description of project, or failure to have the prospective donor feel comfortable with the organization's ability to carry out the proposed project's objectives.

This book will provide tips and guidance to aid in researching potential donors and institutional funders more effectively. However, before you get started, you should first draw a clear profile of your organization and its objectives, and develop a long-term strategic plan. These will be key items to have internal consensus on before you begin asking others to support your efforts. Strength in institutional planning will aid in establishing credibility with potential funders.

With this book you will be able to stop the highly ineffective and time-wasting practice deployed by so many, that of blanket, shotgun, or scatter-approach funding requests, whereby requests are sent to a wide group of individuals, foundations, and corporate prospects. The authors have assembled strategies that, once deployed, will help end these ineffective strategies that ultimately only serve to damage your organization's credibility.

Successful prospect research can be viewed as a five-step process: identification, gaining insight, reviewing and segmenting, nurturing hot prospects, and solicitation and stewardship.

Step One: Identification

The first step in your research is to compile a list of various types of funders—individual, foundation, corporate, private, and governmental—whose areas of interest are aligned with your organization's goals. To develop this list, build on your organization's previous experience and knowledge. Keep your selection criteria fairly broad. If in doubt, include the prospect in your list until further research tells you otherwise.

Using both in-house and online databases, you are seeking to narrow the field to potentially interested prospects. At this point you are not assessing ability or strategy, just a broad list of potentially interested parties.

By the end of this phase, you should have a fairly good idea of what funding resources are available for your type of work. Now you are ready to proceed with the next step—the in-depth research.

Step Two: Gain Insight

In-depth research should expand your knowledge and understanding of the ability and interest of the potential funders on your initial list, and should provide you with insight into their funding interests, potential strategy approach, and, most important, ability.

Many resources and strategies are provided in this book to help you narrow the field of prospects. Depending on the number of staff and volunteers you have, you should be seeking approximately 25 qualified prospects for your project or campaign per volunteer and 100 per actively involved staff person.

Step Three: Review and Segment

Review data with staff and volunteers. The key at this stage is to understand and interpret the data while beginning to develop a strategy for approach. Keep in mind that researched data is just data; the information will guide you toward qualified prospects but will not do the fundraising for you. Assign those staff and volunteers who will be responsible for developing the cultivation of this prospect.

Step Four: Nurture Hot Prospects

Fundraising is not a one-shot deal. Through multiple contacts and approaches over a short or long period of time, contact with the donor will be the final key research step. The education and cultivation process is all about listening and learning. As you take steps to draw the prospect closer to the work of your organization, be certain to focus on the hopes and desires to help. While you may have identified significant wealth in your earlier research stages, now you verify available wealth and determine interest in supporting your projects.

Step Five: Solicitation and Stewardship

Keep in mind, the research process never ends and your best prospect for future support is your last donor. Once a gift is solicited and received, a tremendous amount of information will be learned. This information will be key to working toward your next gift as you move from stewardship right back to cultivation.

Just because someone has money doesn't mean they will give it to your organization.

THE BEGINNING OF THE GLORY DAYS

The glory days of successful major donor prospecting, cultivation, and solicitation have not faded. They are about to begin. For many decades a privileged few charities have had the resources that allowed them to target their efforts toward those prospects they not only suspected might have the resources to give large sums, but had the research and data to back up those efforts. This allowed them to be more targeted, more focused, and more successful.

The Internet and database-mining techniques are now making it possible for charities both large and small to target their efforts on those with identified resources and demonstrated interest.

While information resources have grown, expectations for higher standards have grown exponentially. Charities can now successfully collect information about prospective donors—literally mining information that will help fine-tune their cultivation and solicitation efforts, generating a maximum return on investment.

KNOWLEDGE MANAGEMENT AND ETHICS

In the age of ePhilanthropy, your organization will come into possession of an unprecedented amount of information. Some of this information will be sensitive and confidential. In this book you will learn how to prepare to receive, store, and utilize this information based on the best practices from around the world, while appropriately protecting the privacy rights of your donors and prospects.

GLOBAL STRATEGIES

It seems the world keeps getting smaller and smaller, while the geographic fundraising territory for most charities gets larger and larger. The Internet has allowed even some of the smallest charities to become global. Understanding international strategies is increasingly important to successful major donor prospecting. Our local prospects may have business and investment interests around the world; some of our prospects may live in other parts of the world. This book will assist you in maneuvering through these complicated matters to success.

RESULTS AND EVALUATION

In this book, authors share some of the very best advice that will help you establish processes that will allow you to evaluate your efforts and determine if you are getting the sort of results you should. There is a lot of art to the long process of major donor cultivation, but the process must also be measurable to ensure the efficient and effective use of limited resources.

Major donors will help nonprofit managers, staff, and volunteers around the world to develop online and offline database prospecting strategies, making this strategy an important and valuable part of their overall and major gift fundraising plans. Authors will share real-world successes and failures, allowing the reader to learn from others around the world.

The skilled authors of this book are among the most respected fundraisers and researchers in the field today, and they have shared their best insight into successful donor communication and major gift solicitation, based in management issues familiar and relevant to anyone active in the nonprofit community.

The Internet has changed everything, making it possible for every charity to gain insight into major gift prospects. The key to success is how this tool is used—how the data can be wielded to make a true difference in the lives of donors and the institutions they support.

This book provides tips and suggestions that will help you get the most out of your existing online and offline fundraising efforts.

Major Donors cracks the code for successful major donor fundraising in the age of ePhilanthropy.

CHAPTER 1

Prospecting for Major Gifts

Pamela Gignac and Ken Wyman[1]

"Set your sights that much higher and remember that to have faith is to have wings, and to have wings is to be able to choose both the time and manner of your arrival."

—Patrick Walker, *Evening Standard*,
London, England, March 21, 1994

INTRODUCTION

It is more important than ever to find out who our donors are, what their interests might be, and to match those interests to our projects and institutional goals. With the greater demand for funds and an increasingly competitive search for funding, it is crucial that we do our homework: we must line up the right person, in the right place, at the right time, with the right project.

Penelope Burk, president of Cygnus Applied Research, and leader in the area of donor-centered revolution states:

Many of us assume we know what motivates and appeals to donors but as donors are beginning to signal their desire for change, they are also revealing their willingness to give more money. Cygnus' research discovered that 70 percent of donors would increase their giving—even in times of economic restraint—if they got what they really needed instead of what charities think donors want.[2]

---

[1]Preparation for this chapter was aided by expert advice from Professor Ken Wyman, CFRE, program coordinator, Fundraising and Volunteer Management Postgraduate Program, School of Media Studies & Information Technology at the Humber College Institute of Technology & Advanced Learning in Toronto, Ontario, Canada (email: ken.wyman@humber.ca and www.humber.ca) and research professionals Amy Rotteau, Development Officer Research, Royal Ontario Museum Foundation, Toronto, Ontario, and Stephanie Jonescu, MLIS, director of stewardship, Hamilton Health Sciences Foundation, Hamilton, Ontario.
[2]Visit www.donorcentred.ca for more information on Penelope Burk, Cygnus research, and Penelope's publications on donor-centered fundraising.

Therefore, there is an increased need to have more and better information about a prospect's philanthropic interests to ensure that these are being matched by the work of the nonprofit itself. This is crucial to overall success as well as to eliminate inappropriate approaches and wasting anyone's time—yours or the prospect's. There are now new techniques in prospect research, donor development, moves management, database mining, the Internet as a two-way source, and strategic analysis and evaluation that can be implemented to enable this to happen. So, how do we implement these new and powerful resources into our fundraising?

PROSPECT RESEARCH: BACKGROUND AND KEY ELEMENTS

History of Prospect Research

Prospect research as a profession began at universities and colleges in the 1980s. It was largely an administrative or clerical position that commonly fell under "other duties as assigned." Over the last several years, the profession has grown to be recognized for what it is—an integral and crucial part of our success in building better relationships with our donors, prospects, and the community. Researchers can be central figures in fundraising, and invaluable participants when prospect strategy and development is discussed.

While many organizations have made great strides in raising the profile of this research, more can be done to ensure that it is a dynamic and vibrant component of all our fundraising activities, including its strategic value in the fundraising process. The profession has worked hard to ensure that the field remains strong and highly skilled through the Association of Professional Researchers for Advancement (APRA) and the Institute of Fundraising's Researchers in Fundraising group.

Definitions

    R Read everything that you can get your hands on and more

    E Evaluate all of the details discovered

    S See people, listen, open up dialogues, and find out more

    E Expand on information found and make it grow

    A Approach those close and accessible

    R Review on a regular basis

    C Capture the information in an organized manner

    H Hold to the ethics and best practice of the profession

Association of Fundraising Professionals' (AFP) Definitions   *Prospect research,* according to the AFP, is the process of identifying, interviewing, and involving persons and organizations with the potential to become donors in your organization.

Prospect is a possible source of support whose philanthropic interests appear to be a match with your organization, but whose ability to give, interests, and linkages have not been qualified through research.

Qualified prospect is a prospect who continues to qualify throughout a research, evaluation, and cultivation process as a logical source of support for your organization.

Research Supports Fundraising   More than ever, it is important that we do our homework to ensure our information on prospects and donors is both up to date and as comprehensive as possible. This can be a daunting task when you have tight budgets, numerous deadlines, limited resources, and never enough time. Nevertheless, the key to all of our success depends on effective prospect research.

Research is the cornerstone of any fundraising operation. It:

- Leads to finding the right person, in the right place, at the right time, with the right approach
- Increases the probability of success by doing your homework
- Increases opportunities for cultivating positive responses
- Guides you to ensure that you focus in the right directions
- Assists you in building relationships with your known donors
- Targets new prospects
- Opens up new avenues and ways to turn prospects into supporters
- Matches prospects' interests with your work as connecting your donor to your mission is still key
- Builds confidence and trust through knowledge and information and adds a certain power to drive fundraising for all involved

The Role of Prospect Research

It is widely understood that research plays a significant role (some believe it can represent up to 80 percent) in the work involved in securing a gift. This applies to individuals, companies, and foundations. The fundamental success of research often depends on a well-developed relational fundraising database system and the procedures to manage the flow of information. As new donors are secured, new avenues to prospects are opened up. An effectively planned research program consists of a number of different tools besides a database. These include desk research, market research, Internet research, strategic targeting, and the preparation of background documents such as profiles, briefings, and approach strategies.

Exhaustive research leads to networking, which ensures that the right approaches are taken in the best way possible. This includes the ongoing input, maintenance, and updating of information held on a relational database, which is critical for targeting and analysis of prospective and current donors.

Consistent use of reporting systems and an infrastructure of two-way communication between all levels of your organization locally, regionally, and nationally, from staff to volunteers and board members is crucial. Collate the information captured as quickly as possible and remember that you are accountable for your research and the details entered on your database. These can include personal information such as a prospect's interests, or who knows whom, and how well (see Chapter 9, "Using Gathered Information Effectively within Your Staff and Volunteer Teams" as well as Chapter 10, "Moving from Prospect Identification to Making Friends for Life").

Case Study: The Campaign for the University of Toronto

The campaign for the University of Toronto (U of T) has been a tremendous achievement not only by Canadian but by American and British standards as well. In fact, the U of T reached a historic milestone, raising $1 billion since the launch of the campaign in 1997. The campaign for U of T has been the most ambitious fundraising effort in Canadian university history, and its billion-dollar goal was accomplished more than a year ahead of schedule.

The U of T embarked on its campaign in 1995 under the leadership of Dr. Jon S. Dellandrea, vice-president and chief advancement officer. Dr. Dellandrea's commitment to the U of T and his vision for fundraising clearly led the way for others to share in his successes and lessons learned. An integral part of the campaign's success came from Dr. Dellandrea's belief that research is a crucial part of fundraising for major gifts and well worth the investment.

> *Institutional advancement is a deeply personal process that requires in-depth understanding of our supporters, and the degree to which specific aspects of our own priorities reflect our donors' personal aspirations and interests. Prospect research is indispensable to this process and to identifying possible supporters from thousands of possible donors—it would have been impossible for the University of Toronto campaign to have succeeded in the absence of our investment in prospect research.*[3]

---

[3]Quote provided directly by Dr. Jon S. Dellandrea, former vice-president and chief advancement officer, University of Toronto, Ontario, Canada (to find out more visit www.utoronto.ca or www.giving.utoronto.ca/index.asp). Now the first ever development director, Oxford University, England.

The team, including Dr. Dellandrea himself, often brought back something to enhance the research and make for a successful ask–approach strategy.

Small Shop or Large Campaign: Anyone Can Do Research

Prospect research can be within anyone's reach, whether you are a small shop or a large campaign office. This can be achieved by using some of the ideas and techniques outlined in this book. Remember, it sometimes is better to take some risks, test out new ideas, and be creative rather than accept the cookie-cutter approach. While the level and depth of research are directly affected by budget size, some basics can be implemented in smaller shops through good planning.

For example, training all staff to be more creative in looking and finding out information about donors and prospects—such as reading local newspapers—helps to catch details about community individuals, business transactions, and philanthropic activities within your organization's reach. In addition, train volunteers, such as retirees, who already often go through every inch of their favorite newspaper, particularly the births and obituaries, in what can be useful information. In other words, share with others your need for information, and they will gladly respond because you have given them a purpose for their time spent reading.

It's not only vital to know how to retrieve information but also to make sure this knowledge remains central to organizational memory and that the foundation is set to have the ability to research prospects into the future.

Some key points to consider are:

- Success is not only how to retrieve information but also where to store it.
- Adapt techniques, theories, and experiences from elsewhere and implement new ideas as appropriate to meet specific goals and resources, however limited or small they might be.
- Yes, you can and should start to implement some new ideas to capture information.
- Try out your own six degrees of separation to find out who knows whom, who can open doors for you, and who can provide you with advice.
- It will be a challenge to always perform the amount of research desired to fully capture the necessary information on prospects and donors. There will be times when you must move forward without doing all the homework or planning needed, but some research is always better than none at all.

PROSPECT RESEARCHERS AND FUNDRAISERS TOGETHER

What Makes a Good Researcher?

Good researchers can be so much more than profile producers; they are also strategic partners, managing the moves for the fundraisers, just like the fundraiser moves prospects.

The educational and experiential background of researchers is quite varied. Many researchers grew into their positions over time, some coming from a library and information sciences background and others having completed fundraising courses or earning diplomas in this field. We know good researchers have worked in journalism, sciences, geography, political sciences, human resources, and more.

The common thread among all good researchers is the ability to think critically, and analyze data effectively with a strong understanding of people as well as commitment. Good candidates for this position include people who are capable of backroom work as well as up-front management (people and strategy).

Fundraisers Are Researchers and Researchers Are Fundraisers

Fundraisers are researchers, often conducting field research and gathering knowledge essential to the donor relationship. Researchers are also fundraisers, contributing equally to the bottom line of the organization. All fundraisers do a large amount of research themselves on their donors and potential donors. Executives and board members can also do the same—they just need to know how to look, where to look, and what to look for, and then how to capture and assimilate this information into a central repository that can be accessible to all those who need it. This process can even be fun, as all of us like to be a wee bit nosey—but everyone should take gossip for what it is!

Researchers and Fundraisers Together Creating Strategic Partnerships

Fundraising is a process that involves five main stages in a continuous and ongoing cycle as follows:

1. Identification
2. Qualification
3. Cultivation
4. Solicitation
5. Stewardship

Researchers have a valuable contribution to add to each stage; how-ever, traditionally research tends to be considered as stages 1 and 2, and fundraising, is the rest. The actual level of involvement will depend on resources, strategic plans, and goals as well as the experiences, skills, and interests of the staff. It also may take a little bit of vision and understand-ing to work together.

An understanding of the activities and benefits of research makes for better fundraisers. This is a fact that many instinctively know but not all outwardly recognize. Researchers and fundraisers working more closely together will only enhance and grow success and opportunities for build-ing better relationships with donors and prospects as well as our commu-nities and images overall.

In fact, research can have a positive impact on your organization as a whole and should be linked to operations rather than just development and fundraising. It has also a role to play in communications—to develop and then measure the positive image that your organization wants to portray.

Researchers are often separated from fundraisers. This is both physi-cal, due to lack of office space, and ideological. Research is seen in some organizations as support of, rather than as partner to, development. It is more than time to break down the barriers and provide a forum for regu-lar integration of research with fundraising. Researchers don't just read newspapers and surf the Internet, in the same way that fundraisers aren't always at events schmoozing and having fun.

Good Strategies for Integration   Developing solid partnerships between research and fundraising starts by breaking down barriers of time, work-load, poor communication, budget, and even proximity (separate offices, floors, or buildings). The most basic step is to educate each area of the organization about the type of work being conducted and how all of the functions in the organization impact each other.

The researcher should build relationships within fundraising like the relationship a fundraiser builds with a prospect. The researcher should conduct discovery meetings to learn about needs and projects, understand the case that the fundraiser is working to fund, and their database needs. The researcher can also create opportunities for fundraisers to locate information on their own, and ensure that they receive proper training and support as required.

This strategy serves to educate fundraisers about the type of informa-tion they can locate themselves and the amount of information they need to conduct a visit. It also frees up research time to focus on more complex requests for information.

Conversely, the researcher should be involved where possible in fundraising, such as attendance at key meetings where strategy is created and discussed. Further, they could be involved in events, participating with the purpose of gathering information. When possible, a researcher should participate on a fundraising call to get a sense of what actually occurs and how their work is utilized.

BIG GIFTS AND MAJOR GIFTS

How Big Is a "Big" Gift?

Ken Wyman, a well-known fundraiser and trainer says:

> How big is a "big" gift? For some groups, such as universities and hospitals, nothing below $100,000 is a "major gift"—and many receive multi-million dollar contributions. For other nonprofit groups $100 would be huge. For many of us, the definition remains open—whatever your group would consider a breakthrough. However, many of the techniques require a considerable investment of time and money, and that can only be justified by a comparable return on investment.

Also, the Institute of Fundraising's (IOF) Major Donor and Major Donor Fundraising Code of Practice (www.institute-of-fundraising.org.uk) states that a major donor is one who has:

> [T]he potential to make or procure a gift which would have a significant impact on the work being conducted, who is approached and/or cultivated using personal relationship development fundraising techniques for the mutual benefit of the organization and the donor. The gift may be of capital, revenue, time, or influence.

Annual versus Major Donor

The definition of an annual gift prospect versus a major gift prospect differs according to the size and needs of an organization. Today's annual donors are good prospects for future major gifts. Keep them on your list to be further researched in the future.

Integrating Major Gifts Fundraising

Our fundraising success depends on the right approach, to the right person, with the right project—all at the right time! It is based on building relationships with key selected donors and prospects (see Exhibit 1.1). Strength lies in utilizing the assistance of peer-to-peer contacts and the orbit or spheres of influence and network of contacts that surround each

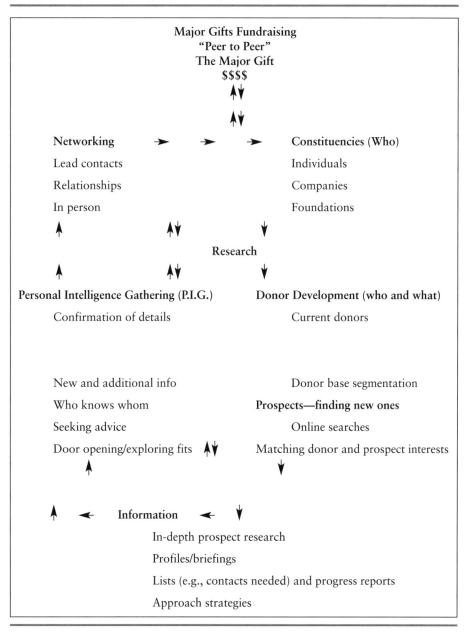

EXHIBIT 1.1 Relationship Management Cycle—Research Is the Foundation of Major Gifts Fundraising. Created by Pamela Gignac.

of them by asking for their help as door openers and gatekeepers. Look to them for advice as well as a gift.

Gifts can be a donor's personal gift as well as those from companies and foundations and can include gifts in kind, cash, and stock. An approach strategy should be developed for each prospect that includes who will ask, what to ask for, and when to ask. At all times it is important to be respectful of both contacts and prospects and to manage the process in a highly professional manner. All approaches should be coordinated and planned out carefully in advance.

Approaches to companies and foundations should be planned to meet the specific criteria required for each one—integrating annual giving with major giving where appropriate. As part of a corporate approach, look at all the avenues of potential support including alliances, partnerships, or sponsorships as well as its community donations program, employee fundraising, employee volunteering, and matching gifts programs. This approach may or may not involve specific applications or contracts with each one. Foundations, on the other hand, usually involve a more straightforward application procedure and a specific process that needs to be followed.

PROSPECTING

What Is a Prospect?

What is a prospect? Someone you think *might* support your work. Not just because they might have money but because their interests match those of your organization.

Can donors be prospects? Yes, they are your best prospects.

Where to start? Start with current donors and close friends. Then go to others who support similar work.

Potential prospects could include any of the following:

- Prospects with stated interests that match your work
- Past and current donors and supporters including board members and volunteers
- Donors and supporters to similar campaigns and charities
- Major corporate and community donors
- Wealthy individuals and high-profile individuals
- Companies, organizations, and individuals who have been approached without success in the past
- Suppliers to your organization
- Clients/alumni/audience

11 Steps That Lead to Prospecting Success

Step 1. Resources required to support an effective research program include press articles, directories, the Internet, subscriptions to online databases, and in-house files (paper and electronic).

Step 2. The fundraising database acts as an anchor for information capture and flow. A good relational database for research and analysis makes all this more efficient, effective, and *easier!*

Step 3. Analyze your database and the Internet for information to build strategies to meet both short-term and long-term fundraising objectives.

Step 4. Identify prospects starting with your own donors, research their background, and find ways to approach them.

Step 5. Manage and regularly update your information to be able to coordinate, facilitate, and search for links through relationships for prospects and donors as well as to avoid blind duplicate approaches.

Step 6. Grow relationships with donors and develop their support.

Step 7. Devote time to find new prospects beyond your donors.

Step 8. Match prospect interests with your own.

Step 9. Use personal intelligence gathering (PIG) and experience to confirm your research and find out new details and names.

Step 10. Always look for the best ask—right person, right place, right time, with the right project.

Step 11. Maintain reports, including contact reports, prospect progress reports, campaign reports, and so on. These are vital for sharing, revising, and analyzing information from all of the previous steps.

RESEARCH TECHNIQUES AND INFORMATION SOURCES

Key Words Can Help You Focus

Key words, as in the same ones used on Google or Yahoo! when surfing the Internet, are helpful not only for searching for information but also as a way to get others to understand what you are trying to achieve. Asking volunteers, board members, program staff, donors, and colleagues what key words they think of when they think of your organization not only gets them involved but often excited and can generate ideas.

Develop an organizational key word list through the following:

- Establish a list of key words based on your organization such as health, research, disability, a particular location or region, and so on.
- Use the case for support and mission to find them, including themes and specific projects.
- Ask your volunteers and board members what words come to mind for them.

- Put together words that would match a prospect's interest with your work.
- Keep these words in mind when doing research and put together a list of key prospects.
- Always look for any mention of a person or company's name with the dollar or monetary sign and amount next to it.

Seeking Answers to Questions

It is important to line up all approaches as close to a match as possible. The right person, at the right level, usually makes the most successful match at the right time. That's why it is vital to spend so much time and effort on careful planning and research.

Coordination of all approaches is crucial for not only your sake but also because the reputation of your volunteers depends on it. They rely on you for top-quality and accurate research information. In order to achieve this, it is extremely helpful to compile a list of questions to be answered when researching prospects:

- Are they new prospects or current donors?
- If they are current donors, then look at these questions:
  - Patterns of giving—has the gift size increased?
  - Are we as an organization meeting their needs?
  - Are they board members, senior staff, or volunteers?
  - Are they high-end users of your services?
  - Do you have volunteers that can leverage the gift?
- To find or explore new prospects or to add to what you know about your current donors, look at these questions:
  - What companies or foundations have an easily identified interest in our type of organization? Or our projects and programs?
  - How closely do we match with their known interests and criteria?
  - Do we need to find out more about them?
  - If we do have a good match and the right contact, could we go for a larger gift or support package?
  - What would be our best approach strategy?
  - On a first approach, which source (or sources) would we seek support from?:
    - Personal wealth
    - Corporate gift and/or sponsorship
    - Foundation grant
  - What type of individuals would be interested in our work? For example, corporate executives, directors, entrepreneurs, self-employed, younger, older, local, etc.

- Who have they given to in the past? Who do they currently support?
- What is their range of giving? The average gift size? Largest known gift given and to whom?
- What are their donations' policies? What are their restrictions?
- When do we apply and what is their application procedure?
- Do we hold out for the right approach? Is it potentially worth our while to do so and if so, how long do we wait? Three months? Six months? One year or longer?
- If we make preliminary approaches, which "home team" member or partner should make the approach and at what level can contact be made (e.g., chief executive, corporate affairs, marketing)?

Information Sources

Identify and select sources of information that are most suitable for your organizational goals, resources, and budget. Check the following:

- Personal contacts—valuable information can be gained from:
  - Personal conversations and interviews with prospects and donors as well as their peers, friends, and family.
  - Donor surveys.
  - Conversations at events.
  - Remember to beware of gossip and maintain caution regarding privacy rights, confidentiality, and other issues.
- Using technology and paper sources of information:
  - Interrogate your database and check in-house files, lists for attendees and program participants who might become donors through research and further cultivation and solicitation.
  - Check public sources of information, including newspapers, magazines, books, directories, and media as well as a wide variety of sites and information that can be found on the Internet.
  - Use Internet sources and online searches, and corporate/foundation searches through key words.
  - Search local, regional, national, and international sources for press, business, professional and trade journals, social directories, and magazines.
- Annual reports for companies include:
  - Philanthropic and community involvement.
  - Financial statements including proxy statements for top director salary disclosures.
- Salary information—disclosure lists online for government positions and proxy statements for public companies as well as salaries mentioned in press articles.

- Other nonprofit sources of information:
  - Annual reports.
  - Newsletters.
  - Special event brochures and programs.
- External research providers:
  - Identification and research services to provide electronic screening.
  - Specialized services such as online prospect research databases.

Six Degrees of Donor Development (Relationship Management and Spheres of Influence)

The probability of success increases by sharing researched names with people and finding out about their personal contacts and their six degrees of friends, family, and colleagues. Sharing a list is better than a blanket question (e.g., Who do you know?), as it gives them something to focus on. It will generate comments more easily and show them the scope of what you are trying to achieve. Ask for their advice and look for answers to these questions:

Are there any prospects within their reach?

Do they have any additional information?

Can they open doors?

Is it appropriate to be directly involved in the approach?

Contacts are important. Ken Wyman explains why:

- Donors sometimes bend the rules when the right person asks.
- Some donations are made because of who asked and not what the nonprofit does.
- Some supporters can open doors if you find the right ones.
- Anything less and you are just another little-known group in a large pile.
- Corporate employees can often get matching gifts for nonprofits they support with time or money.
- It's harder for a company to say no to a customer asking for support.
- Service clubs and unions often respond to members and their interests.

How do you find connections? Ken Wyman suggests the following:

- Ask those closest to you, such as your board members, volunteers, staff, family, friends, donors, members, and clients, for their advice and information. Try getting them to fill in a survey about where they work and live, clubs they belong to, where they worship, and their hobbies.

■ Ask selective donors if they can suggest others with similar interests such as companies, foundations, or groups. Find out if they would be willing to open the door and offer advice on securing support from them.

■ At events and public gatherings, ask people if they would drop off their business cards, perhaps to win a prize. Or fill in raffle forms that ask for email addresses as well as their names, phone numbers, and addresses.

■ Create your own business council and ask it to raise funds from peers. Include business owners, managers, and franchisees. Don't ask them to attend committee meetings. Their job is to give and get others to give.

■ Ask for assistance in finding contacts from your own peers and another or larger nonprofit organization.

■ Set up a speakers' bureau and talk to potential donor groups such as service clubs, churches, schools, and so on. Collect business cards and names of people you meet and talk to about your nonprofit and its work. Set up information sessions about the work of your nonprofit for a local company and their employees.

■ Choose the companies with the largest number of employees in your area (you should be able to get a list from your local government or other publications). Call them to ask the name, position, and contact information for the person responsible for donations and community support. Don't approach them yet. Confirm the spelling and any information you might already have. Develop and implement a file of information on the company to be used as a guide in making an approach.

■ If you can't find any contact information, a cold call might be necessary. Although it will be less successful, it could still turn out to be worthwhile.

Calling to Find Out More

A one-on-one call will need to be made to a prospect sooner or later. You will need to call to find out information, confirm or update your research, or determine their current status on giving. For example, they may have already made all their commitments for the year and you need to find that out and decide if you should apply next year. If you don't call as a researcher, you will certainly need to as a fundraiser.

Prepare yourself:

- Who are you calling? Is it a company or foundation?
- Why are you calling? Application deadline looming? Information to prepare for an upcoming meeting or presentation? Or has an employee, friend, or relative given you an introduction to them?
- What do you need before you make the actual call?
  - Information found through your research including a list of sources and dates.
  - A telephone script based on your research and a discussion with your fundraiser.
  - A brief discussion with your fundraiser (if it's not you) to:
    - Determine the scope of your conversation.
    - Find out what the initial approach might be.
    - Explore how much info you should give them.
    - Determine any possible follow-up, who should be involved, etc.
    - Find out what other, if any, contact has been made.

Who you should talk to is not always necessarily who you will get access to. A lot depends on the organization, but it could be any one or more of the following:

- Donations person
- Application secretary
- Marketing person
- Public relations person
- Main receptionist
- Chief executive or other director's assistant
- Human Resources

How much should you tell them?

- State clearly who you are and why you are calling.
- Speak clearly and avoid jargon as much as possible.
- Assume that they are very busy people and that they likely know little about you (unless they are a donor who is close to you already).

What can happen?

- They will give you the information you are looking for such as:
  - A person's name, giving policies, and application details.
  - They will ask you to send in a formal application and/or want to set up a meeting.

■ You may have some inaccurate information and they will want to know where you got it. Deal with this courteously and try not to blame your sources, but ask if you should pass on the correct information.

■ They may not have the time or inclination to talk to you. Deal with this courteously.

■ They may offer a donation immediately.

■ They may tell you they will not donate to you.

Prospecting Lists

As a rule, there are two types of lists used to share your prospect names. One is often called a circle of friends and is usually a basic list drawn from your database. These names have had little or no research to refine them and are typically your current or lapsed donors. Expect to see between 250 and 500 major gifts prospects or around 10–20% of your database or more. In this case, you have contact with them and need research to determine an approach strategy.

The other list is known as a contacts needed list. This contains more in-depth research information on current donors and new prospects. This list needs to be kept to a manageable size relative to the target and number of gifts you are trying to secure; a typical list will consist of 100 to 250 names. Any more than that is too difficult to manage and tiresome for your volunteers to review.

In this case, you have the research basics but you need the contact to determine the right approach strategy. This might include donors with known interests in your area but, no known past with you.

Both lists support your strategic program to build relationships; these are the donors to concentrate on. The ultimate purpose is to increase gifts from current donors and/or to secure new, larger gifts from new prospects.

These tools and other techniques are also discussed in Chapter 9, "Using Gathered Information," as well as Chapter 10, "Moving from Prospect Identification to Making Friends for Life."

Prospect Qualification

The three main components of prospect qualification are:

1. How likely is it they will give (if all was in the right place, how likely is it that they would support you)?
2. How close are they to you?
3. How close do you match their interests?

Unlike the United States, many countries have limited access to information regarding wealth, ownership of property, and financial holdings. While certain sources will provide some detail (e.g., proxy circulars, inside trades), overall this type of information is unavailable for the typical prospect. We have developed other ways to evaluate or qualify a prospect; one major Toronto advancement shop relies on a prospect's giving to other institutions to understand gift capacities and comfort. This information, put together with a rating system that determines connections and affinity to the organization, is a good tool to qualify prospects.

When the information is available, it is important to consider other factors—number and age of children, financial commitments that are not always detectable, and generally how the industry in which that individual is working is performing. Understanding this type of information can help determine whether the prospect is feeling rich or poor.

A rating system should be simple and easy to understand. It should measure affiliation and the monetary value of a potential gift. It does not have to measure capacity, as capacity will have little bearing on an actual gift if the affiliation to the organization does not exist. Coding prospects using an alphanumeric structure, wherein A/B/C etc. equals affiliation and 1/2/3 etc. equals the projected gift size, can assist in segmenting the database. This information, coupled with other data tracked on the database (lifetime giving, frequency of giving, and participation in activities with the organization), can go a long way in determining the right person making the right ask at the right time.

WHERE DO WE GO FROM HERE?

Taking what has been discussed here and elsewhere in this book, determine what is appropriate for your organization, including your goals, resources, and budgets. Plan your steps, needs, and responsibilities including internal and external communication. Decide on the criteria to identify top prospects, establish procedures, and set guidelines to serve privacy and accountability. Make sure that research is addressed in your fundraising planning, and design individualized approach strategies.

Implement research and personal intelligence gathering (PIG) to share information with others in a confidential manner and revise your approach strategy accordingly. Use the information you have gathered in a respectful, responsible, and accountable manner.

Overall, review, plan, coordinate, execute, evaluate, report, record, inform, communicate, and go out and ask—and do it all over again and again! Most of all, do it.

CONCLUSION

Research is an invaluable activity for any organization. It ensures that you are not wasting your time and that of the donor or prospect. Any investment made in research for major gifts, individuals, companies, and foundations will enhance and support your fundraising activities; time and money spent on research will be recouped as more successful approaches are made. But research only works when organizations make the commitment to do it effectively and responsibly.

It takes practice to know where and how to look, and it can be a challenge to make it interesting for those doing it. It is also important to ensure that colleagues and others are enthusiastic about its relevance. So plan on investing time and money before you get proficient at research, and remember that your own knowledge will grow and so will the possibilities of where it can take you. You will develop an instinct about where to look and when to stop based on experience.

Remember that doing good research allows you to do good works for your community. Yes, you, too, make a difference through your dedication and efforts; you really do.

Happy prospecting and fundraising!

CHAPTER 2

Knowledge Management, Data Mining, and Prospect Screening

Jeff Gignac and Chris Carnie

"Hi, Jeff."
"Hi, Chris. Howya doing?"
"Great, thank you. How's the weather over there in Toronto?"
"Oh, you know, the normal; gray. How's Barcelona today?"
"Sunny, but there are big clouds building. It's August, so it's likely to turn into torrential rain this afternoon."

INTRODUCTION

Jeff and Chris are exchanging knowledge. Not just the facts about the weather ("gray," "sunny") but their interpretation of the facts based on years of learning, observing, remembering. Jeff knows that gray is normal. Chris accurately predicts an afternoon of rainstorms.

Knowledge is like that—apparently banal exchanges of information given depth and relevance by the people making the exchange. Just think of any recent fundraising event you have attended and the conversations that occurred. Consciously or not you were probably picking up a load of biographic and demographic data about your donors and prospects in those brief verbal exchanges, and more if you were able to pick up the speaker's tone, appearance, and posture.

This chapter is about the practical applications of knowledge in fundraising. How we find it, where we keep it, and what we do with it. Along the way we will introduce you to your knowledge ambassador. We will cover three key areas:

1. Knowledge Management
2. Data Mining and Prospect Screening
3. Tracking Prospects

The first section, on knowledge management, explains the key concepts in this new and important discipline, and shows how they can be applied to the world of fundraising. The second section details techniques that identify the best of your prospects. Section three shows how to track these prospects.

DEFINITIONS

We have tried to avoid jargon here, but some key words need definition.

In this chapter we will refer repeatedly to *knowledge* and *knowledge management*. There is no one universally accepted definition of these concepts. For the sake of clarity we define knowledge in the context of a nonprofit organization as the sum of

- Information
- Skills
- Learning

   On or about:

- Stakeholders (including donors, volunteers, customers, and suppliers)
- Markets
- Products
- Governance
- Internal processes

   Knowledge management can be defined as the acquisition, sharing, and use of knowledge with organizations, including learning processes and information systems.[1]

> *Knowledge is about the ability to understand context, see connections, and spot significance when dealing with information . . . Knowledge management . . . promotes an integrated approach to the creation, capture, organization, access, and use of an enterprise's Intellectual Capital on customers, markets, products, services, and internal processes.*[2]

KNOWLEDGE MANAGEMENT

The Holistic Approach

Knowledge refers to the whole organization. It is not something that you put in a fundraising database (that is data), and it is not simply the know-

---

[1] Business Processes Resources Centre, University of Warwick.
[2] Marc Auckland, chief knowledge manager at BT, quoted in *Competing with Knowledge,* Abell and Oxbrow, Library Association, London, 2001.

how of the development and fundraising team. It includes the knowledge of the people you raise funds for—your research scientists, health workers, animal-care specialists, or ecologists. These are the people delivering the nonprofit's work on the ground, and their knowledge is equally valuable. They know about your projects, so you use them already to write up your case statements and budgets. They also know about people in their field, and some of these could be major donors.

A useful example comes from a major London museum. The development (fundraising) department was two floors above the museum offices, and the door that divided them seemed never to open. But the museum's curators knew all sorts of people who were potential major donors—people who collected Japanese ceramics or Greek sculpture. The museum set up staff exchanges between the curatorial staff and the development office, and a monthly open evening (wine and snacks in the development department) to which key curatorial staff were invited. As the direct result of these actions, a number of key donors were identified and persuaded to invest in the museum's future.

This whole-organization approach goes beyond senior staff. Your quiet but charming receptionist, who has been in post these last 20 years and has seen all sorts of people coming and going through your door, is a valuable source of knowledge. She knows your former staff, the early volunteers who shaped the organization and keeps in touch each Christmas with the young former volunteer who is now the CFO in a significant downtown enterprise.

In knowledge management, everyone is a knowledge manager just as in fundraising everyone is a researcher, everyone a fundraiser.

The Model

A straightforward model to understand knowledge in organizations is to consider knowledge as a flow—flowing into your organization, through it, and out. The model looks at the ways in which knowledge arrives at the organization, how it is stored, how it is shared between colleagues, and how it is produced.[3]

---

[3]This approach is derived from *Information Management in the Voluntary Sector,* ed. D. Grimwood-Jones, S. Simmons, ASLIB, London, 1998, as well as other texts.

Knowledge Capture   In most organizations, knowledge arrives:

- With new staff
- From external sources mediated by prospect researchers:
  - Data screening
  - Press and media sources
- From leadership
- From donors themselves (e.g., word of mouth)
- With new donors, volunteers, inquirers
- From field or operational departments
- From consultants and other suppliers

Fundraising needs all of these knowledge sources, because each has its own special quality.

Word of mouth—from a donor phone call or a board member's hint—can give valuable information about a person's motivation or interest in your nonprofit. Word of mouth is current, fast, and fun, and it delivers high-quality informal information about prospects and suspects. But it is difficult to manage and measure, and does not give the comprehensive and comparable results that fundraisers need in order to do their job. Too often, word of mouth information is stored in the heads of those who collect it and is not shared with those who can act on it.

Prospect research, the subject of this book, offers structured, comprehensive information about potential donors. Prospect research requires dedicated human and computing resources, time, and money. Its product is the steady, consistent research that creates a pipeline—the prospect pipeline—of suspects, prospects, and then donors. Prospect researchers use data mining and prospect screening to understand and add to their data; we deal with these topics next.

Managing Knowledge Capture   The first step in managing knowledge as it arrives at your organization is to work out what is happening now. Take a large sheet of paper, a mug of fresh coffee, and a sharp pencil, and start to draw up a map of the knowledge and information flow around your major donor fundraising process. As you'll see from the brief outline in Exhibit 2.1, it all becomes quite complicated.

You can find out more about the technique of process-based knowledge mapping in a number of specialist titles on the topic.[4]

---

[4]A good general starting point is K. Dalkir, *Knowledge Management in Theory and Practice,* Butterworth-Heinemann, 2005; or try A. Abell and N. Oxbrow *Competing with Knowledge,* Library Association Publishing, 2001.

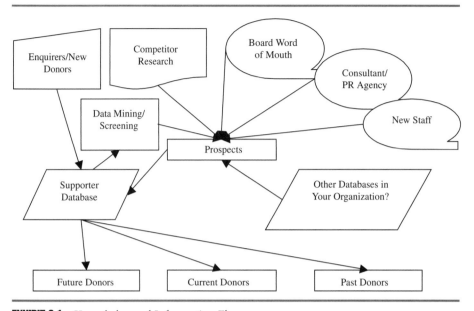

EXHIBIT 2.1   Knowledge and Information Flow

Knowledge Store   Your people are the most important part of your organization. Why? Because the knowledge of the organization rests on their shoulders, literally. In their heads is the knowledge of projects, personal connections, background, someone-I-met-once-who-might-be-useful, and, in the case of skilled fundraisers, of the techniques for approaching, asking, and recruiting a new major donor.

People, like machines, codify the knowledge in their heads. They think of old Mrs. Smithkins as "the person who sits next to me at the synagogue" or of young Jake Starborgling as "that gangly kid I used to play football with." So when you ask them casually, in the canteen, if they know anyone who might become a major donor to your institution, they say, "er, I don't think so." In fact Mrs. Smithkins is the stunningly wealthy Tupperware-to-headlamps inheritor and Jake Starborgling is now the boss of Global Private Banking, Inc.

This situation is reversible—there are well-established knowledge management techniques that you can apply to release this internal knowledge. Running through lists of prospects with colleagues—prospect review—is sometimes enough to spring names and connections from inside the heads of colleagues. It is good practice to do this as a managed process—explaining to colleagues why you are doing it, and detailing the steps you are taking to guarantee the confidentiality and security of any data they share with you.

Knowledge Ambassador   Consider nominating a colleague as your knowledge ambassador. This is a fun job, probably the best fun you will ever have in the office, because it involves talking to people. Your knowledge ambassador is the person from your department who can rove around your organization, having a coffee here, sharing a joke there, talking about the weather or local politics with the CEO's personal assistant. Like a real-life ambassador, they are personable, easygoing, and attentive. They know when to shut up and listen, and that is their job—to act as the informal link between your fundraising or development department and the rest of the organization. They complement the formal links (the senior management meetings, the memos, the reports) with informal knowledge and information—about new staff, people's backgrounds, what's up, and who's down. This has to be a two-way exchange—they're not a spy—so that other colleagues in the office hear about the fundraising team and its news, stuff they could not (or did not bother to) read in an interdepartmental memo. Your knowledge ambassador represents your department's views in an informal way with other people in the organization.

The Database   The other great information store is your database, and we'll talk about data mining and screening in a moment. Bear in mind that when we talk about database we mean all your databases. Because a common problem with the knowledge store is that it is made up of silos—unconnected heaps of information. Alongside your donor database you probably have a press office database (useful contacts), a field office database (including a directory of other nonprofits working in your sector), a volunteers database (listing the people who care about you most of all), and, behind the stern gaze of her personal assistant, a contact-rich Outlook database full of the people that your CEO lunches with. Don't forget the paper files—current and archived files on people and organizations linked to yours.

Managing the Knowledge Store   It's back to the paper and pencil routine, this time to draw up a table of all the places in which data is stored in your organization, including brief details on the numbers of records, a sample record from each, and a commentary on the possible applications of that knowledge store to your major donor program. This is a first and essential step before considering data mining or screening for your organization.

Knowledge Out   *Knowledge out* is not a phrase you'll find in textbooks—they tend to talk about knowledge sharing, knowledge application, and knowledge exchange. But it conveys the idea behind a key step in the process—getting the knowledge out to the people who can use it.

Major gift programs typically produce knowledge in the form of:

- Lists of prospects for reviews
- Prospect profiles
- Tracking reports, indicating who should be contacted when, and about what
- Performance analysis and reports to leadership

There are standard models for each of these kinds of knowledge products. See C. Hogan, *Prospect Research. A Primer for Growing Nonprofits,* for useful examples.

The key to useful knowledge products is to understand how they will be used. A 14-page prospect profile including detailed financial analysis of three private companies is no good if you are trying to read it quickly in the back of a taxi on the way to the prospect's Manhattan penthouse. The tiny typeface, the columns of detail, the size of the sheets of paper, not to mention the distractions of the driver's monologue on, say, horse racing, are enough to render the most beautiful, painstakingly prepared profile utterly useless. Much better would have been a Rolodex-card summary (it fits in your jacket pocket) showing the key points in Times New Roman 12-point font and suggesting one question that your fundraiser could ask of his important new prospect.

Managing Knowledge Out   Print out an example copy of your department's reports, notes, and profiles relevant to major gift fundraising. Take them to your colleagues who are meant to read or act on those reports. Ask them how they used the documents, where, when, and under what conditions; ask them about ease of use, readability, information overload and information gaps, about security and confidentiality of personal data, and about their ideas for improvements. Use their comments to develop new reports, formats, and content. Think laterally; would color card or color ink help? Could we do that in a brief email? Could we put that straight into their handheld device, or mobile telephone?

Building a Prospect Pipeline

These techniques come together in major donor work when you build a *prospect pipeline.* This is the delivery mechanism for new prospects for your fundraising team, and it's based on the knowledge-in–store-out model described previously.

Your fundraisers need a continuous supply of new prospects. Depending on which major gift strategy they are following, that might mean anything from 10 to 10,000 new prospects per annum. To find those

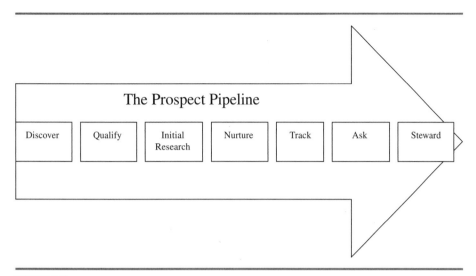

The Prospect Pipeline

| Discover | Qualify | Initial Research | Nurture | Track | Ask | Steward |

EXHIBIT 2.2 The Prospect Pipeline

prospects, someone must sift through many times that number of potential prospects, or suspects. She will then want to select the best of those, find out more about them, and push them through a process that involves nurturing or developing the prospect, tracking, asking, and stewardship. It can be summarized as shown in Exhibit 2.2. Planning the prospect pipeline is part of the job of the knowledge manager.

Becoming a Knowledge Manager

We prospect researchers are naturally humble people. We like our books and our quiet research corner, and we tend to avoid showy titles. But this is one title that every prospect researcher should have in his sights: to become the knowledge manager for your organization or at least for the fundraising and development part of your organization. You are probably already doing many of the activities that a knowledge manager would do—just maybe not in the coherent, proactive way that the title implies. That is the big step, to move from reactive researcher to proactive manager.

Becoming a knowledge manager means analyzing the flow of knowledge in your organization; devising new ways of gathering, storing, and processing information; building a truly organization-wide knowledge store; helping colleagues understand and code information so that everyone can use it . . . in fact the whole paraphernalia of knowledge processes introduced previously. The impact on your organization will be immense—in the commercial sector the current estimate is that knowledge management will save $31 billion in annual re-invention costs (the cost of thinking up a solution that someone else in your organization has already devised) at Fortune 500 companies.[5] At your organization, knowledge management will mean new and better donors, happier colleagues, and smoother working practices.

INTRODUCTION TO DATA MINING AND PROSPECT SCREENING

What Is Data Mining?

According to Microsoft the definition of data mining is:

> *An information extraction activity whose goal is to discover hidden facts contained in databases. Using a combination of machine learning, statistical analysis, modeling techniques, and database technology, data mining finds patterns and subtle relationships in data and infers rules that allow the prediction of future results.*

In other words, data mining means discovering, within a database, records that show particular patterns. Donors that give each year at Christmas, donors who only respond to certain types of appeals, donors who fall into certain age or social categories, and combinations of these factors.

Data mining is also:

- The starting point on the road to finding out more about your donors and potential prospects.
- A method used to interrogate and analyze your customer databases based on a set of statistical facts and numbers.
- A broader look at your database from a big-picture perspective.
- Usually more effective with larger numbers of records and databases.

Data Mining Results

Data mining provides you with reports based on averages and selected statistical information and criteria. A detailed report is provided based on these averages. It is not an exact science. It provides better information to make qualified decisions as to whom you should approach. It doesn't provide finished prospect research reports or even partial profiles.

In fact, additional research is usually required to flesh out the information from data mining, and to match your strategic objectives and

---

[5]Y. Malhotra, "Integrating Knowledge Management Technologies in Organizational Business Processes," *Journal of Knowledge Management 8*, 1, 2005, 7–28.

needs. The results of any data mining should, however, point you in the right direction toward identifying which of your prospects warrants additional research. For example, your organization has a donor database of 50,000 names. One goal of a data mining exercise could be to identify which are your best 1,000 prospects based on their patterns of giving, their recruitment history, and wealth or demographic indicators.

It is important to note that no matter what the investment made in data screening, it is crucial to involve researchers and fundraisers as a coordinated team effort to make sure any results actually get used. Please see appendix B for a sample checklist that can be used as a good starting point that people can use as a foundation to develop their own process specifically tailored for their needs. For further information contact Carol McConaghy Thorp, Senior Applications Consultant, SunGard BSR Inc (*carol.thorp@sungardbsr.com*) and (*www.sungardbsr.com*).

Data Mining or Prospect Screening?

Just because someone has a certain level of wealth indicated by the data mining process does not mean they will necessarily support your work. Prospect screening takes it to the next step. It uses the technique of data mining and fine-tunes it for a more appropriate application to be used in the nonprofit sector.

Prospect screening is considered a more holistic and specialized approach to the analysis of the results found in searching a database and your donor records. The questions this process seeks to answer are much more sophisticated, specialized, and customized than those asked during general data mining. As a result, the information found is more applicable and can be implemented faster.

How Does It Work?   Prospect screening compares the data from your database against other data. Years ago, this meant painstakingly comparing a donor database against a paper list of names, such as a *Who's Who*. Nowadays it is, of course, all done electronically.

What Is the Point?   Prospect screening selects people with potential. In fundraising, the focus is on finding people who have the potential to become major donors. So we screen donor data against data about wealth, power, or philanthropy (such as lists of property owners, business directors, and foundation board members). The advantage of this method is that it picks out people who have the potential to make a major gift irrespective of their giving history; they may only give you $10 per month, but they have the *potential* to give you $10 million.

Using the Results   Even for those who have invested in prospect screening of their database, a bigger challenge remains—taking the results and strategically implementing them by putting it all into action. Sometimes the report ends up as a large document put away in a file drawer. Thus using a specialized service provider for the nonprofit sector may ensure that this valuable information is put to good use quickly and efficiently. As this is a relatively new area for fundraising, the number of providers, their services, and options will continue to grow.

Key Nonprofit Prospect Screening Companies		
Company Name	Web Site	Country Served
Blackbaud Analytics	www.blackbaud.com	US/Canada
Charity Consultants UK	www.charityconsultants.co.uk	UK
Factary	www.factary.com	UK, Europe
Foundation Search	www.foundationsearch.com	US
Fundraising Research Consultancy (FRC)	www.frandc.co.uk	UK
Grenzebach Glier & Associates, Inc.	www.grenzebachglier.com	US
Hep Development Services	www.hepdevelopment.com	US
JMG Solutions Inc.	www.jmgsolutions.com	Canada/US/UK
P!N	www.prospectinfo.com	US
SunGard BSR, Inc.	www.sungardbsr.com	US
Wealth Engine	www.wealthengine.com	US

TRACKING PROSPECTS

Really Simple Syndication

In today's world, nonprofits can utilize many new innovations to assist them with their daily chores. One such innovation is something called really simple syndication, or RSS, and it sends you updated web content. RSS is an extensible markup language (XML) format for content distribution. You don't need to know much about XML except that it gets the information to talk to your computer.

An RSS feed can help you track your prospects. An RSS looks complicated and unreadable if you click on the link to open it in your web browser directly. However, there are many programs that you can use that will decipher the code for you and deliver real-time up-to-date news to your computer.

Each web site will provide a subscription page. It may end in XML, RSS, or some other extension but will all follow the same format. Many web sites will use the XML or RSS icon. Many of today's blogs provide RSS links back to their content (*blog* is short for weblog and is a web-based communications tool, often described as an online journal).

What Is XML?

XML (extensible markup language) is a new form of HTML, the technology that allows you to view web sites. By using XML you can have real-time personalized news delivered to you on the Internet. In the past you were required to watch TV newscasts, read the newspaper, or go in search of news on the Internet. Now you don't have to visit each news site to get your syndicated news. It comes to you whenever you want it to.

How to Get Started with RSS

Step One Download and install a RSS news reader or news aggregator.

A Selection of Current News Readers		
News Reader	Web Site	Platform
AmphetaDesk	www.disobey.com/amphetadesk/	Windows
Bloglines	www.bloglines.com/	Web
Feed reader	www.feedreader.com/	Windows
NetNewsWire	http://ranchero.com/netnewswire/	MAC OS
NewzCrawler	www.newzcrawler.com/	Windows
SharpReader	www.sharpreader.net/	Windows
Straw	www.nongnu.org/straw/	Linux

Note that some news readers are free, while others might require a small fee.

Step Two Once you have your news readers installed, you can subscribe to a news feed. There are many content providers, and more are added all the time. Just look for the RSS icon or link on your favorite web sites.

Examples of RSS feeds you might want to subscribe to include:

Provider	RSS Feed
About Nonprofit Charitable Orgs	http://z.about.com/6/g/nonprofit/b/index.rdf
Global Fundraising Innovation	www.fundraisinginnovation.com/?feed=rss2
Librarians' Index to the Internet	http://lii.org/ntw.rss
Nonprofit Matrix	www.nonprofitmatrix.com/rss.asp

Examples of prospect research blogs you might want to link to include:

Provider	Web Site Address
Prospect Research Blog	http://stevenhupp.typepad.com/prospectresearch/
ResearchBuzz	www.researchbuzz.com
ResourceShelf	www.resourceshelf.com
Sandra's Prospect Research Blog	http://larkinresearch.blogspot.com
Search Engine Watch Blog	http://blog.searchenginewatch.com/blog

Step Three   When you have opened the RSS feed in your browser and see the XML data, then highlight the URL of that feed and copy it. Paste the link into the appropriate section of your RSS news reader and select Subscribe.

Please consult the documentation for your RSS reader for more information on how to add a new subscription.

Step Four   You are free to start receiving information!

An example of a print screen using a news reader is shown in Exhibit 2.3.

How Can Nonprofits Benefit from This?

Currently many researchers and fundraisers are using either Google News or Yahoo! News to keep track of their prospects. Many are also using Yahoo! Finance for updated financial information.

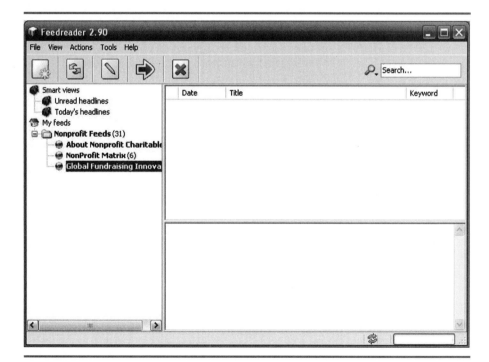

EXHIBIT 2.3   Newsreader Example

With RSS, you can now have all this information in your news reader and the reader will do all the work in searching for new content.

Example #1: Keeping Track of a Prospect with Google News   Let's imagine that Bill Gates and the Bill and Melinda Gates Foundation are prospects, and you want to know when they are in the news. You already have a subscription to Google News so you receive a daily email (sometimes two) whenever your prospect is in the news. If you have 10 prospects, that is a lot of email to review.

By using our news readers, we can set up the Google News RSS feed and each day we will only have one item to review.

The following are some basic steps for accomplishing this:

Step 1. Go to Google News (http://news.google.com/), enter your prospect name (in our case Bill Gates), and click Search News.

Step 2. When the results appear, there will be an RSS link on the left-hand side. Click this link.

Step 3. Copy the URL and add it to your subscriptions in your news reader.

Step 4. Repeat this for each prospect.

An example of a print screen from a news reader showing this is shown in Exhibit 2.4.

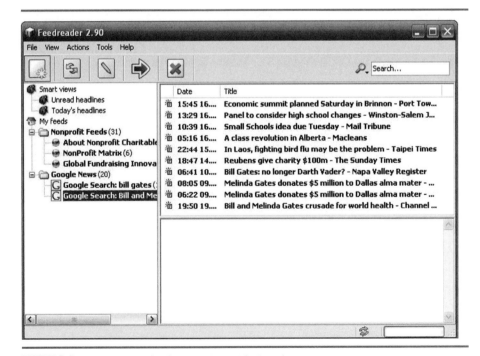

EXHIBIT 2.4   Keeping Track of a Prospect with Google

Example #2: Keeping Track of a Prospect through Yahoo! In addition to Bill Gates, you are also tracking Microsoft with Yahoo!, which allows you to subscribe to RSS feeds for the different public companies you are tracking. The following are some steps for setting this up:

Step 1. Go to the Yahoo! Company News web site (http://biz.yahoo.com/rss.html).

Step 2. Scroll down to the section titled "Yahoo! Finance Company News RSS URL Generator."

Step 3. Enter the stock symbol for the company you are tracking (MSFT in our example).

Step 4. Yahoo! will automatically generate the XML/RSS feed link you can enter in your browser (in our case: http://finance.yahoo.com/rss/headline?s=msft). An example of a printscreen using newsreader is shown in Exhibit 2.5.

Step 5. Copy this link and paste it in the subscriber information in your news reader. An example of a printscreen using a newsreader is shown in Exhibit 2.6.

Step 6. Repeat for each public company you are tracking.

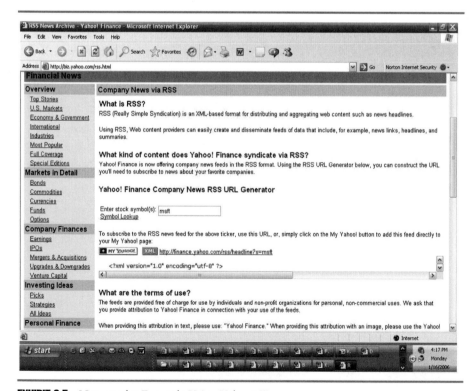

EXHIBIT 2.5   Newsreader Example Using Yahoo! Finance.

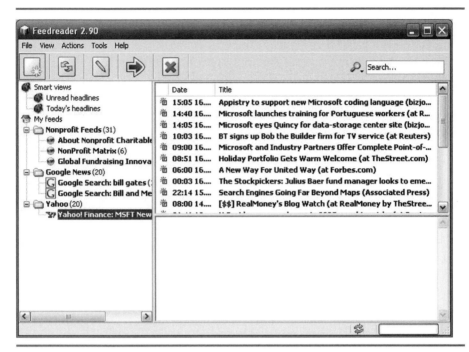

EXHIBIT 2.6 Newsreader Example with Company News Results

Short Glossary of Terms	
Term	**Short Definition and/or Examples**
Blog	Short for weblog and is a web-based communications tool, often described as an online journal, and regularly updated.
Feed readers or news readers	Examples are: Bloglines (www.bloglines.com) NewsGator Online (www.newsgator.com/home.aspx) My Yahoo! About Page on Feed Readers (http://email.about.com/od/rssreaderswin)
Feed sources for news alerts	Examples are: Topix.net (www.topix.net) Yahoo! News (www.yahoo.com) MSN Search (http://search.msn.com) Google Alert (http://googlealert.com) PubSub (www.pubsub.com)
Permalink	Is what makes a blog a blog
Ping	Sends a message through a network
RSS	Sends updated web content known as feed readers or news readers
Trackback	Tells someone that you've linked to them
XML	Is a feed-friendly markup language

CONCLUSION

The techniques described in this chapter—knowledge management, data mining and screening, and automated prospect tracking—are designed to make your job easier and more productive. Today's fundraisers and researchers are very busy people, working in an increasingly competitive environment. These tools, used selectively, can help nonprofit staff use their scarce time and resources effectively.

CHAPTER 3

Why Bill Gates May Not Be Your Best Prospect

Peter B. Wylie and David M. Lawson

Ninety percent of high-net-worth individuals support philanthropy. That simple fact means that the most likely reason you are not receiving support from an individual has nothing to do with the person's philanthropy, but rather her interest in your particular organization.

What we want to do in this chapter is help you generate a list of individuals who are not yet on your radar screen (i.e., they haven't yet made a major gift to your organization) but who meet these three criteria:

- They have the financial means to make a major gift.
- They have a high degree of attachment to your institution.
- They have a high degree of affinity to your institution.

Once you do that, we'll offer suggestions on how these individuals can best be approached. We can't guarantee each of them will welcome your appeals with open arms and large checks. Some may even turn you down as flatly as if you were a pesky telemarketer who calls in the middle of dinner. But some will offer to help. And some will surprise you: "Where have you been all these years? I love the _____. I was just waiting for someone to ask me for money."

Will these folks make as big a gift as Bill Gates would if he were a supporter of your institution? No, probably not. But, frankly, what chance do most organizations realistically have of getting a major gift from Bill Gates? With these folks, you'll have an excellent chance.

THREE IMPORTANT CONCEPTS: ABILITY, ATTACHMENT, AND AFFINITY

Shortly, we'd like to take you through some basic steps using examples from an actual higher education institution. Although some of it can be applied to your nonprofit, other points—regardless if they are applicable or not—should provide you with some ideas, insights, and direction. First let's talk about ability, attachment, and affinity, three important concepts that will guide your efforts to find good prospects for your institution's upcoming campaign.

Ability

On the face of it, ability to make a major gift seems pretty straightforward. Unless a prospect has the wherewithal to make the gift, it doesn't matter how well we research and cultivate that person. However, we think there are three factors worth considering when you assess someone's capacity to make a large contribution to your campaign:

- Volatility
- The prospect's sense of wealth
- Type of wealth

Volatility: The When of Asking

When you ask for a gift is influenced by many factors, some of which are internal, such as the timing of your campaign and your travel plans. If you are an East Coast charity, those San Francisco prospects are going to have to wait until you make the West Coast swing.

The problem is that a prospect's capacity to give can fluctuate a lot more than caring for your institution. They may love you when you arrive, but they may have a lot less money to show that love.

Let's look at three types of wealth:

- Public stock
- Private company
- Professional (e.g., lawyer or physician)

A quick look at today's winners and losers section of the stock page will tell all you need to know about the volatility of publicly traded stock. Sometimes the reasons are obvious: the company's earnings are down or the economy is affecting sales. Other times it makes little or no sense, but the stock falls out of favor and down it goes. If your prospect has most of their wealth in a particular stock and that stock loses half its value, your chance of success has fallen dramatically.

The ups and downs of a private company's fortunes don't get reported in the stock pages, but they can change just as dramatically. A big customer might decide to go with a competitor, or that competitor might create a new product that forces your prospect to put their assets into product development rather than your mission.

A lawyer's or a physician's fortunes depend on a combination of abilities, the value of the particular specialty, and competition. Personal injury attorneys have extremely volatile wealth; it rises and falls with the success of each case. A lawyer can spend years working on a case with little or no income, win the case and receive millions overnight, or lose and be out all the expenses with nothing to show for it.

The Prospect's Sense of Wealth

Closely tied to volatility is the prospect's sense of wealth. Over the years we have witnessed million-dollar asks turn into $50,000 gifts despite every indication that the prospect loved the mission, was ready to be asked, and had significant capacity. As we started to look at when the ask was made, we often found that the prospect's wealth had undergone a dramatic change since it was first identified. In one case a prospect had lost half the value of his publicly traded stock. He still owned $500 million in stock directly, but that same stock was worth a billion when the campaign started. Examples like this led us to realize that it was the prospect's sense of wealth, not the actual wealth, that was determining how much was given.

Type of Wealth

There are a lot of ways to become wealthy in America: winning the lottery, selling a business, and picking the next Microsoft before it's on the cover of *Business Week* are just a few. This is in addition to the people fortunate enough to inherit their wealth and/or marry into it. The way someone made money can have significant impact on that prospect's ability to give and also the type of gift likely to be made.

Let's start with an easy one: the lottery winner. Here is a person who was most likely not wealthy before and now suddenly has a whole lot of cash. The government is going to take its piece right off the top, so what's left is liquid wealth. A cash gift is the most likely vehicle for this individual in the short term. However, a number of lottery winners actually go bankrupt within three years. It would be a good idea to park some of that cash into planned giving vehicles that will ensure a lifetime of income and tax-free growth.

While most people do not win the lottery, the new generation of wealth has a lot in common with these lucky individuals. Eighty-three percent of today's millionaires is first-generation wealth. This means that the person who will be a major donor to your next campaign is more likely to be someone who is relatively unknown in your community.

The best example is the private company owner, also known as "the millionaire next door" we hear so much about. This prospect has about 20 percent of his wealth in liquid assets after owning the business for more than five years. That means 80 percent is tied up in the business. How do you unlock this wealth? If the person sells the business, you receive a gift of stock prior to the sale (for cash) and your institution (rather than the prospect) sells the stock. This saves capital gains and gives a tax break on the full value. Another scenario is a transfer of ownership to the next generation. A gift of stock can be made and then the next generation purchases the stock from you, again saving the prospect capital gains and giving a tax break.

For the prospect that bought the next Microsoft, giving is very easy. They're sitting on highly appreciated stock with a low-cost basis—the perfect conditions for a gift of stock. This may be outright or as part of a planned gift, depending on the prospect's age, family, and overall financial condition. A lot of donor-advised funds have been set up by this type of prospect, which means your institution will have to wait until the fund makes disbursements. Smart institutions are setting up their own donor-advised funds whereby a prospect can gift the assets, take the deduction, but wait to make a gift. The institution may stipulate that a certain percentage of the fund must ultimately end up being given to it.

Wealth comes in all types, sizes, ages, races, and both sexes. No two people worth the same amount of money are ever going to be quite the same in terms of ability. Knowing the implications of the type of wealth can help you craft a proposal that makes sense not only for your organization, but also for the prospect.

Attachment

In philanthropy, there is no single, widely agreed upon definition for attachment. This chapter defines attachment by breaking it down into two major components:

- Duration of giving
- Frequency of giving

Let's work through some examples from our sample data (from an actual higher education institution). We're looking at 7,000 prospects closely for our upcoming campaign.

- Over 1,600 of these prospects have never made a gift to our institution, so (obviously) their attachment is low. They have no duration of giving and no frequency of giving.
- We have about 400 prospects whose duration of giving is less than two years, but we've got over 250 prospects whose duration of giving is 28 years.
- We have about 400 prospects that have given us one gift, but we have a handful of prospects that have given us over 100 gifts.

If we're looking for people with high attachment, then clearly those folks who've given over a period of 28 years and have given upward of 100 gifts have very high attachment to our institution.

Affinity

Like attachment, affinity is a concept that has no widely agreed upon definition in philanthropy. If anything, it's a fuzzier term than ability or attachment because it does not involve any measure of dollar amounts (either of wealth or of giving).

So what exactly is affinity, anyway? In our view, affinity is an indication of a prospect's likelihood of giving to your institution even if she has never ever made a gift. "But," you say, "how can that be? How can you know someone's likelihood of giving if she doesn't have any history of giving?" Good questions; they get at the heart of a relatively new field in fundraising called data mining and predictive modeling. The basic logic of affinity goes like this:

In any fundraising database, there is nongiving information on each record. At the very least you have fields such as:

Prefix

First name

Middle name

Last name

State/province

Zip code/postal code

But even in small nonprofits you're likely to also have such fields as:

Home phone number

Business phone number

Email address

Date of birth

And if you're an independent secondary school or higher education institution, the number of nongiving fields can be lengthy indeed. To name just a few:

Year of undergraduate degree

Year of advanced degree(s)

Marital status

School within university where degree was received

Greek membership

Number of reunions attended

Volunteer activities

Well, as it turns out, a lot of this information is highly related to giving. Let's work through an example. Take a look at Exhibit 3.1, which shows the percentage of alums at a large university who fall at three different levels of lifetime giving: $0; $1 to $74; and $75 or more. (By the way, if you're surprised at how poor this giving picture looks, take a look at what it is for your own school. You may be unpleasantly surprised.)

Now take a look at Exhibit 3.2. It shows the difference in the percentage distributions at each of these three levels of giving for alums who have a home phone listed in the database versus those who don't. Clearly, alums who have a home phone listed are better givers than those who

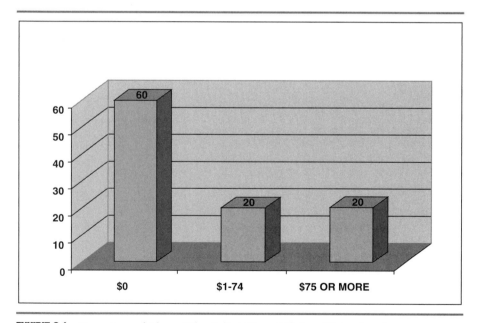

EXHIBIT 3.1 Percentage of Alums Who Fall at Three Lifetime Giving Levels

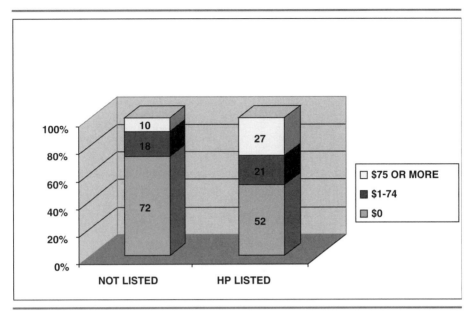

EXHIBIT 3.2 Percentage of Alums Who Fall at Three Lifetime Giving Levels by Whether Home Phone Is Listed

don't. Of those with a home phone listed, 48 percent have given something to the university (however little). Of those without a home phone listed, only 28 percent have given anything.

So let's imagine you're appealing by mail to alums who have not yet given your school anything. Let's further imagine that all you know about these nongiving alums is that they have a home phone listed or not. Which group do you think you'd be more likely to turn into first-time donors? The ones with a home phone listed or the ones without a home phone listed? That's what data mining and predictive modeling is all about: finding pieces of information in your prospect database that are related to giving and then combining them together into a score.

If you have any doubts about this, here is a little research project we recently undertook. For each of 10 four-year higher education institutions we created a simple score for a large random sample of alums based on these five pieces of information:

- Whether a home phone was listed in the database for an alum
- Whether a business phone was listed in the database for an alum
- Whether an email address (either personal or business) was listed in the database for an alum
- Whether an alum was either in the oldest or youngest 25 percent of alums
- Whether an alum was listed as missing in the marital status field

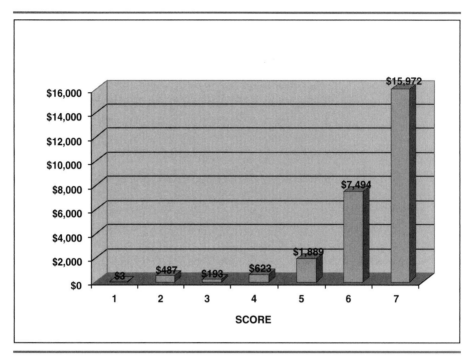

EXHIBIT 3.3   Mean (Average) Lifetime Money Given by Score Level at School A

If you're interested in the scoring formula we used with these data, you can look at the footnote.[1] Basically, the scores for each school ranged from 1 to 7 or 8. Exhibits 3.3 to 3.5 show the very strong relationship between these simple scores and lifetime giving at three of the 10 schools. The results showed the same kind of patterns for the other seven schools in our study.

Our point here is that affinity is a forceful concept whose time has come in philanthropy. To continue ignoring the powerful relationships between information in our donor/prospect databases and giving is unacceptable. Now that the Internet is part and parcel of our home and office lives, the concept of affinity is even more important. The traffic on our fundraising web sites is increasing at an exponential rate. A recent study showed that 65 percent of donors consult an organization's web site before making a gift. This provides an opportunity to learn about

---

[1]SCORE = HOME PHONE LISTED(0/1) + BUSINESS PHONE LISTED(0/1) + EMAIL(home and/or business) LISTED(0/1) + OLDEST GRAD CLASS QUAR-TILE(0/1) − YOUNGEST GRAD CLASS QUARTILE(0/1) − MARITAL CODE MISSING(0/1) − SINGLE(0/1) + 3
(The constant of 3 is simply a way to avoid negative and zero scores that just confuse people.)

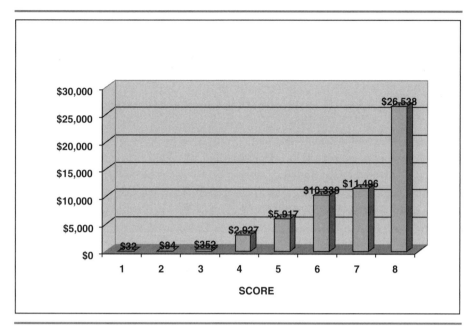

EXHIBIT 3.4   Mean (Average) Lifetime Money Given by Score Level at School B

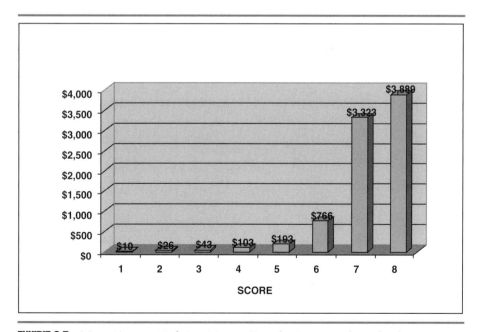

EXHIBIT 3.5   Mean (Average) Lifetime Money Given by Score Level at School C

prospective donors from the donors themselves. Many people believe that only the young are using the web, but the reality is that people 55 and older are the fastest growing users on the Internet. More important to you, a Pew Research study showed that 92 percent of people making more than $100,000 per year are actively on the Internet.

To not develop such behavioral indices based on these web interactions and turn them into predictors of giving is just leaving precious money on the table. Here are just a few that we can start to track:

- The number of emails from us that a prospect has opened
- How many times a prospect has clicked through to our web site after receiving an email
- Whether a prospect has registered as a member of our online community
- The average amount of time a prospect has spent exploring our web site after each log-on

HOW TO GENERATE A LIST OF HIGH-QUALITY PROSPECTS FOR YOUR CAMPAIGN

Up to this point we've explained the concepts of ability, attachment, and affinity, and we've tried to bring these concepts alive with concrete examples. That's great; but how do you take these concepts and generate a list of high-quality prospects (who've not yet made a major gift) for your upcoming campaign?

Admittedly, the details involved in creating such a list can get a bit complicated. No question about that. Nevertheless, we think the basic process for coming up with such a list is simple and straightforward. What we'd like to do in the rest of the chapter (for more information see Chapters 1, 2, and 9) is take you through some abbreviated steps in that process (using the actual pool of prospects mentioned earlier). Specifically, we'd like to show you how to:

- Isolate a group of prospects who have the ability to make a sizable gift
- Isolate a group of prospects who have high attachment to your institution
- Isolate a group of prospects who have high affinity to your institution
- Isolate a group of prospects who belong to all three groups (high ability, high attachment, and high affinity) but who have not yet made a major gift to use as your preliminary list of prospects

Isolating High-Ability Prospects

At this point in the process we're looking for a rough measure of ability to make a major gift. For the moment we're not concerned about the subtleties of volatility, the prospect's sense of wealth, or their type of wealth. So let's use a measure of overall ability provided by a reputable vendor screening company.

You'll remember that we're starting with a list of slightly over 7,000 names that are alums (most of them over 50) that we'd like to whittle down to a manageable list of prospects. Our vendor screening company has provided us with data that indicate that 569 of these alums have an estimated total wealth in excess of a half million dollars. This is clearly a group that has the wherewithal to make a large gift to our school. Several of them already have, but half of them have given us less than $2,500 lifetime, and about 6 percent or so have given us nothing at all.

Isolating Prospects with High Attachment

Earlier we defined attachment by breaking it down into two major components: duration of giving and frequency of giving. To simplify things here we've arbitrarily identified a group of slightly over 1,000 alums who have made a minimum of 19 gifts to our school and whose span of giving is at least 24 years. To us, that satisfied a reasonable criterion of high attachment.

As you might imagine, within this group there are some alums who have already given huge amounts to the school. However, well over 400 have given us less than $5,000 lifetime.

Isolating Prospects with High Affinity

With some quick analysis we were able to establish whether an alum was married or not, whether an alum had a business phone listed in the database, and whether an alum had attended at least one reunion since graduation were 3 dichotomous variables highly related to lifetime giving. Combining these variables into a very simple affinity score that went from 1 to 4, we identified 533 alums with a score of 4 who had a mean average lifetime giving of well over $100,000. However, at least half of these alums had given less than $5,000 lifetime, and close to a hundred had given less than $1,200 lifetime.

Isolating a Group of Prospects Who Belong to All Three Groups

Now we're ready to start narrowing in on prospects who belong to all three groups (high ability, high attachment, and high affinity) but who

	NUMBER OF PROSPECTS	MEDIAN LIFETIME $
ABILITY CUT	569	$2,925
ATTACHMENT CUT	114	$12,993
AFFINITY CUT	34	$23,350

EXHIBIT 3.6   Number of Prospects and Median Lifetime Giving at Each Cut

have not yet made a major gift to use as our preliminary list of prospects. Exhibit 3.6 shows the narrowing process we'll go through.

Since sports and reality show competition are so much a part of our culture, let's refer to this narrowing process as a series of cuts:

- Our first cut is the ability cut. As we said earlier, we've isolated 569 alums who have an estimated total wealth of at least $500,000. The median lifetime giving for this group is $2,925. That means at least half of this group has given our school less than $3,000 lifetime.
- Our next cut is the attachment cut. We've now narrowed the 569 alums down to a group of 114 who have an estimated total wealth of at least $500,000 and who have made a minimum of 19 gifts to our school and whose span of giving is at least 24 years. The median lifetime giving for this group is $12,993. That means at least half of this group has given our school less than $13,000 lifetime.
- Our next and final cut is the affinity cut. We've now honed the 569 alums down to a group of 34 who have an estimated total wealth of at least $500,000, who have made a minimum of 19 gifts to our school, whose span of giving is at least 24 years, and who were at the highest level (4) on our affinity score. The median lifetime giving for this group is $23,350. That means at least half of this group has given our school less than $24,000 lifetime.

Okay, so where are we here? Let's take a look (see Exhibit 3.7) at the lifetime giving of each of these 34 alums.

Kind of interesting, isn't it? If we look at alums #1 and #2 . . . everybody knows who they are, right? If they aren't already under serious stewardship, we have no business asking anyone for money. Let's work our way down the list to alum #14. That person has given us just under $50,000 lifetime. Is he on our radar screen for the upcoming campaign? Maybe. Probably not. Should #14 as well as everybody below that person

ALUM	LT $ GIVEN	ALUM	LT $ GIVEN
1	$22,332,998	18	$20,304
2	$ 7,748,129	19	$19,372
3	$ 521,669	20	$15,872
4	$ 287,659	21	$13,979
5	$ 245,190	22	$12,727
6	$ 229,407	23	$12,422
7	$ 220,575	24	$10,818
8	$ 207,621	25	$ 9,683
9	$ 175,443	26	$ 9,160
10	$ 115,641	27	$ 9,160
11	$ 58,606	28	$ 8,768
12	$ 58,606	29	$ 4,677
13	$ 50,436	30	$ 4,471
14	$ 49,707	31	$ 4,142
15	$ 43,987	32	$ 3,198
16	$ 31,483	33	$ 3,081
17	$ 24,892	34	$ 1,195

EXHIBIT 3.7   Lifetime Dollars Given by 34 Alums in Descending Order

be on our radar screen? We think so. Each of them has satisfied our criteria of high ability, high attachment, and high affinity.

At this point you may be thinking that this particular data sample is special. We can assure you it is not. What is special is any one individual's affinity and attachment. Their wealth has nothing to do with the organization, but affinity and attachment certainly do!

Should our research team do some more digging on these folks, keeping in mind the concepts of volatility and the prospect's sense of wealth and type of wealth as well as geographical location, etc.? Yes, of course; but any way you cut it, these alums are good prospects. Some of them are just waiting to be asked for a major gift, and we're pretty certain that they will give us a warmer welcome than Bill Gates when we go knocking on their doors.

We are living in a time of unprecedented wealth creation. For philanthropy this should mean that money would be donated to educate, heal, help, and work to solve the many challenges we face. Why, then, is philanthropy growing so slowly? We believe it is because we are so focused on the Bill Gates type of prospect, aka the usual suspects, that we are missing the Bill and Mary Smiths who are hiding in prospect databases waiting for someone to look beyond their current giving to see their ability, affinity, and attachment.

One final note: we both want to thank Bill Gates for his extraordinary philanthropy. There are a lot of children around the world who are healthy because of his efforts.

CHAPTER 4

Prospect Research Policy, Privacy, and Ethics

Stephen Lee and Susan Mullin

POLICY, ETHICS, AND PROSPECT RESEARCH

Prospect researchers are often the first point of contact with prospective major donors and play a crucial role in the identification and management of the donors' research profile throughout the life of support to the cause.

Good marketing, moral obligations, transparency, honesty, and the protection of individual privacy rights, together with an increasing incidence of legal regulation backed by financial, in some cases, criminal and other sanctions, make it imperative that all organizations engaged in structured research of donor personal information establish clear strategies and acceptable practices for the collation and management of data.

The Role of Prospect Research

Structured research into the giving capacity of key donor prospects has always been important to truly effective major gift solicitation.

The school endowments by Plato in Athens and Pliny at Como were carefully sourced: early committed giving schemes inspired by the emergence of the great religious faiths were recorded and analyzed by clerics to ensure full compliance according to means. The detailed fundraising strategies that ushered in the completion of the cathedrals of northern Europe required concerted investment in sophisticated prospect research techniques, while the creation of the great endowments and subsequent grand fundraising designs at Oxford, Cambridge, Harvard, etc., all found their grounding in the persistent application of individual prospect research undertaken and managed through informal, peer-to-peer networking programs.

In the modern idiom, the effective segmentation and management of donor intelligence systems are only made a practical reality through the application of systematic, detailed, prospect research techniques supported by the development of complex relational computer programs.

The Standing of Prospect Research in the Contemporary Context

In the contemporary context, the alliance between the power of the techniques available to researchers, the potential for intrusion that they afford, and the lack of public regulator and fundraising practitioner understanding the appropriate boundaries of practice has resulted in scrutiny of the methods employed in prospect research and the intention that it supports. This scrutiny has resulted in a growth of prohibitive regulation designed to inhibit proactive prospect research practice on both sides of the Atlantic.

This chapter outlines the nature of the privacy and data protection regulation that has sought to fill this prescriptive void, designed to protect the privacy rights of individuals. We start with an appreciation of the ethical and professional practice concerns that should be addressed when formulating strategies for major donor prospect research.

ETHICAL AND PROFESSIONAL PRACTICE CONSIDERATIONS

An Imbalance of Power

Marketing theory and the evidence of successful fundraising practice both demand that effective segmentation and targeting strategies are grounded on tested, empirical data best developed from detailed and highly personalized prospect research. Properly researched, appropriately targeted and supported solicitations create donors who are more content; they are more appropriately involved with their organization(s) and causes of their choice; and their commitment is properly recognized for the gifts they have made.

Major donor stewardship guides donor prospects through this process—a process often of self-awareness for the donor that, when it works well, is benign in nature and idealistic in motivation.

However, it is important to reflect on the fact that stewardship remains a highly prescriptive means-to-end-based process. When properly viewed from the perspective of the underlying motivation of the researcher and the organizational needs they are seeking to meet, it is focused upon the need for the donor to give to the maximum of her self-expressed capacity.

This is not to suggest that this process should always be viewed with suspicion in the mind of the donor or regulator, nor that it should be regarded as inappropriate activity on the part of the researcher, fundraiser, and the organizations that they serve. When applied properly, sophisticated marketing research and prospect research techniques can do much to enhance donor satisfaction and goal attainment.

Rather, this more considered view of the prospect research process and its place within the broader donor stewardship context simply reasserts the fact that an imbalance in power, skewed as it often is toward the information owner, characterizes the nature of these relationships. Without the development of appropriate safeguards, the potential for inappropriate practice is ever present.

This deeper understanding of the nature of the relationship between researcher/fundraiser and donor/prospect creates obligations on the part of the researchers/fundraisers and their institutions in the design, implementation, management, and accountability of their prospect research programs.

Prospecting organizations must decide before prospect research commences where the line should be drawn, in practice, between further intrusion into personal information and lifestyle of their existing and potential supporters and the enhanced ability that this might afford to raise levels of giving.

It is the responsibility of the prospect researcher and fundraiser to communicate the parameters of acceptable research practice across the organization before research and marketing activity commences. Researchers and fundraisers must act in accordance with these parameters at all times—monitoring, training, and managing often-disparate parts of the organization in the collation and analysis of prospect research data in a structured, transparent, and accountable manner.

Key Components of a Prospect Research Code of Practice

The practical outcome of these ethical and professional deliberations should lead to the development of a published framework, or code of practice, that supports all prospect research undertaken throughout the organization, or by third-party suppliers acting on its behalf.

Important elements contained within any such framework or code will necessarily be specific to the organization concerned. For example, matters pertaining to the nature of the cause served, the specific characteristics of the beneficiaries associated with the cause, the particular needs of special categories of donor prospects, the past history of fundraising activity and the place of prospect research within that history, the nature of the fundraising methods to be employed, the geographical scope of research prospecting, and a published policy position with regard to confidentiality and the uses to which data might be applied should all be outlined in the document in terms of their impact on prospect research practice.

There will also be the need to ensure that certain basic ethical principles are contained within the document and that these principals link directly to acceptable behaviors that will govern actual research practice. The essential elements that should be addressed in such a framework or code are set out in Exhibit 4.1, alongside the accepted behaviors and outcomes that they should be designed to invoke.

Major Donor Fundraising Code of Practice Including Prospect Research

The Institute of Fundraising in the UK (IOF) has developed an extensive category of fundraising codes and best practices (www.institute-of-fundraising.org.uk) that takes a look at some of the techniques utilized by fundraisers but mainly focuses on respecting and adhering to legal regulations and accountability issues. It does not cover how to do the fundraising, but the main points to be considered to ensure transparency and accountability to donors, prospects, and the public at large. All fundraising and prospect research professionals, regardless of the country they are based in, can benefit from this code of best practice. The IOF Major Donor and Major Donor Fundraising Code of Practice states that:

> *Major donor fundraising is about people and relationships. It involves the entire organization from the chief executive officer to the administrative assistant working as a team to secure the gift. It also involves the family, friends, and associates of the major donor informing the timing, size, regularity, purpose, and method of the gift and requires the fundraiser to be resourceful and responsive. Major donor fundraising is not an isolated process but a team effort, which yields a mutually beneficial outcome for all, yet it is very rarely done in an overt way. There are no broad-brush techniques and it can often be difficult to define the next step.*
>
> *Major donations aren't always planned. Nor are they always made for philanthropic or altruistic reasons, but, whatever the circumstances, the major donor should take pleasure in making the gift and the fundraiser or organization be pleased to receive it.[1]*

Prospect research best practices plays a big part in how we present ourselves and operate in a legal, ethical, and accountable manner whether

---

[1]Institute of Fundraising's Code of Practice for Major Donor Fundraising, September 2005, www.institute-of-fundraising.org.uk.

Best Practice	Professional Behavior
Content within a code of prospect research best practice should address:	Adherence to the code will promote professional behavior that ensures:
	✔ Truth-telling
✔ Respect for the value/dignity of individuals	
	✔ Promise-keeping
✔ Openness and honesty	
✔ Accountability to donors and donor prospects	✔ Transparency
✔ Tolerance, diversity, and social justice	✔ Fairness
✔ Prudent application of resources	✔ Respect for the wishes of the data subject
✔ Compliance with law and regulation	✔ Respect of personal privacy and confidentiality when requested
✔ A commitment beyond self-interest (individual and institutional)	
✔ A commitment beyond law	✔ Fidelity of purpose
✔ A commitment to the public good	
	✔ Security of the information held

EXHIBIT 4.1   A Framework for Prospect Research Code of Best Practice for All Fundraisers and Researchers

you are a fundraiser, researcher, executive, board member, or volunteer. For prospect researchers to be effective in their work and to ensure that donor satisfaction is not compromised, there is a need to be secure in the knowledge and implementation of the research methods that each non-profit utilizes.

Specific codes of accountability and codes of ethics have been and are being developed and implemented to adhere to current legal regulations and to meet expectations of donors, governments, and the public. Further information can be found in Chapter 11 by Jim Greenfield as well as The ePhilanthropy Code of Ethics found in the Appendix.

In the United Kingdom, the Institute of Fundraising (IOF) Code of Practice for Major Donor Fundraising identifies the following key skill requirements of proficient prospect researchers:[2]

- Understand how to analyze sources and data
- Understand the motives behind charitable giving
- Understand the fundraising and stewardship process
- Be proficient in locating and processing relevant information
- Understand and recognize wealth indicators

---

[2]Institute of Fundraising's Code of Practice for Major Donor Fundraising, September 2005, www.institute-of-fundraising.org.uk.

- Understand relative strengths and weaknesses of the sources they utilize
- Corroborate research findings where possible from multiple sources
- Cite sources used
- Be committed to applying information that is securely held, up to date, and relevant

Respect at all times for requests of confidentiality and donor anonymity is of the utmost importance if sustainable relationships are to be cemented and the stewardship process not compromised.

Poor Compliance Equals Lost Donors

Ensuring conformity to codes of best practice in this area is not simply a matter of determining what is right and wrong practice. Compliance with the basic principles and assured behaviors that comprise these codes also lies at the heart of what constitutes effective relational marketing and relationship fundraising theory and practice.

Poorly applied prospect research leads to the wrong request being made, at an inappropriate time, to the wrong donor. Donor prospects who are lied to, who have promises broken, or who are uncomfortable with the information held about themselves or their family and friends will quickly become donors who are less than satisfied with the stewardship relationship and will take their support elsewhere.

The Challenge of Data Protection Legislation

The explosion of access to personal information afforded by advances in information technology, the emergence of the Internet, and the growing sophistication of interrelational computer databases have cemented the importance of prospect research to contemporary major donor acquisition and development programs.

Across the globe there has been a steady growth in data protection legislation that has created a complex framework of regulation designed specifically to protect individual privacy rights and to constrain the capacity of marketing research in favor of those rights.

Nonprofit prospect research is not immune from the majority of provisions that have been imposed upon marketing research and consumer intelligence data gathering by these frameworks. Designed to address perceived inequities in the ability of commercial enterprises to amass personal information, these frameworks often pay scant attention to the specific concerns of the major donor prospect researcher and the stewardship processes they serve.

DATA PROTECTION REGULATION: THE EUROPEAN APPROACH

The European Community (EC) has led the world in the development of contemporary data protection legislation, spurred on by the construction of a single European trading entity.

Historically, with some notable exceptions, European regulators have maintained a broadly liberal view on the need to protect the general public from potentially abusive use of personal data by third-party organizations.

For example in the UK context, the Data Protection Act of 1984, while establishing a wide-ranging regulatory system impacted the management of personal data for marketing purposes, it did so in a largely benign manner.

At its core, compliance for fundraising, marketing, and prospect research purposes was achieved by the presence of an opt-out statement at the point of data acquisition on all relevant fundraising and marketing communications. Having provided the data subject with the clear opportunity to opt out of the intended processing, should the opt-out opportunity not be exercised by the data subject, the nonprofit organization could then legitimately acquire and hold the personal information for the purpose of fundraising in practice for as long as it felt it needed to.

Implementation of the EC Data Protection Directive

The European directive addressing data protection (EU Dir. 95-46 EC) changed the nature of the obligations placed upon marketers and researchers under the new regulations and expanded the scope of regulation to include both computerized and certain types of manually held personal data, together with provisions affecting data acquired and processed electronically (by telephone, email, or Internet) at home and abroad.

The new measures were approved in 1995 and required all member states of the time to implement complementary national legislation within a three-year period.

Only limited areas within this overriding regulatory regime were left to national interpretation in order to support equality of trading practice throughout the single market.

European Data Protection Legislation: Key Requirements Impacting upon Prospect Research

At its heart the regulation revolves around new and expanded definitions of what constitutes personal data and the processing of that personal data: compliance with the identified Data Protection Principles; the protection of data subjects' rights during the course of processing; and compliance by Data Controllers with the Fair Processing Codes established within the legislation.

Central to the interpretation of these new definitions and concepts for prospect researchers are the breadth of scope of what constitutes personal data caught within the regulations; obligations to register the nature and scope of fundraising for which personal data will be acquired; obligations placed upon researchers with respect to the acquisition of personal data—not least in the nature of the *consent* required in each instance and in the attainment of personal data from third-party sources; the lawful management of international personal data flows; procedures for data retention and archiving; requirements ensuring subject access to data held about them; and provisions for ensuring data accuracy and security.

NOTIFICATION AND REGISTRATION

In each case, national governments have established broadly complementary procedures for the notification or registration of data processing intention by data controllers. Registration/notification of intent is mandatory in nature and more often than not legitimizes the right to engage in data collection and processing activity specific marketing function, by function.

Fundraising organizations will need to ensure therefore that each of the specific marketing functions that comprise their overall fundraising and marketing activities achieves appropriate registration. Marketing research, and in this particular context, the engagement in prospect research, forms one such specific function alongside fundraising, trading in data, and marketing more generally applied in the nonprofit context.

The purpose of these registration schemes is to ensure that members of the public have some public recourse to be aware that specific organizations have registered to engage in specific types of data collection and processing activity. It follows that in most cases, while nonregistration is itself an offense to be avoided, registration alone does not secure effective compliance with the data protection regulations.

CONFORMITY WITH DATA PROTECTION PRINCIPLES

While specific national interpretation of the EC directives varies somewhat between individual states, key principles associated with the maintenance of appropriate data protection practice have been established across the community.

Regulation invariably identifies, in statute, the core requirements or basic data protection principles that must be achieved and maintained by organizations processing personal data at all times. In the United Kingdom, for example, there are eight such principles reflecting the scope of the regulation originally envisaged in the European Community directives:

Personal data shall be:

Processed fairly and lawfully.

Obtained only for one or more specified and lawful purposes, and shall not be further processed in any manner incompatible with that purpose or those purposes.

Adequate, relevant, and not excessive in relation to the purpose or purposes for which they are processed.

Accurate and, where necessary, kept up to date.

Processed in accordance with the rights of data subjects identified in the Act.

Held in secure manner at all times.

Personal data shall NOT be:

Kept for longer than is necessary for any purpose or purposes.

Transferred to a country or territory outside the European Economic Area, unless that country or territory ensures an adequate level of protection of the rights and freedoms of data subjects in relation to the processing of personal data.[3]

Fundraising organizations must comply with each of these requirements, in full, in every aspect of their acquisition and management of a donor prospect's personal information.

Clearly there are specific challenges for the prospect researcher engaged in preemptive prospect research undertaken prior to any formal contact having been made with that prospective donor.

Further challenges emerge in the ongoing management of personal information—how broadly defined can the nature of the personal data held on a major donor prospect be, given that data can only be held legitimately if it is deemed *adequate, relevant, and not excessive* to purpose and retained for a limited time span?

Fundraising organizations will need to ensure that all personal data is held in a secure manner at all times. This presumes that prospect research undertaken to support local major gift campaigns within a national or

---

[3]*The Data Protection Act 1998*, HMSO 1994.

international NGO's are subject to rigorous management that affords effective compliance in all cases.

It will also require diligence on the part of the prospect researcher tasked with managing personal data acquired from volunteer sources, often in an informal manner.

It presumes an obligation upon prospect researchers that where major donor personal data is acquired and transported across international boundaries by means of personal contact, written material, or use of electronic media, the fundraising organization will ensure that effective compliance procedures, similar to those in operation in the European Community, have been used in data capture.

Prospect researchers need to be clear about what constitutes the rights of major donors/prospects when constructing their research databases. Data subject access (a right of access to all personal information held on a person) is enshrined within the European Directive. Prospect researchers will need to ensure, therefore, that their administrative systems are structured in such a manner that they can comply with information requests about the nature of the personal information held by them from major donors and prospects. Failure to comply is in most instances a criminal offense.

It is important to note that effective compliance with subject access obligations may, in itself, lead to committal of further, unrelated offenses (i.e., slander or libel) if the information held is deemed offensive or excessive by the data subject. Given that donors and prospects have the right to see *all* the personal information that you hold on them, it follows that prospect researchers will want to review and screen the quality of data held across the entire prospect research database to ensure that inaccurate, idiosyncratic, or offensive data, when viewed from the perspective of the data subject, is not recorded!

CONSENT

The issue of achieving consent from the data subject for the purpose of acquiring and holding personal information that pertains to them is central to the achievement or otherwise of the continuing overall legitimacy to hold their personal data at all.

The original EC Directive defines *consent* as[4]:

> *... any freely given specific and informed indication of his wishes by which the data subject signifies his agreement to personal data relating to him being processed.*

---

[4]EU Directive 95/46/EC.

By any interpretation this is a harsh test and one that fundraisers and prospect researchers will need to meet in practice with all donors and volunteers if personal information is to be held over an extended period of time.

In the United Kingdom, further guidance on the interpretation of the practical obligations placed upon fundraisers and prospect researchers with regard to achieving consent identifies that simply doing nothing . . . remains a dangerous option.

> *The fact that the data subject must "signify" his agreement means that there must be some active communication between the parties. A data subject may "signify" agreement other than in writing. Data controllers cannot infer consent from nonresponse to a communication, for example from a [donor's] failure to return or respond to a leaflet.*[5]

More generally, through the European continent, prospect researchers will want to feel comfortable that appropriate communications exist with current major donors and identified prospects to ensure that they revalidate legitimate use of personal data held for fundraising and marketing purposes in an active, ongoing, and measurable fashion.

The Practical Achievement of Consent

In practice, prospect researchers have two alternate options to choose from when deciding how, in practice, to ensure that the major donor or prospect concerned has consented to the holding of their personal data in a legitimate manner.

At the point of first contact with the individual (remember this might well be a contact achieved by the prospect researcher, a fundraiser, a board member, or volunteer), the individual concerned should be offered the opportunity to either opt in to the holding of their information by the organization, or given the explicit opportunity to opt out.

Should the data subject decline the opportunity to opt in or exercise their right to opt out, the prospect researcher will need to ensure that all personal data relating to that individual is removed from records held by the organization, save for the retention of sufficient skeletal information necessary to ensure that if further information becomes available at a later date pertaining to that individual, it is not inadvertently introduced into the organization's records.

Across Europe, the pattern of reliance between the prescribed use of opt-in communications as opposed to opt-out varies nation by nation. Germany, Denmark, Sweden, Finland, and Italy all require opt-in compliance.

---

[5]Data Protection Act 1998: Legal Guidance, p. 29.

Elsewhere, opt-in arrangements are still normally required for personal information regarded as sensitive in nature (i.e., information relating to sexuality, medical condition, religious or political convictions, etc.). Nonsensitive personal data can be held legitimately through provision of an opportunity made to the donor at the first point of contact to opt out of the relationship.

Here again, prospect researchers need to develop institutionalized guidance to take account of differing circumstances. A religious-based fundraising organization may feel it is particularly important to record personal details of a religious nature; similarly, in order to avoid embarrassment or upset, an organization established to address a medical condition may wish to record incidence of that condition among major donor prospects and those close to them. In each case, determination will need to be made by express, written judgment on the part of the prospect research/fundraiser concerned, whether or not the information held is sensitive in nature and therefore requires an opt-in response as opposed to an *opt-out* nonresponse from the donor.

Finally, it is important to note that consent should be achieved at the *first* point of contact with the major donor or prospect. This might actually be achieved in circumstances that are not specifically related to major donor development programs at all (i.e., through previous attendance at a fundraising event, a gift in response to direct marketing activity, etc.). It is important, therefore, that prospect researchers ensure that their data protection compliance needs are understood across the entire fundraising function and that compliance statements are carefully crafted to be inclusive of all future fundraising and volunteering activity wherever contact with a donor or major donor prospect might first be initiated.

Personal Information Acquired from Third Parties

Major donor prospect research often records insights and intelligence achieved from sources other than the donor prospects themselves. Where this occurs, the information is clearly already held in the public domain (i.e., from published material such as newspapers, lifestyle magazines, etc.). As long as the material collected is not sensitive in nature, nor regarded as excessive or inaccurate in form and is directly pertinent to the proposed future fundraising activity for which it is held, then that information can be legitimately captured as a precursor to direct contact with the donor prospect in question. Where this practice is undertaken on a routine basis to support ongoing major donor development programs, for example, the nature of the data protection consent statement provided to prospects at the first point of contact should be drafted accordingly.

Great care should be taken when sourcing third-party intelligence, either from individuals with some connection to, or expressed knowledge of, the prospect concerned (as in the case of peer-based, private fundraising campaigns), or where the authenticity of the intelligence offered might be subject to inaccuracy or misinterpretation (i.e., random search engine web-based outcomes, unpublished documents, or published documents whose source might be questioned). Not only might the information achieved be misleading or defamatory, if this is a routine prospect research function within your organization, be mindful of the fact that in some countries all prospects and donors have a right to be aware (and to be made aware) of the personal information held about them that has originated from sources other than themselves.

Retaining Personal Data and Archiving Personal Information

Personal data held on major donors and donor prospects can only be retained for the length of time associated with the specific purpose(s) for which they were obtained. While donors remain active givers as long as the organization revalidates its legitimate use to hold the data by a regular opt-out opportunity for the data subject personal information can continue to be held for that purpose.

Where major donors lapse or when specific, time-limited appeals come to a conclusion, prospect researchers will have to make judgments about the length of time it remains legitimate to retain or add to a donor's personal information file. Prospects and donors, even lapsed donors that have previously agreed to be kept in touch with future funding plans, can be legitimately retained on the prospect file as can past major givers for whom further funding opportunities might be developed in the future. But where personal information is retained on prospects that have stopped supporting or who have never supported, a time line should be established after which their personal data will be removed from the database or archived in a manner that lies outside the scope of the regulations.

Personal Information Acquired via the Internet

Where prospect researchers wish to acquire personal information via the Internet utilizing their own web site or through hosting achieved on other sites, it is important that in each instance the site location provides clear information to the user (the prospective data subject) that personal information is being captured, together with a statement indicating the purpose(s) for which that data is being captured.

This statement should be displayed in a prominent and intelligible manner at *all* points where the collection of personal data might occur. It is not sufficient to simply allude to a privacy statement accessed elsewhere by *click-through* or to rely upon a detailed statement made only once (i.e., on the home page) and removed from the actual point of data capture. To ensure compliance and *best practice,* the statement should be made at all points of potential personal data capture.

When linked directly to fundraising activity, the collection of personal data via your web site must provide an opportunity for the data subject to express their consent either through the application of an *opt-in* prompt or through provision of an *opt-out* alternative, provided at each point of possible personal data capture. Researchers will need to be mindful that the specific regulations applicable in this regard will vary. In each case, the regulations currently applicable where the web site is operated are the regulations that should be followed.

Where contracted suppliers capture personal data on your behalf, on your web site or on other sites (i.e., credit rating services, specialist services associated with the secure electronic capture of donations, etc.), all parties collecting the data must be identified to the donor.

It should be noted that the use of *spiders* or other scavenger-type computer programs used to collect donor prospect *email* addresses is in violation of the ePhilanthropy Code of Ethics (see appendix).

Publishing (Posting) Major Donor Personal Information on the Internet

Care should also be taken when considering publishing major donor personal information on the organization's web site or elsewhere on the Internet. In the European data protection context, there are restrictions imposed upon data controllers transferring data outside the European Economic Area. Publication or free access posting of personal information on your web site potentially offers global access to the personal data and could lead to the transfer of that personal data to inappropriate parties. Where possible, researchers or fundraisers should gain the explicit consent of donors or prospects before any personal information pertaining to them is published or posted on a web site. Security and international transfer issues can be mitigated in certain situations through use of password-protected procedures or alternative restricted access techniques.

Personal Data Capture Undertaken within the EC by Organizations Located Outside the EC

In certain circumstances, prospect researchers engaged in international fundraising campaigns located outside the EC may need to capture personal information pertaining to potential prospects residing within the EC. To do so they might access web sites located with the European community.

Where activity is conducted electronically by Internet or by *email* it will be caught by European data protection regulation if the web site operator located outside the European Economic Area (EEA) uses equipment located within the EEA to facilitate the processing of the data. This might occur when an operator located outside the EEA has a site hosted within a European community nation state(s) or where an international operator places a *cookie* on the computer of a European Internet user in order to facilitate the creation of a profile of that individual's online giving behavior.

Where personal information is captured or processed by international organizations headquartered outside the EEA, if the data processing activity itself is located within the EEA area, it will be caught by the regulations applicable in the state of residence that the organization is using for the purpose of that processing activity.

DATA PROTECTION REGULATION: THE NORTH AMERICAN APPROACH

To remain competitive and transact business in today's global economy, North America has followed the lead of the European Union (EU) in developing legislation and regulation to protect individual privacy rights. Compared to Europe, Canada and the United States are relative latecomers to regulation protecting the collection of personal information.

In 2002, the European Commission ruled that Canada's federal privacy legislation met the adequacy standards of the EU directive, allowing for the continued flow of personal information between Europe and Canada.

As a response, the U.S. Department of Commerce, in consultation with the European Commission, developed the *safe harbor* framework, allowing companies adhering to the framework to avoid experiencing interruptions in their business dealings, including the transfer of personal information, with the EU.

Professional fundraising associations including the Association of Fundraising Professionals (AFP), the Association of Professional Researchers for Advancement (APRA), and the Association for Healthcare Philanthropy (AHP) have been working hard to influence the most restrictive elements of proposed state, provincial, and federal legislation.

The View in the United States

In the United States, the approach to protecting the privacy of individuals has taken many forms, from self-regulation to legislation.

Information deemed to be highly sensitive, including personal health information, is protected by federal legislation. The Health Information Portability and Accountability Act (HIPAA) of 1996 lays out rules on the collection, use, and disclosure of personal information, including addressing how this information may be used for marketing and fundraising.

With nonprofits organized under state law, U.S.-based fundraising professionals must refer to both federal and state law to fully understand the regulatory framework under which they must operate. However, for the most part in the United States, the charitable and nonprofit sectors rely on self-regulation and codes of professional practice and ethics to guide their privacy and protection of personal information business practices.

The View in Canada

In January 2001, new privacy legislation took effect that would ultimately impact all organizations, including charities. The new act, the Personal Information Protection and Electronic Documents Act (PIPEDA), establishes ground rules on collection, use, or disclosure of personal information in the course of commercial activities "including the selling, bartering, or leasing of donor, membership, or other fundraising lists." The direct inclusion of specific fundraising activities in the legislation caused the charitable and not-for-profit sector in Canada to carefully consider how PIPEDA would impact fundraising activities, including prospect research.

Defining Personal Information (Canada)

Personal information means information about an identifiable individual, but does not include the name, title, or business address or telephone number of an employee of an organization. It includes factual and subjective information that may be used to identify, distinguish, or contact a specific individual including religious affiliation, opinions, beliefs, financial information, birth date, memberships, home address, education, etc.[6]

Canadian organizations are not governed by federal legislation alone. To date, Quebec, Alberta, and British Columbia each have passed privacy laws deemed by the Federal Privacy Commissioner to be "substantially similar" to PIPEDA. Additionally, many provinces have specific legislation

---

[6]Adapted from *Complying with the PIPED Act,* Office of the Privacy Commissioner of Canada.

dealing with personal health information that impacts the fundraising data collection activities of these organizations.

Sanctions for organizations that are found by the Privacy Commissioner of Canada (or the province where substantially similar legislation exists) to have breached the legislation range from recommendations for changes to information management practices to application for recourse at the federal court where any manner of orders to correct practices, public notices, and award monetary damages may be applied.

This complex web of federal and provincial privacy legislation has resulted in a heightened awareness and commitment by charities and not-for-profit organizations to protect the privacy rights of individuals. Organizations that work across provincial, territorial, and national boundaries are being forced to comply with different and, in some cases, conflicting sets of regulation. More important, organizations recognize that individuals—their major donors and prospects—have heightened expectations of accountability and transparency from the organizations they choose to support.

It is within this context that Canadian organizations have implemented privacy policies to protect the personal information they collect, use, or disclose in support of major gift and other fundraising activity.

The CSA Model Code: Privacy Principles

Federal and provincial privacy legislation share one common element: they are built around 10 privacy principles outlined in the Canadian Standards Association (CSA) Model Code for the Protection of Personal Information (see appendix for the list of principles and definitions in the code). These principles provide the framework on which professional fundraisers approach prospect research and data collection.

Compliance with these principles provides confidence that organizations meet the federal requirements of PIPEDA, and other provincial privacy legislation.

The Privacy Code covers two broad issues: the manner in which organizations collect, use, disclose, and safeguard personal information; and the right of individuals to access personal information about themselves, and, if necessary, to have that information corrected.

APPLYING PRIVACY PRINCIPLES
TO PROSPECT RESEARCH

Understanding what personal information an organization already collects and for what purpose is a good first step to applying privacy principles such as those contained in the CSA Model Code. An audit of the current personal information within a fundraising organization's control will provide many insights into aligning business practice with key privacy principles. In the case of PIPEDA, personal information collected prior to the enactment of privacy legislation is governed by the same set of rules as information collected since the legislation came into force. For activities covered specifically under PIPEDA, all personal information, regardless of date of collection, must be treated the same.

Legislation and the privacy principles require that individuals may withdraw consent at any point and that organizations must provide meaningful opportunities for donors and prospects to do just that on an ongoing basis. In the case of major donor prospect research, implied consent may be assumed. This relies on the premise that a prospect would reasonably expect an organization to have gathered certain personal information prior to a first or other contact. The data subject must be given an opportunity at first contact to opt out or to withdraw this consent.

With potentially sensitive personal information, researchers must carefully assess the appropriateness of recording this information without the data subject's express or opt-in consent. This may include information provided by volunteers in the context of prospect review, or information gleaned from unsubstantiated sources, including some Internet sites.

Prospects and donors have the right to view, within a reasonable period of time, all personal information in their files. Organizations must provide access to all print and electronic files, including central and *working* files held by staff. One test for the appropriateness of personal information collected by an organization is to consider how a data subject would react to seeing this information in their file.

Information in the Public Domain

In the age of the Internet, it is easy to assume that information obtained through a simple online search of a data subject would be considered *public domain* and therefore open to be collected and retained without consent. PIPEDA does include some consideration for information in the public domain, but it should be noted that this information is relatively limited in scope. First, the principles of limiting collection to that which is necessary for the intended purpose (in this case major gift cultivation and solicitation) and of limiting use, disclosure, and retention of personal information to the purpose for which it was originally collected (at the source of collection) preclude some information in the public domain from being collected, used, or disclosed. Furthermore, personal information that appears in a publication, including a magazine, book, or newspaper, in printed or electronic form, may only be considered *public* if the individual has provided the information. This may include an interview with, or a quote from, the data subject, but not an opinion piece written about the data subject.

The fact that information may be found in the public domain does not preclude researchers from considering the ethical principles related to its collection, use, and disclosure.

Assuring Compliance with Regulation and Best Practice

The capture and management of personal information for marketing and fundraising purposes is a sensitive and important strategic issue for any nonprofit organization engaged in major donor fundraising and prospect research.

In the context of nonprofits, it is likely that the core values underpinning the vision and mission of the organization at the strategic level will require or command the existence of a published privacy policy that directly addresses the needs of beneficiaries, donors, and other key stakeholder groups. This should be the first step for the prospect researcher in the design and application of a prospect research strategy and code of professional practice. It should provide practical demarcation of the acceptable boundaries for recording donor personal information.

If such a policy does not exist, prospect researchers should work with fundraisers and other key professionals within the organization to ensure board and senior management commitment to the adoption and implementation of such a policy.

General privacy policy apart, the fundraising and marketing functions will need to develop a combined framework or code of acceptable practice designed to govern market research activity in general and to ensure full compliance with data protection regulation across all pertinent activities undertaken throughout the organization.

THE ROLE OF PROFESSIONAL ASSOCIATIONS AND INTERMEDIARY BODIES

There is an increasing background of guidance and advice designed to support major donor prospect researchers in the design and implementation of effective and appropriate prospect research strategies.

- International fundraising professional associations (AFP, AHP, IOF, SAIF, and the ePhilanthropy Foundation) provide general codes of fundraising practice that can be tailored and applied to the prospect research function.
- International fundraising professional associations also provide more specialized guidance on major donor research strategy development

and data protection regulation compliance, often compiled by research practitioners experienced in the practical application of policy to the field.

- ■ National marketing and direct marketing professional associations provide guidance on data protection policies and the generation of appropriate privacy statements applicable to the management of manual, computerized, and Internet and e-based marketing activity.
- ■ International trade bodies, nonprofit and commercial, provide guidance and advice on the international transfer of personal data developed for marketing and fundraising purposes.
- ■ Governmental agencies with responsibility for the regulation and enforcement of data protection regulation provide guidance and support on effective compliance procedures.

Above all else, the effective and appropriate prospect research professional will start with the vision, mission, organization, and fundraising strategy of the institution they seek to serve and will construct a major donor prospect research strategy that ensures the security of trust and confidence from existing and potential major donors at all times, and which promotes the construction of individual donor research profiles that are rigorous in development, relevant to the needs of the organization to raise funds in an efficient and effective manner, and which enables major donors to meet their own expectations through the gifts they make with freedom of choice.

CHAPTER 5

U.S. and Canadian Strategies

Pamela Gignac and Kristina Carlson

A TALE OF PERSPECTIVES

There is a story of two stonecutters sitting amongst a pile of stones, chipping away at small blocks. They were asked what they were doing, and one said, "I am cutting stone" while the other replied, "I am building a cathedral." (Another version of the stonecutter story involves a man cleaning the floor for an office at the NASA space center. When he was asked what he was doing working so late at night he replied: "I am helping to put a person on the moon.") This sense of a goal and perspective on your work adds a new dynamic to the activities you undertake. It is the dynamic of purpose in what you are doing.

Effective fundraising and research determines not only the direction but also the success of securing support for the work of your charity. Even when there is no recognition for the work of a researcher, it is important to remember that the researcher is the stonecutter building the cathedral.

This chapter emphasizes the importance of research in fundraising success and looks at strategies for research and development across the United States and Canada.

It's a Small World

When it comes to finding information on our donors and prospects, it truly is a small world. Many prospects have business and/or personal interests in various countries around the world. This is particularly true of those prospects connected to public or private companies, but it can also include other high-profile individuals as well as celebrities and sports personalities. More and more, we are finding that we have much to learn about prospect research and fundraising from other nations.

In North America, we are intricately involved with our closest neighbors, particularly between the United States and Canada. Individuals may own property and split time in various countries. Businesses might have employees in more than one country. So, it is highly possible that U.S. sources of information might have information on a prospect that you could not find in Canada and vice versa. The same could be true in the United Kingdom, Europe, China, and Japan. It depends on the business and/or the individual as to which ones would be applicable to them.

Being aware of strategies and techniques used in other countries enhances our professional understanding, conduct, and growth and helps us learn from each other about legislation and fundraising ideas that work. For example, privacy and accountability are a growing global concern, not the least due to the Internet and availability of information. Legislation limiting access to information in one country could impact what we experience at home down the road. This topic is covered in greater detail in Chapter 4, "Prospect Research Policy, Privacy, and Ethics."

This chapter focuses on specific U.S. and Canadian prospect research strategies, sources, and techniques. The next chapter, "International Strategies—Europe and Asia," covers the international perspective in more detail.

STRATEGIES FOR RESEARCH AND APPROACH

Organizations seem to have an unending need for funding and a multitude of options for raising funds. Yet successful organizations with strong fundraising programs understand the importance of framing their efforts with measurable goals and objectives. A whole industry exists in methodologies for setting plans and objectives that are measurable. Keep everyone focused with objectives that are SMART—Specific, Measurable, Attainable, Realistic, and set in a Time frame.

Prospect Research Strategies

So how do you focus prospect research? First, understand the key components of a strategy that are applicable to any organization, of any size, in any country.

Here are five main areas that need to be addressed within a basic research strategy:

1. What are our objectives?
   - Financial
   - Development
   - Organizational growth or change
2. How will new prospects be identified, and how will we learn more about our current donors?

- Planning and implementing an effective research program
- Identifying and using the resources available
- Finding ways to approach prospects
- Defining preliminary approach strategies
- Revising approach strategies

3. What resources will be required?
   - Press cutting service
   - Internet searches and information retrieval including press articles, using free sources whenever possible
   - Access to some specialized fee-based online information and service providers
   - Library of key directories
   - Fundraising database system
   - Staff and volunteers to do research

4. How will the information be managed?
   - Manage and regularly update information
   - Database and filing systems
   - Coordination, facilitation, and searching of links through relationships for prospects and donors
   - A relational database
   - Analysis of information by researchers and fundraisers
   - Identify prospects and their contacts for short-term and long-term fundraising needs

5. When do we need more in-depth research, and how will it be accomplished?
   - Research and first-hand experience constantly add to the approach strategy
   - Collation, coordination, and implementation of intelligence learned
   - Sharing information with others—staff, volunteers, board members, and fundraising team

Using Research to Develop Approach Strategies

With an overall prospect research strategy in place, you can begin to research specific prospects in order to identify the best approach for solicitation. What you actually apply will be based upon what is known about prospects, how close they are to you, and how closely you match their interests. You also must consider whether they are new prospects or current donors, and identify someone respected by them to assist you in your approach.

In order to determine the individual approach strategy for each prospect, you should answer these questions:

- How do their interests match the work and mission of your organization?
- Who within your organization has the best access to them?
- How will you touch them (communicate, contact, ask, fundraising, etc.)? In what way?
- Is additional cultivation needed before a solicitation? If so, what steps will you take them through—what various actions should you implement to capture interest and maintain support?
- What contact vehicles will you use and in what combination (if any)?
  - Telephone
  - Written communication
  - Face-to-face meetings
  - Electronic communication
- Is your research valid? How often will you update it? How long should it be maintained and kept on file?
- Are you maintaining prospect progress reports? Will they be kept in a central confidential file? Who will be responsible for updating this information on the database?
- Who will have primary responsibility for managing the relationship with each prospect? Who will be the coach? Who will manage the process? Who will ask? When?
- What stewardship will apply? Is the prospect interested in recognition levels?
- How will you thank them and ensure that they know who you are and what you are doing? How will you share successes with them and keep them informed?
- How will you activate relationship-building communication?
- How will you advance their donor development to the next stage of giving?
- Do you know when to approach again if unsuccessful?
- Can they open doors for you to other potential donors?
- Are you thanking them again and again?

As you answer these questions, keep in mind that impersonal data gathering has its limits. At some point, someone will have to meet with the prospect in order to really understand what approach will lead to a significant gift.

The Approach Strategy

The fundraising elements of approaching donors are covered in Chapter 10, "Moving from Prospect Identification to Making Friends for Life." Here we deal with the research elements of the approach.

An approach strategy is an organized way to plan your work with a prospect. How are you going to approach this donor, keeping in mind your objective of securing a major gift? What will you do to get your donor ready and most likely to say yes to your ask?

Think of yourself as a director of a play. Your prospect is the star of the production. Your key actors are the others involved in the approach—your staff, volunteers, board members, and other donors.

Your approach strategy is the script. It should include:

Stage One:
- What are you going to do to line yourself up to be ready?
- What is your production outline?
- What do you need to be ready to put on your production or play?
- Who are your actors, players—partners?

Stage Two—Making the Ask:
- What is your open, introductions, purpose, intent, and close?
- How will you design your scenes?
- What lines are assigned to your actors?

Stage Three:
- What follow-up is required?
- Have you kept a prospect progress report?
- What stewardship will apply?
- What are the appropriate recognition levels?
- How will you activate relationship-building communication?
- How will you advance donor development to the next stage of giving?
- When should you approach again if unsuccessful?
- Have you asked them to open doors for you?
- Have you thanked them again and again?
- How can you keep them involved and informed?

Approach Strategy Report   This research report is like a profile report. It contains information regarding the most recent approach strategy. It gives the essential information as a briefing for yourself or others acting on your behalf (leaders, volunteers, or partners). The report is designed for a specific initiative such as cultivation or making the ask. It consists of the following information:

Prospect name

Date, time, and place of meeting

Objectives of meeting or activity

Detailed background about the prospect—broad view and specific background

Analysis of the prospect's interests relating to each objective

Contact details for the fundraiser assigned to this prospect

Approach Strategy Report Example

Name:

Position:

Organization:

Contact details (address/tel/email/web site address, etc.):

Meeting/telephone/lunch/dinner/reception/w-end/other (circle)

Contact date:

Key individuals to be present (name and title):

Any known interests:

Other known contacts (name, title, key organization):

Who knows well enough to approach (highlight the best asker):

Known donor history/contact history:

Detailed background about the prospect—broad view and specific background:

Analysis of the prospect's interests relating to each objective:

Advice on how to progress:

Strategic objectives:

Target amount: $____ over ____ years

National project: yes/no

State/provincial/regional/local: yes/no. If yes, location:

Particular project or fund, e.g. research: yes/no. If yes, which one:

Objectives of this meeting or activity:

Comments:

Action required: follow-up letter/tel/visit/further research/hold for closer asker:

Date to be completed by:

To be carried out by:

Approach strategy prepared by:

Date prepared:

Further research required: yes/no

> To be completed and sent to: (insert fundraiser or researcher contact details here including phone, email, and instructions such as circulation to fundraiser, researcher, data entry, etc.)

SOURCES

The most valuable information you can gather about a prospective donor is obtained through personal contact. So the organization's records regarding how a donor first got involved, why they gave, what events they attend, who their primary contacts are within the organization, and when they usually give can often tell you much more than any data gathered via the Internet. Your best prospects for giving are people who already have a connection to your organization.

Yet, external sources are needed to supplement internal knowledge. For example, it can be quite telling to learn that a $500 donor to your organization just contributed $500,000 to another organization in another country.

When a prospect has broader interests or connections, checking out American and British sources for business and personal information can help you find interesting information that would have been missed otherwise. Fortunately, the Internet opens up the possibilities of accessing this information for little or no cost (except for your valuable time!). For example, you could check out British newspapers for stories that include your prospect and find out something not covered in North American media sources.

When to Use International Sources

Do you have prospects that might remotely be involved elsewhere and should you look there? More and more of our potential large donors have interests in more than one country—whether those are business, philanthropic, family, or social interests. Looking at international sources for both professional and prospect research purposes, you will find a world of insights, opportunities, and discoveries surrounds you.

We have listed here a selection of key sources for the United States, Canada, the United Kingdom, and Australia. See Appendix N for further sources. These and other sources are also listed on the ePhilanthropy Foundation web site, www.ephilanthropy.org/global.

U.S. Sources	Free	Fee-Based
Great first-step sources	www.google.com www.dogpile.com www.ask.com	www.newslibrary.com www.philanthropy.com
Sources for finding contact information	www.anywho.com www.switchboard.com www.411.com	www.knowx.com www.privateeye.com

continued

Continued from previous page

U.S. Sources	Free	Fee-Based
Sources for finding philanthropic information	Use your favorite search engine such as www.google.com and enter the following phrases: "name of donor" + gift "name of donor" + donation "name of donor" + donor "name of donor" + contribution	www.donorseries.com www.fundraisinginfo.com www.prospectinfo.com
Sources for finding relevant wealth information	www.sec.gov www.crimetime.com/online.htm www.wingsonline.com—for airplane owners www.greatlodge.com—for boat searches	Asset search on: www.knowx.com Also: www.hoovers.com
Sources for finding relevant biographical information	www.martindale.com—for lawyers www.ama-assn.org—for doctors www.vote-smart.org—for politicians	

Canadian	Free and Fee Sites
Search engines	Canada 411 at www.canada411.com Canadian Yellow Pages at www.yellow.ca Infospace Canada at www.infospace.com/canada Yahoo! Canada at www.yahoo.ca Altavista Canada at www.altavista.ca
Newspapers and magazines	Globe and Mail at www.globeandmail.com National Post at www.nationalpost.com Canada Newswire at www.newswire.ca Canadian Jewish News at www.cjnews.com Canadian Business at www.canadianbusiness.com Maclean's at www.macleans.ca Profit at www.profitguide.com Canadian Business at www.canadianbusiness.com Toronto Life at www.torontolife.com Chatelaine at www.chatelaine.com/read/work/entrlist.html
Stock, disclosure, and insider information	System for Electronic Document Analysis and Retrieval (SEDAR) at www.sedar.com Factiva (Dow Jones and Reuters Company) at www.factiva.com Carlson Online at www.fin-info.com Stockwatch at www.stockwatch.com Strategis at www.strategic.ic.gc.ca/engdoc.main.html CanCorp Canadian Financials (DIALOG File 491) at www.dialog.com

continued

Canadian	Free and Fee Sites
Researching Canadian individuals	Canada's *Who's Who* visit http://utpress.utoronto.ca/cww/cw2w3.cgi Directory of Directors visit www.financialpost.com/product/directory.htm *Who's Who in Canadian Business* visit www.canadianbusiness.com/whoswho/wwbusiness.htm or visit www.canadianbusiness.com/whoswho/women.htm *Who's Who of Canadian Women* www.canadianbusiness.com/whoswho/wwbusiness.htm Canadian Medical Directory www.southam.com/Magazines/dental.html
Researching companies (in addition to various U.S. sites)	Blue Book on Canadian Business at www.bluebook.ca Scott's Directory at www.scottsinfo.com Canadian Key Business Directory at www.dnb.com Dun & Bradstreet (Canada, U.S., U.K., etc.) Dialog File 520 www.dnb.com/
Popular fee-based sites	BIG Online Research Database at www.bigdatabase.com Foundation search at www.foundationsearch.com Prospect Research Online (iWave's PRO Online Research database)—PRO Online at www.iwave.com Directory of Foundations and Grants at www.ccp.ca NewsCan at www.newscan.com InforGlobe-DowJones Interactive www.djinteractive.com NewsCan www.newscan.com CBCA: Canadian Business and Current Affairs Fulltext (DIALOG File 262) www.dialog.com
Other useful sites	Canada Newswire http://newswire.ca JournalismNet www.journalismnet.com/canada.htm College of Physicians and Surgeons of Ontario www.cpso.on.ca Martindale-Hubbell lawyer locator www.martindalehubbell.com/locator/home.html Bay-Street.com www.bay-street.com

A Sample of U.K. and European Sites:

U.K. and Europe	Free and Fee Sites
Newspapers	*Sunday Times* Newspaper www.Sunday-times.co.uk *This is London* www.thisislondon.co.uk/dynamic/news/business/top_direct.html *Times* Newspaper www.thetimes.co.uk/ *Independent* Newspaper www.independent.co.uk/news/Business/ *Guardian* Newspaper www.guardian.co.uk/

continued

Continued from previous page

U.K. and Europe	Free and Fee Sites
Business	Companies House www.companieshouse.co.uk
Fundraising and nonprofit	Institute of Fundraising (in the U.K.) www.institute-of-fundraising.org.uk Fundraising U.K. www.fundraising.co.uk Directory of Social Change www.dsc.org.uk/ Charities Aid Foundation www.caf.org.uk/ Association of Charitable Foundations www.acf.org.uk/ Association of Chief Executives of Voluntary Organizations (ACEVO) www.acevo.org.uk/main/index.php?content=main Association for Research in the Voluntary and Community Sector (ARVAC) www.charitynet.org/arvac/index.html Alliance of European Voluntary Service Organizations www.alliance-network.org/ European Association for Gift Planning (EAPG) www.plannedgiving.co.uk/
European Union	Europa—Gateway to European Union www.europa.eu.int/index_en.htm

Australian Philanthropy Sites:

Australia	Free and Fee Sites
Philanthropy and giving	Philanthropy Australia www.philanthropy.org.au/ Council for the Encouragement of Philanthropy in Australia (CEPA) www.cepatrust.com Centre for Philanthropy and Nonprofit Studies http://cpns.bus.qut.edu.au/ Givewell www.givewell.com.au/ Auscharity www.auscharity.org

CASE STUDY: RESEARCHING A MAJOR DONOR

How you research a major donor has a lot to do with where you are based. The following tells the stories of two researchers, both looking at the same major donor prospect. One researcher was in the United States and the other was in Canada. Read their stories to see how their journeys differ.

From Florida

Kristina's client in Florida asked that research be conducted on a man who had recently attended their organization's open house. Here's what they knew: the gentleman owned substantial real estate in the community. He had a British accent (in fact, his accent was actually Canadian and his wife's British), and he threw elegant parties at his home that were attended by celebrities and British royalty.

The research began with a local focus. We went to the county assessor's web site and researched the man's property holdings. Needless to say, they were vast and quite valuable. (To find out if a U.S.-based property is in a county that posts its data to the Internet, visit http://indorgs .virginia.edu/portico/personalproperty.htm.)

The real estate records also revealed two other important facts: the name of the gentleman's spouse and the name of the trust in which some of the properties were owned.

At this point, the information flowed. We conducted some typical queries on www.google.com and www.dogpile.com using the gentleman's name, his spouse's name, and the trust name.

These initial searches revealed that Forbes (www.forbes.com) estimated the gentleman's wealth at more than $60 million, claimed he collected avant-garde art, and suggested he was very connected to the British royal family.

Initial queries on search engines provided information about the spouse's vast political and philanthropic interests as well as possible business connections that needed to be investigated.

We also conducted a few newspaper archive searches, particularly focusing in areas where the gentleman had either business or personal interests. These searches helped identify the primary people with whom he associated.

As our client had the gentleman's contact information already, we did not feel too much more information was needed at this point. We knew his wealth, his philanthropic interests, and his closest associates.

From Canada

Students attending the Fundraising and Volunteer Management Postgraduate Program at Humber College Institute of Technology & Advanced Learning, Toronto, Canada, are asked to put together a profile and presentation on an assigned prospect. The assignments asked the students to do so in two parts: preliminary research, followed by a presentation on their assigned prospect.

This is student Scott Wight's journey as he fully researched his first prospect, who is the same person that Kristina's team researched for their Florida-based client.[1]

---

[1] Interview with Scott Wight, graduate of the Fundraising and Volunteer Management Postgraduate Program at Humber College Institute of Technology & Advanced Learning, Toronto, Canada, August 2005.

Scott's Personal Journey	Comments
Steps Taken	Scott started with information from the Canadian Business Magazine's Rich 100 (list of top 100 wealthy Canadians at www.canadianbusiness.com) as the prospect was on this list.
	This information then needed to be checked, updated, and added to accordingly.
	It was crucial to find more than one source to verify the accuracy of the details listed as well as to find any other bits of useful information.
	Scott conducted preliminary research on the Internet through Google, news sites, news searches, and some other search engines including Yahoo! and All the Web. Searches were not limited to Canadian or American sites and included some European and U.K. sites.
	The prospect's corporate web site and foundation web site were reviewed.
	Deeper research was done through:
	BIG Online research service (www.bigdatabase.com)
	iWave PRO Online Research service (www.iwave.com)
	Both of these sites have Canadian and U.S. information.
	Also used Imagine Canada's Canadian Directory to Foundations and Corporations (www.imaginecanada.ca).
	Foundation Search www.foundationsearch.com.
	All of the research was assembled and Scott weeded out irrelevant information to get what he felt was the most appropriate for this particular report.
	Initial notes and first drafts were written.
	Scott returned to the three major research sites (BIG, iWave, and Imagine) to search again, ensuring that nothing was missed during the initial searches.
	The next draft was written and edited, followed by a final version, which included a PowerPoint presentation as a summary of the report.
Resources used	Google, Yahoo!, All the Web, Google News.
	Including U.K. versions of the above for searches resulting in further sites to visit.
	BIG Online Research service (www.bigdatabase.com), iWave PRO Online Research service (www.iwave.com), Imagine Canada's directory (www.imaginecanada.ca).
Challenges	The biggest challenge by far was deciding what information was most relevant for the report. The prospect had a lot of information available, even on the free sites such as Google.
	Assimilating the information, digesting it, and putting a report together of the details to ensure that they were clear and precise was difficult when there was clearly so much to find and analyze.
	It was especially difficult to decide when to stop for the purposes of this report.
	Determining what articles and so on were considered too old and would need further investigation for verification of details, for example, anything pre-2002, was challenging.

continued

Scott's Personal Journey	Comments
Challenges	Assembling the data in a logical and readable order and format proved difficult!
Frustrations	Too much data! Way too much data!! But still difficult to find details such as home addresses.
Successes	So much data available even on the free sites made searching exciting and fun. It was easy to determine that the search results were actually referring to the prospect the student was looking for, as it was not a common last name and there was continuity of information from various sources. The majority of information found was relevant to the report. The pay sites were absolutely fantastic. All of the information was in one place. Resources were great and worth paying for, as they take the researcher to a good starting point of data to be reviewed and updated. BIG and iWave were also easy to navigate. It was important to find alternative sources for verification and validity as well as additional information. I enjoyed doing the research and was pleased by how it was received by my professor and the class through the presentation and also through the written report read by the professor and other students. I am glad to have been able to do this research.
Scott's teacher, Pamela Gignac, notes	Scott's work was very thorough and well prepared, which enabled him to make an outstanding presentation on his findings and analysis of his prospect.

The British Angle

The prospect to whom we have been referring is also a prominent name on many British prospect lists due to his interests, contacts, business, and family history. This prospect's background makes him an appropriate prospect for different organizations, not only in his home country of Canada but also in the United Kingdom. His interests and connections include the British royal family, and he is known to have a passion for polo, a popular sport among the royalty.

Finding information on global prospects is crucial to putting together complete background profiles on prospects. The range and quality of U.K. sources are increasing all the time, with business, charity, and agency sources available. A good starting point is the U.K. researchers' discussion list prospect-research-uk (prospect-research-uk@yahoogroups.com).

PRIVACY

In addition to understanding what information sources are available for researching prospects, we also need to understand the importance of knowing what other countries are doing related to donor rights, accountability, and privacy. Take a close look at Chapter 4, "Prospect Research Policy, Privacy, and Ethics."

TRENDS

When conducting prospect research, it is important to take a look at what other countries are doing in the profession of fundraising as well as legal regulations they have or could have down the road. These national differences may:

■ Impact future legislation in your own country
■ Contribute to your profession's perspective of relevant issues
■ Change your donors' and prospects' perception of what is and is not proper

For example, some of the legislation in Canada was founded on the same principles as the Data Protection and Charities Acts in the United Kingdom. Our peers through the Institute of Fundraising and Researchers in Fundraising in the United Kingdom have been acutely aware of legislation and contributed widely to discussions before and after enactment to ensure that nonprofit professionals act responsibly as well as trying to make their views known.

By watching what is happening not only across our own country but also overseas, we will be better informed, forewarned, and prepared to present our views to the appropriate parties and governments when it comes to legislation that greatly impacts our work. It is also useful, as it could be a strong indicator as to where we might be heading with regard to legal regulations on privacy, accountability, the Internet, and other areas that impact our work.

Keeping our eyes open and recognizing the potential value of looking elsewhere will only increase the probabilities of success as fundraisers and researchers in gaining support for our causes. It will also help us grow through our own professional development. To find this out, we can ask ourselves the following questions:

■ Should prospect researchers in other countries look at trends being implemented in the United States? As well as elsewhere?
■ What can we learn from each other?

It truly is a small world.

CHAPTER 6

International Strategies— Europe and Asia

Chris Carnie and Sarah Boodleman Tenney

INTRODUCTION

Our prospects and donors come from all over the world. Many of them come from many parts of the world, all at once: family in Europe, stocks in a Japanese company, close friends in India, and a favored charity in Mexico. Changes in the way we travel, work, and build families mean that our prospects will increasingly be multinational people.

This chapter is designed to meet that challenge. We are going to help you find and understand prospects and donors in two key geographic markets: Europe and Asia. In each market we'll be looking at:

- History
- The big numbers
  - Wealth and giving in Europe and Asia
- Philanthropic culture
- Getting the basics right
- Getting into depth with prospects
- Getting over the barriers
  - Language
  - Privacy
  - Culture
- Places to look for information

EUROPE

History

Europe has a long and generally heart-warming history of philanthropy. Indeed, it was here, in Greece, that the word was invented. The Greeks glued *philos*—friend—to *anthropos*—human being—and gave the name to an activity that had been going on since Cro Magnona helped her friend Homo Habilis with some hand-me-down wolf skins.

All across Europe, and in all cultures, there is evidence of philanthropy. It has probably always been there, although the evidence we see today is that which has survived in our monuments and schools, our hospitals and theaters. These survivors of early philanthropy point to the importance of royalty in early European philanthropy.

Rather, royalty and religion, as exemplified by the abbey of Sant Joan de les Abadesses (Saint John of the Abbesses) in the mountains that separate Spain from France. The abbey is a simple symmetrical stone building with a church and a cool, quiet quadrangle at its heart. It was founded in 887 A.D. by a warrior baron descriptively named *Guifré el Pelos* (Hairy Geoffrey) who created the Benedictine abbey for his daughter Emma. Like all church buildings of the time and most since, the construction depended in part on the finances of the baron and in part on philanthropic donations by his friends.

Inside there is proof of that in the form of a stone tablet that records the names of the landlords and ladies who donated stone, earth, food, and wine to the construction project. Early philanthropy, and early donor recognition, too.

As Europe developed, so too did its philanthropy. With the horror of the Crusades came the need to provide medical services for combatants on both sides of the religious divide. The Order of St. John of Jerusalem (www.orderofmalta.org) was founded in Palestine around 1050 as a semireligious order dedicated to the care of the sick and injured. Today, almost 1,000 years later, St. John's still provides volunteer services at sports events and public meetings.

Don't imagine that all of this had to do solely with the Church. Synagogues and mosques also provided a focus for philanthropic activity, and the wakf (charitable foundations) of Arabic Spain or of Muslim Turkey were early providers of food and healthcare to the local population.

Move ahead a few hundred years to the point at which Europeans start to look overseas and we see new motives for philanthropy: progress and the science that goes with it were the subjects of royal patronage. Famously, Cristóbal Colón (you'll know him as Columbus) had to rely on the patronage of the Royal Treasurer to King Ferdinand in order to equip his tiny transatlantic bathtubs. He would not even have started on his journey had Henry The Navigator (The Duke of Viseu, Portugal) not made a major endowment gift to found the Navigators School in Sagres, from whence came Colón's maps.

This big-scale philanthropy, for the betterment of the human condition, continued from the fifteenth century to the present day. Founding schools— Eton was founded by King Henry VI in 1440, creating observatories in

Greenwich in 1675, and establishing centers for science—were all important ends for philanthropic giving in Europe. Not forgetting the giving, often tithing, of charity for the poor.

Fast-forward to the turmoil of twentieth-century war. Vaster, bloodier, powered by weapons of awful destructive power, war crushed Europe and then came back and crushed it again. Sandwiched between the wars was the Great Depression.

It was at this time that Europeans handed philanthropy to the State. All across Europe—from the National Health Service in Great Britain to the nationalized theaters of Austria—governments took over activities that had previously been carried out by the nonprofit sector. Hospitals and schools (previously the domain of the Church), museums and universities (held by foundations), and social care for the elderly and infirm all became the responsibility of the State and were paid for by taxes. The notion that you, a member of the public, could donate philanthropically to a local hospital became outmoded and later actually distasteful.

In most parts of Europe the idea that you should give to support a university or a hospital is at best politically incorrect and at worst an abuse of democracy. The people have voted for public ownership and control of their social, medical, and educational services (albeit nowadays in a mixed public–private partnership), and they don't want that taken away, thank you very much.

Britain is, as always, a bit different. The U.K.'s universities have entered the fundraising and philanthropic world with gusto and are running large U.S.-style campaigns. British hospitals and museums are following suit. But their continental European counterparts are not. At least not yet.

Getting the Basics Right

Names. From a prospect research point of view, the Spanish have the most useful naming convention in Europe. Spaniards carry both their fathers' and their mothers' names, and best of all, Spanish women don't change their surnames on marriage. So the Sr. José García López in your alumni database is the son of a Señor García and of a Señora López; the first of the surnames denotes the father, and the second the mother. His wife, Sra. Maricruz Colell Romero was given that name when she was born, and has not become "Mrs. García." Tracing your female alumnae or donors in Spain is thus immensely easier than doing the same job in the rest of Europe. For your database, do please bear in mind the importance of accents. It's José, not Jose.

Other naming conventions are not so helpful. Titles, common across most of Europe, can cause you and your database a nasty hiccough. For example, drs Hans Western (yes, the lower case drs is purposeful) is simply an Austrian with a university degree. Mlle Nadine Lebrun is a single Frenchwoman (her married mum is Mme Lebrun) and Lord Bartington, the 4th Baron of Entwhistle would be known as "Mr. Bartington" if his dad had not been the 3rd Baron; his is a hereditary title.

These types of naming conventions are important details in first identifying then approaching potential major donors. You will cause offense by confusing your Don with your Doña or your Herr with your Frau.

Addresses.   Your database will also have to cope with a wide variety of address formats. The address in Spain is an example of the problems faced with European addresses; the country name is in the local language, and the post code comes in at least two formats (see Exhibit 6.1), one beginning with an E-, the other not. Worst of all, the address is in fact a postal box—widely used in continental Europe—so don't try to drop in.

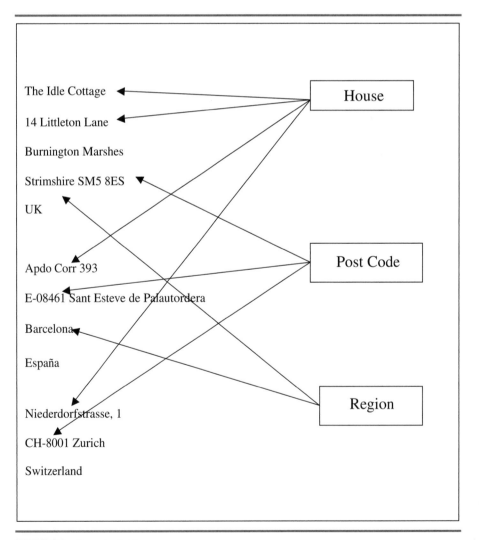

EXHIBIT 6.1   Sample Addresses

On the subject of addresses, it is good to agree on one language for addresses. Your alumna who reports her address as "Genf" lives just down the road from the alumnus who comes from "Genève"— and both of them live in Geneva, where the multilingual Swiss have a number of names for each city. Similarly, you'll probably know "Den Haag" better as "The Hague." Agreeing on a language for your addressing protocol avoids a lot of confusion.

A number of sources can help with all of this. The front section of the *Who's Who* for the country in question may explain naming conventions. The embassy web site might carry the information; if they don't, try *The Economist* at www.economist.com for country guidance.

Companies: Types

Company Names. Like surnames, company names give us clues about structure and origins, which give us a load of useful information about our potential major donor. There's a world of difference between a privately held German GmbH and its bigger brother, the public AG. So it's worth taking time to learn about company naming conventions in Europe (as a guide, a few of the main types are listed here).

Name	Place	Full Name	Type
AG	Germany, Austria, Switzerland	Aktiengesellschaft	Larger stock corporation. May be quoted or private.
BV	Belgium, Netherlands	Besloten Vennootschap	Limited liability company.
e.V.	Germany	eingetragener Verein	Nonprofit society.
GmbH	Germany, Austria, Switzerland	Gesellschaft mit beschrankter Haftung	Company with limited liability. Always private.
NV	Netherlands, Belgium	Naamloze Vennootschap	Larger company. May be quoted or private.
SA	Belgium, France, others	Société Anonyme	Normally, larger company, which may be quoted or private.
SpA	Italy	Società per Azioni	Limited share company.
Srl	Italy	Società a Responsabilità Limitada	Limited liability company.

Sole Trader.   Also known as an *autonomous trader,* this is the basic form of business in most of Europe. A Sole Trader trades solely on her own behalf, making simple returns to the tax authorities. Millions of electricians, architects, doctors, and builders across Europe are Sole Traders. From a prospect research point of view this group is tough to research; generally they don't have to record their name in a public register, so there is little data available. The professionals among them will register with a trade body, but they are unlikely to report anything more than their name, title, and address.

Partnership.   Groups of sole traders form partnerships, and there is a wide variety of this business formed across Europe. It's especially prevalent in Switzerland, where a signing partner can be a powerful individual in a leading international law firm.

Private Limited Liability Company.   The basic limited liability company format—a GmbH in Germany or a Ltd in the UK—normally carries some legal reporting requirements. At last we can get hold of company information about our prospect. Countries vary in their requirements—some have a national register (Companies House in the United Kingdom, for example) while others have regional or local registers on business. These registers are starting to post their information online (www.companieshouse.co.uk/), although the level of detail available can vary hugely. Compilers such as Dun & Bradstreet, Hoovers, or Reed Information Services will also provide the data you need; the cost may be slightly higher, but the consistency and ease of use often justify the extra budget.

Public Company.   The public or quoted company—one whose shares are available to the public—is the easiest to research. It has a web site, and the investors' area of the site will generally carry recent news and a downloadable annual report. The company will also be the subject of endless analysis, and stockbrokers, the financial press (*Financial Times,* for example), and business magazines such as *Bilanz* or *Trends* will all carry information on the business. Compilers carry data, too—in addition to those previously listed you could try Yahoo!'s finance section at www.yahoo.com—and even campaigners, typically from the antiglobalization side of the political divide, will provide some information. Take a look at the Campaign Against the Arms Trade (www.caat.org.uk) or www.transnationale.org for examples.

Foundations: Types

Like companies, foundations in Europe come in a wide variety of types, depending partly on the laws of the country concerned and partly on their traditions. These differences can be surprising for prospect researchers and fundraisers brought up in the more homogeneous market of North America.

Some foundations in Europe look quite like their U.S. counterparts; these are the large grant makers with a more or less stable income, a more or less independent board, and a grants program. Volkswagen Stiftung, one of Germany's largest funders of scientific and social research, is an example.

These U.S.-model foundations occur in most European countries, and many are members of the European Foundation Centre (www.efc.be), the umbrella body that is promoting this model of managed grant-making practice. The EFC is also promoting the community foundation movement in Europe, with great success.

Move away from these familiar models, and things start to look very different indeed. It's impossible to give you the whole story in a mere chapter, but some examples illustrate the diversity.

Austria has foundations—some 1,500 at the last count—but don't look here for grants. Although they carry the foundation (or, in this case Stiftung) label, very few are philanthropic foundations, and only a tiny handful actually make grants. In fact, a number are used simply as tax-avoidance vehicles.

Move across Europe to Spain, and the picture changes. Spanish foundations are innovative, philanthropic, and expanding both in number and in assets. Fundaciones in Spain include significant grant makers like BBVA Foundation and active fundraisers like Fundación Intermón Oxfam, the humanitarian aid organization. Fundación La Caixa, another significant grant maker, illustrates a phenomenon that has occurred in Spain, Italy, and France: it is closely linked to a savings bank, an institution set up to encourage savings and to provide loans for house purchasers. These savings banks enjoy special status but must give 25 percent of profit to social causes; in La Caixa's case that meant €185m in 2004.

Switzerland has a number of substantial foundations, and its laws allow foundations to conduct family investment business. So if you visit the web site of the Sandoz Fondation de Famille, you will see that its primary activity is to protect the assets of the founding family. Grant making is only a minor concern for this asset-rich pharmaceutical concern.

FINDING EUROPEAN PROSPECTS

Foundations

Foundations in Europe are becoming easier to find thanks to a concern for financial transparency. In most European countries they are listed in a government register (visit the Charity Commission in the United Kingdom, for example, www.charity-commission.gov.uk). Most countries don't yet have a foundation directory, but the foundation associations—generally set up with the encouragement of the European Foundation Centre— are beginning to list foundation members on their web sites. Outside of the United Kingdom only a few European foundations have a web site, but we can expect to see more of these soon.

People

Biographic Information.   *Who's Who* directories are available for most of Europe, although in some countries such as Belgium the publishing frequency can mean that you are looking at a five-year-old version. Most follow the familiar format: name, date of birth, biography, and contact details. Some, such as *Who's Who en France,* even use an English title. Few of these biographic directories are currently available online—Germany's *Wie ist Wie* is the exception. Sutter is a leading English-language publisher that offers some online directories.

Philanthropic Histories.   This is an area of extreme frustration for prospect researchers in Europe. In general, no philanthropic histories are available for anyone, anywhere beyond the database of the specific cause that the donor supported. Donations in Europe are a private affair, and even news reports on gifts are limited to the really spectacular donations.

Connections and Links between People.   Europe is a small place, with 379 million people squeezed into a space equivalent to just two Alaskas. So people know each other—from shared schooling, careers, board affiliations, or interests. Mostly this is researchable, just as it is in the United States. The painstaking process of using corporate and foundation information, plus biographic directories, to identify the links yields information. In the right setting with a trusting board member or other volunteer, you can expect good results from a contacts and connections review. Make sure that you stress the security and confidentiality of your data-handling techniques, and don't expect to hear much bad stuff about the prospects you are reviewing.

Corporate Information

Finances and Ownership.   Your regular supplier of corporate information (e.g., Dun & Bradstreet, Lexis Nexis, or Hoovers) will give you good coverage of the major European companies. That's the good news. The bad news is that a huge part of the European economy is based on mid-sized privately owned businesses (the German *Mittelstand*). Your prospects' holdings in these companies, and the wealth they are generating from them, will be harder to establish because European accounting standards vary, and some do not require disclosure of useful markers such as directors' remuneration.

Boards. Commercial compilers such as D&B and the government registers on which they base their information, are good sources of board information. In the United Kingdom, for example, Companies House will provide directors' names and home addresses for any registered company for a small fee.

GETTING OVER THE BARRIERS

Before you reach for your passport and get on the plane to Europe, you should consider some of the barriers that make fundraising in Europe such a challenging (and thus fun) profession.

Sprechen Sie Europe? We speak lots of languages, and lots of dialects, too (don't expect to hear the same things in Bavaria as you hear in Frankfurt). While it is now true that a European elite does commonly speak some English, it is also true that most people don't. So be prepared to do your prospect research in German, Swedish, Dutch, and French, and have your foundation applications, brochures, or letters translated into the language of the country you're writing to. Maybe get a local to give you a hand.

Privacy. It doesn't take much imagination (bear in mind what happened to Jewish people, Roma people, and homosexuals in 1939 to 1945) to understand why Europeans are cautious about data protection and privacy. We don't allow anyone to record our religion, our sexual preferences, our ethnicity (except in special circumstances) in their databases, nor our politics or labor union membership. We don't allow data to move out of the EU, except in special circumstances, and we are limited in many other ways from holding or passing on personal information. There is more on privacy in Chapter 4, "Prospect Research, Policy, Privacy, and Ethics."

Philanthropic Culture. The history of philanthropy in Europe has helped to create a distinct culture. Attitudes to money vary widely, depending on background and culture. It is notoriously difficult to talk money in France and the Netherlands, for example. Bringing up the idea of a major gift, and particularly asking directly for one, causes severe headaches. Persuading colleagues in one energetic Paris-based nonprofit to ask for €10,000 proved to be impossible until we asked the nonprofit's patron, a priest, to do the deed for us, and this type of thinking is commonplace. Even experienced fundraisers in continental Europe are wary of asking a donor, to his face, for a substantial gift.

EUROPE: A VALUED FRIEND

Europe has long been a source of funding for U.S. organizations—with a European Foundation Center study in 1997 estimating foundation gifts from Europe to the United States totaling US$35 million per annum. This study did not account for the gifts from U.S. expatriates in Europe, from Europeans supporting their U.S. alma mater, and from European government bilateral aid programs supporting U.S. nonprofit activity.

Europe is a valued philanthropic friend of the United States, so do it the honor of dedicating time and resources to research and strategy.

AS FOR ASIA

During a dinner gathering of friends one evening at our home in Hawaii, the conversation turned to stories about Asia. The group was an intergenerational mixture with a magnificent blend of tales, including tours of duty during World War II, fantastic new foods from Korea, student exchange mishaps in China, and vacationing in Vietnam. One of the well-traveled guests concluded the evening by stating, "Asia is so large that we could tell a story about a different place each day until the end of our lives and we would still have missed some important areas." This guest's comment perfectly expresses the challenge in providing information on how to prospect for major gifts in Asia.

This section provides professional fundraisers and researchers a valuable reference to look at Asia and familiarize oneself with the elements to cultivate major gift prospects. It demonstrates the value of looking at other sources no matter which country is considered *home*, provides a better understanding as to who Asian prospects are, and gives insight into the expectations one may encounter when prospecting in Asia.

Defining Asia

Technically, Asia is the world's largest continent and it spans from the edge of Europe to the Pacific Ocean. It is large enough to be commonly referred to in segments, such as North Asia, South Asia, Continental Asia, East Asia, and even Asia Minor. As our dinner party guest pointed out, the key challenge to discussing prospecting for major donors in Asia is an endless combination of factors and location issues, which ultimately impacts philanthropic prospecting in Asia.

During my tenure with MeesPierson, the private wealth management division of Fortis, my role as the Head of Philanthropy Services for North Asia was to help build a new philanthropic consulting division. Working with this European, yet Asia-based, financial institution provided exposure to major donors, discussions with government officials, competitive vendors, advocates in educational institutions, and experiences with cultural expectations. The focus for Asia will be on two city-states, Hong Kong and Singapore, which are areas with concentrated philanthropic activity. If a major gift prospector can master the basics of these two areas, then any prospecting for major gifts in Asia will be enhanced.

Global Trends Impact Major Donor Prospecting

What is intriguing about Hong Kong and Singapore is how philanthropy flourishes despite the incredible historic tensions between those who determine the system of rules and those who are part of the masses who follow or contest the development of such rules. In fact, philanthropy spawned in different forms despite natural or man-made tensions, and it is a professional's responsibility to develop appropriate methods to seek major donors within the tensions that exist. Asia's importance in global trends is increasing, and so is its impact for successful prospecting. For instance, the following examples show how recent global trends may seriously impact a prospector's work and focus in Asia.

Trend 1: The 1997 Asian Financial Crisis.   This crisis put multiple Asian countries in economic turmoil. Overnight, the currencies of nations lost their value, and business owners and investors began pulling investments out of Asia. Businesses closed down and special public services were eliminated to ensure that basic services like electricity, refuse, and food were available. Funding from government agencies required additional reports and proof.

Trend 2: Fighting Terrorism.   During my tenure with Fortis, we received a weekly email that contained a list of names and entities that had been identified and dispersed by the U.S. Treasury Department. If any of the names on the list were our prospects or clients, we were to immediately notify supervisors and a process would take place to turn over information to the authorities. The terrorist activities on September 11, 2001 in the United States changed the banking processes and requirements across the globe and forced banks to define "Know Your Client" programs. Traditionally, banking in Hong Kong and Singapore focused on the transactional elements and allowed privacy management to take place at the banker level. Now, the monetary authorities of nations are subject to tracking and regulations to assist the apprehension of terrorists. This ultimately influenced banks to ensure that wealth managers could prove the source, location, and level of knowledge of their clients.

Trend 3: Global Response to Catastrophes.   In Hong Kong, on December 26, 2004, the *South China Morning* relayed the horrific news that more than 20,000 people had died in the Asian Tsunami overnight. I remember the shock this number gave me, as losing more than 3,000 people on September 11th was still a vivid tragedy, and then the inconceivable casualty increased on the front page of the paper each day thereafter. To have more than 100,000 dead in one single event of nature impacts the way philanthropy operates, and prospecting for major donors must anticipate change.

Prospecting for major donors requires a specific focus and familiarization with global trends and decisive commitment to revise a previous strategy to move forward. For example, during the 1997 Asian Financial Crisis, a donor profile would be heavily dependent upon approvals and relationships with government agency funding. In the aftermath of the September 11th event, managing an individual knowledge of the board directors or fiscal agents was increasingly required and heavy emphasis was placed on balancing privacy requirements with prospecting strategies. In the wake of the Asian Tsunami, a major gift prospector would need to be familiar with changing regulations, such as tax incentives in response to gain funds for Asian Tsunami support. Knowing an individual's propensity to give to emergencies as well as annual personal interests is key during times of major global events. It also requires an astute knowledge of global trends and events and the ability to implement strategies accordingly that work.

GETTING THE BASICS RIGHT

Individuals, companies, and foundations all give major gifts in Hong Kong or Singapore. Let's review some of the basics in communicating and interacting with them based on philanthropic culture and where to start to get information on prospects.

Philanthropic Culture

Infrastructure.   Hong Kong or Singapore has a long history of philanthropic giving, but only recently have their governments begun to put formal infrastructures in place to advocate philanthropic activity. Special taxation divisions focusing on philanthropy, support for accredited university degree programs, and introduction of certified fundraising executives are good examples of government and educational infrastructures. Previously, infrastructures were more likely to be seen as practices imbedded in customs, relationships, and networks. Therefore, it is helpful to keep the following in mind.

Gift Amounts.   Many areas in Asia have a monthly individual income that is less than US$400. Therefore, the definition of a major gift in Asia expresses very differently and is often seen as a concentrated and focused effort rather than an outright cash gift. Programs in Hong Kong, like the "Caring Company" program, document companies that have committed gifts and specific support to entities in need.

Familiar and Formal.   Major gift donors in Hong Kong and Singapore give to what is familiar to them. Public demonstration of gift giving is highly accepted in close business circles and in formal celebrations such as Chinese New Year or a family wedding. It is rare to see major gifts given without a history of relationship or interaction.

In Groups and Out Groups.   In both Hong Kong and Singapore, *in-group* versus *out-group* rules apply. In-group contacts consist of family, lifetime friends, and close business associates or vendors. Examples of *out-group* contacts often consist of professionals who are paid to assist, new employees, foreign language speakers, and prospective clients. During meetings and parties it is important to realize which group you are part of in relation to the host and act accordingly. There are specific practices of politeness such as offering tea and sharing bilingual business cards that are crucial for successful meetings.

Naming Functions.   Businesspersons in Asia have the option of using their birth name or choosing one in the local language to use. Anticipate doubling the prospecting time for candidates who have registered several names or have been married three or more times.

Company Basics.   Philanthropy and business go hand in hand. This is due to the entrepreneurial environment of family-owned companies. As generations evolve into family ventures, philanthropy from the business is usually advocated by the decision maker or the lead family business. Even for corporations, it is important to know the family that started the entity and any philanthropic focuses of the family.

Governance. The Sarbanes-Oxley Act has changed the face of business in Asia as well. Since the Enron and Worldcom financial failures, Sarbanes-Oxley has segmented businesses into two groups: those who aim to meet the Western standards and those groups who deny U.S. influence in their affairs. Exhibit 6.2 shows the change in governance commitment by Asian countries from 1997 to 2004.

1997	Official Governance Code?	Laws about Independent Directors?	Required Audit Committees?
China			
Hong Kong	Yes	Yes	
India			
Indonesia			
Japan			
Korea			
Malaysia		Yes	Yes
Philippines			
Singapore		Yes	Yes
Taiwan			
Thailand			

2004	Official Governance Code?	Laws about Independent Directors?	Required Audit Committees?
China	Yes	Yes	Yes
Hong Kong	Yes	Yes	Yes
India	Yes	Yes	Yes
Indonesia	Yes	Yes	Yes
Japan	Yes	Optional	Optional
Korea	Yes	Yes	Yes
Malaysia	Yes	Yes	Yes
Philippines	Yes	Yes	Yes
Singapore	Yes	Yes	Yes
Taiwan	Yes	Yes	Yes
Thailand	Yes	Yes	Yes

EXHIBIT 6.2   Change in Governance Commitment in Asia.

Getting into Depth with Prospects

To find someone in Hong Kong or Singapore, it is as easy as picking up the telephone or using the Internet.

1. The information directories speak a host of languages, and all digital directories offer English. Basic biographic information is possible to find if you know someone who knows something about the prospect. Within one day, a veteran prospector should be able to find the major gift donors' schools, marital situation, number of children, and employment record.

2. For immediate prospecting needs, it's difficult to find detailed public information that easily quantifies propensity to give and the time frame for an appropriate major gift. This requires time and dedication to familiarize with the prospect.

3. Both Hong Kong and Singapore divide their residents into two groups. A resident is either a *local,* someone born in the city-state, or an *ex-pat,* an ex-patriot who moved to the city-state and will most likely move away once business objectives are accomplished. To search for biographic information on an individual in Hong Kong or Singapore via the Internet, an understanding of local versus ex-pat web sites is recommended. This will familiarize you with the availability of professional services and products used by both groups.

SPECIFIC THINGS TO KNOW

The following are effective things to know to get you started.

Know a Method to Initiate

A private wealth banker taught the following method to me, and it works effectively in Hong Kong and Singapore to start a profile with three key concepts:

1. International living in Hong Kong and Singapore is initiated or usually focused on a business connection. Search the navigational resources in key industry web sites. Business-related web sites not only help find a prospective candidate, they clarify if the candidate is a person who is involved in or respected by the selected industry in which she works. Established names in associations and groups are clear symbols of respect and acceptance.

2. Determine if the major gift candidate resides in more than one Asian country. International Directory Inquiries Service from PCCW helps you find overseas phone numbers. If you place your telephone number query via email, the International Directory Inquiries Service will email the result to you at a charge of less than US$2 for each successfully obtained overseas number. International Telephone Listings Directory: www.pccw.com.

3. Map out where a candidate lives. Housing areas in Hong Kong and Singapore are clear determiners of salary or company support. The www.YPMAP.com features a complete set of digital maps of Hong Kong on the scales of 1:1,000 and 1:10,000. The maps can be flexibly viewed by using a mouse for various panning and zooming perspectives. Alternatively, an eight-level bar is provided for viewing at different levels. All maps can be printed. Hong Kong Yellow Pages Map: www.YPmap.HK.

Know the Traditional Industries

Every serious professional who prospects for major donors will match the prospecting strategy to the mission of the organization they are trying to find funds for. The mission of the organization is always connected to at least one industry. In Hong Kong and Singapore, the history behind major successes or failures in the development of an industry gives an idea of philanthropic involvement. The parameters of the philanthropic involvement become a profiling tool for major donor prospecting.

Know the Families: It's Business

I have heard it quoted that in Asia more than 80 percent of all businesses are managed by a specific family. Although some believe philanthropic giving is driven by family interests, it is more accurate to state that philanthropy is given by every family and those with particular businesses are more likely to support philanthropic endeavors that their business affiliates, vendors, and staff support as well.

Know the Women

Traditionally, women manage the home budgets. The loss of spouses or family members does not automatically transfer assets as in other countries. Today, females have more opportunity to be educated and play a role in family businesses. Wives play an important role in business and deciding where family and business discretionary funds will be spent.

GETTING OVER BARRIERS

The barriers that make fundraising in Europe such a challenge are found in Asia as well. During a first meeting in Hong Kong, a Chinese gentleman was impressed that I had a Chinese name, and asked me why I chose "Icy Woman." When he translated the name, I was horrified to find that it meant "icy woman." I later approached my colleagues who helped provide the name, and one innocently asked, "Snowy Princess, does that not have a good meaning?"

- **Language is more than words.** The biggest barrier to prospecting may be ensuring the word you are looking for is the word you want to use. The same goes for symbols. During a meeting, a visiting gentleman showed words connected together with a graphic of a spider web. The visual was supposed to represent a web of information, but later my local colleagues shared that it was an odd picture in the presentation, because a web in Asia is often a symbol representing death or evil.
- **Privacy.** People in Asia understand sharing data is a trade-off for convenience and service in an expedited manner. Cards for the subway, banking systems, shopping, and residences always come with a SIM chip of identifying information. However, if I asked for personal information during a dinner party, it may be considered rude and impersonal if requested in the wrong situation.
- **Culture.** Hong Kong and Singapore are built on international business. Hearing five different languages in one day is not uncommon. The cultures of differing segments of the public have merged to express the do's and do not's for subcultures.
- **Using professionals.** Professionals from overseas are not easily accepted until their expertise is showcased, or a senior manager gives a major signal to announce acceptance. Ensure you have a proper introductory letter or resume to share.
- **Build professional relationships with wealth managers, bankers, or financial experts who work in Asia.** Although professionals will not give specific data on individual clients, they will be able to keep professional fundraisers and researchers familiar with the changes impacting wealthy clients who may have the discretional income available for philanthropic cultivation.

OTHER PLACES TO LOOK FOR INFORMATION

- **Tax registration office.** For a list of philanthropic organizations, go no further than the office of taxation. Both Hong Kong and Singapore provide a list of registered organizations.

■ **Alumni web sites.** School and alumni records are the best resources for finding and updating the status of major donor candidates.

■ **Best business associations.** The Chambers of Commerce for specific countries, such as the Australian Chamber of Commerce, are key networking venues. Industries that require certification, such as legal and accounting membership societies, are also excellent sources for Asian major donors.

■ **Unique philanthropic events.** Attending or volunteering to help special events is a perfect way to mingle or familiarize oneself with major donors in Asia.

CONCLUSION

Asia and Europe require work and patience to produce wonderful philanthropic results. Professional fundraisers and researchers should build a foundation to begin developing strategies to cultivate major gift prospects outside one's home country. The value of familiarizing oneself with global trends, business impacts, and the insight to anticipate cultural expectations in the journey is not to be underestimated. In both Europe and Asia, patient research, good personal relationships, and careful strategic management will take you on an adventure to remember!

CHAPTER 7

Your Web Site—What Does It Say to Major Donors?

Howard Lake[1]

INTRODUCTION

Major donors do not ignore the Internet when it comes to researching and carrying out their philanthropic activities. They research potential recipients of their gifts, examine progress of programs they have already supported, and communicate with fundraising or program staff at nonprofits. Some even make their major gifts online, although others choose more traditional methods.

This is true in North America at any rate, where, in October 2003, online fundraising provider Kintera reported that, according to an informal online poll of its clients, 9 percent of the nonprofits that responded had received an online gift of $1 million or more. Another 4 percent had received a donation of over $100,000, and 13 percent had received a gift between $10,000 to $99,999.

In February 2004 the company reported that 8.3 percent of all donations received online by 3,151 nonprofits during 2003 had been for $1,000 or more.

THE TREND CONTINUES

This trend of online giving, at least in North America, is not new. Some commentators and practitioners spotted the potential of soliciting major gifts online in the late 1990s. In 1997, Adam Corson-Finnerty, Director of Development for the Library of the University of Pennsylvania, and Laura Blanchard argued in "Fundraising and Friend-Raising on the Web" that

[1]Preparation of this chapter was aided by expert advice from Steve Maclaughlin, Blackbaud (steve.maclaughlin@blackbaud.com). His assistance is greatly appreciated.

major gift solicitation should be a prime focus of the fundraising or development office.

> *"One day,"* they wrote, *"a very significant amount of money will be donated to nonprofit institutions through direct transfer via the Internet. But that day may be quite a few years off. At present, we believe that the Web is currently most useful in soliciting and acknowledging major gifts."*

Three years later, writing an update to that chapter, Corson-Finnerty reported that, as a fundraiser, he was indeed generating major gifts through his organization's web site. He mentions a two-year grant from a family foundation worth $50,000. "I have been looking at your web site and I really like what you are doing," said the donor, an alumna of his university. "I am the trustee of a family foundation and we would like to make a gift to your library." At that time, his organization was enjoying particular success at raising major gifts online for, appropriately enough, online projects. "I can add to that," he wrote, "a $300,000 gift from an individual to develop our electronic publishing capacity, a $200,000 grant to create a Shakespeare/English Renaissance teaching site online, a $25,000 individual gift to put illustrated books online, and a $500,000 NEH Challenge Grant to endow our electronic publishing program which we will use to leverage $2,000,000 in additional gifts."

He was not wedded to the online medium exclusively. "I have yet to land a major gift solely by email," he conceded, "but I have negotiated one gift of $150,000, and another of $500,000 primarily by this device." Furthermore, one of his colleagues had "put the final touches on a $10 million gift, all by email."

THE PERSONAL APPROACH

Nonprofit technology and information expert Michael Gilbert approaches the issue of major gift fundraising online from the opposite angle. He argues that the personal approach that should underpin major gift fundraising can and should be extended to all donors. "I have been arguing for some years now that online fundraising, because of the reduced cost of communication, has the promise of allowing us to treat all our donors a lot more like major donors," he argues in "Online Donor Cultivation: The Quest for Metrics" in April 2005. In particular, he felt that "there is lots of potential in translating mainstream major donor cultivation and tracking techniques into online communication."

If Gilbert is right that, by using the Internet, "the potential exists to treat every donor like a major donor," then the online treatment of major donors themselves should be several degrees more advanced than what is offered for the majority of donors. In North America, this is the case with major gift fundraising online, clearly well established in many organizations. By contrast, the United Kingdom has very little activity in this area, even in mid-2005.

Giving in the United Kingdom

In the United Kingdom, according to the Institute of Philanthropy, 6 percent of the population contributes 60 percent of all monies donated to charities. For this reason alone, major gift fundraising should interest and concern many charities.

Yet an examination of the web sites of the top 20 fundraising charities in the United Kingdom during summer 2005 found almost no mention of, ,or active solicitation of, major gifts. These are the charities that are more likely to employ staff dedicated to major gift fundraising. Only one, Cancer Research UK, the United Kingdom's largest fundraising charity, featured any mention of major gifts, and even this was combined with donations from grant-making trusts. Others not only had no information for or about major donors, the online fundraising elements of their sites were evidently not focused on encouraging such gifts.

For example, where charities included a prompted level of giving in their online credit/debit card donation pages, most had a very low top amount. The National Trust's and NSPCC's top figure was £100. Only Comic Relief approached the scale of a major gift, with a suggested level of £1,000. Not all large organizations use a prompted level of giving; Oxfam GB, for example, simply leaves the amount field blank, so there is no opportunity to indicate that major gifts are encouraged or welcomed.

Where organizations offered a shopping list of what different donations could buy, the British Heart Foundation and the Royal Society for the Prevention of Cruelty to Animals (RSPCA) stopped at £50, and the Royal National Lifeboat Institute (RNLI) at £500.

Cancer Research UK's web site does, therefore, stand out from those of the other major charities (www.cancer.org.uk/donate/other_ways_donate/trusts_majordonations/).

It includes its major donor content under an "Other ways to donate" section, which lists "charitable trusts & major donations." It explains that it "has a dedicated team who works closely with charitable trusts and individual donors giving £10,000 or more. We are happy to discuss funding options and ensure that major gifts are allocated according to donors' wishes."

The web site asks for major gifts, and gives examples of what could be achieved with gifts ranging from £1,000 to £314,000. To encourage dialogue, it provides details of named contacts at the charity with their telephone numbers and email addresses.

Although a step ahead of other major U.K. charities, Cancer Research UK's site does not include case studies of successful partnerships with major donors. Nor does it include testimonials from satisfied major donors, or even public acknowledgments of major gifts.

However, it does indicate how it can work with major donors to recognize their gifts and report back on their impact: "in addition to sending progress reports on our work, we would be pleased to recognize your generosity in a variety of ways, and to discuss any options with you." The charity's web site lists four methods of recognition, including "invitations to meet scientists and senior charity staff at lab tours and small receptions" and "naming a laboratory or a research fellowship."

Few Major Gifts Made Online

Given this lack of online promotion of major gift fundraising by the largest U.K. charities, it is not surprising that few report major gifts received or generated online. The online fundraising service "Bmycharity" reports that the largest single amount it has handled online for a charity client to date was £20,000, followed by £8,480, £6,000, and £5,000. A CEO of a major listed company gave the largest gift just before Christmas 2004 to Save the Children. That said, the £6,000 gift was one of four gifts of the same amount, all given over a short period, totaling £24,000. These four related gifts were given to a major international charity by, perhaps not surprisingly, an American donor.

Indeed, *Bmycharity's* analysis of these major online donors shows that, of the top 30 donations by size, 20 were from the United Kingdom and 10 were from the United States, including one U.S. military serviceman serving overseas. For what it's worth, *Bmycharity* added, "Heuristic analysis indicates that the largest donations tend to be made in the afternoon (local time)."

Bmycharity takes a more sophisticated approach to major gifts online. Managing Director Ben Brabyn explains: "Sometimes, major donors don't give large sums online. Yet we have come across well-known names giving reasonable sums online, including high-growth entrepreneurs from the new media industry." Effective and rapid acknowledgment of these gifts could open the way to a future major gift.

Just giving, another online fundraising service provider, reports that the largest donation it has handled to date in the United Kingdom has been £25,000. Yet its CEO, Zarine Kharas, frankly admits that "we don't target or prospect wealthy donors at all." Instead, it promotes sponsored event fundraising by individuals and groups.

This is at the root of why online major gift fundraising is so underdeveloped in the United Kingdom compared to North America. The emphasis in online fundraising has been on quantity of credit/debit card donations and, more recently, direct debit regular payments. The quality in terms of size of these donations has been of secondary importance, it would seem, although many charities have been pleasantly surprised by the higher average gifts received online compared to the average for offline gifts.

NEEDS AND CONCERNS OF MAJOR DONORS

There is also a more fundamental lack of awareness by charities about the needs and concerns of major donors. According to "Managing Major Donors: How Charities Manage Their Relationships with Major Donors," a study published jointly in 2003 by the Institute for Philanthropy and the Ansbacher Group, many of Britain's charities are failing to meet or even understand the expectations of their wealthier donors. The report's conclusions included the analysis that "opportunities for fundraising from major donors remain largely unrecognized and so projects lack appropriate leadership, methodologies, and resources," whether online or offline.

Hilary Browne-Wilkinson, director of the Institute for Philanthropy, said: "Six percent of people contribute some 60 percent of all monies donated to charities. Anything which can be done to improve the understanding of the needs and motivations of this important group can only be of help to the sector as a whole."

Another study published the year before by the Institute for Public Policy Research yielded similar conclusions. " 'A Bit Rich?' What the Wealthy Think about Giving" reported that "what is striking is that there is little evidence of much thought being put into how much the rich and affluent give."

Indeed, no published academic research into major giving online in the United Kingdom seems to be available. Adrian Sargeant and Elaine Jay's "Nonprofit Website Effectiveness: The Role of Donor Relationships" of December 2003, for example, has no coverage of major gifts fundraising online. The regular "Virtual Promise" surveys of U.K. charities' use of the Internet, since their first research carried out in summer 2000, have not covered major gift fundraising online.

ATTRACTING DONORS

So, what content and services should a nonprofit's web site contain to attract and persuade major donors to give? The recommendations on good practice included in "Managing Major Donors: How Charities Manage Their Relationships with Major Donors" and the Institute of Fundraising's 2005 draft code of Best Practice for Major Donor Fundraising afford some useful indications. The Managing Major Donors report offers seven succinct questions that a charity needs to ask of its major donors, which should help online major gift fundraisers:

1. What is the type and frequency of contact?
2. How respectful is the charity?
3. What is the timing of requests?
4. How emotionally committed does the donor wish to become?
5. How professionally do donors wish to become involved?
6. How much public recognition do donors want?
7. Who do major donors wish to meet?

The Institute of Fundraising's code of practice includes other advice, some of which is particularly pertinent given the often-geographical distance between donor and recipient nonprofit. For example, the code advises that the transaction process must offer transparency and a good audit trail: "when completing any major gift, fundraisers must ensure that the charity is provided with sufficient information to enable it to verify to its auditor or examiner and the tax authorities the nature of the receipt." This is designed to help fundraisers comply with legislation regarding offenses relating to money laundering, such as the Proceeds of Crime Act 2002 and Money Laundering Regulations 2003.

Sarah Hughes, former head of New Media at Charities Aid Foundation (CAF) and now founder of charity21, the new media agency for charities, suggests other content for high-net-worth donors: "High Net Worth donors carry out a greater degree of due diligence on a charity, so online they expect detailed financial information and annual reports." They also expect "a sense of impact and dimension of the problem, progress being made against the issue, the big picture."

Sarah offers suggestions to nonprofits for future development in this area. "High-net-worth donors," she suggests, "may require portfolio management services for their giving and these also lend themselves well to online access, for example managing information across a range of projects being supported using a variety of financial mechanisms." She also suggests enabling or encouraging major donors to use the Internet to collaborate and share advice. "Private intranets where high-net-worth donors may share lessons, experiences, and tips and signpost worthy projects or request suggestions for things to fund may also be a future valuable service," she adds. She posits a giving site equivalent to The Motley Fool (www.fool.co.uk), which would act as "a specialist aggregator portal with dynamic, detailed, and financially astute information on giving major gifts, backed by editors from a range of professional backgrounds, including independent advisors, grant makers, and foundations."

Those major donors who opt not to carry out the research themselves can now turn to intermediary organizations such as New Philanthropy Capital (www.philanthropycapital.org) for advice. New Philanthropy Capital "carries out independent research and analysis on where and how funds and resources can be targeted most effectively, bridging the gap between donors and the voluntary sector." It aims to help the "many donors (and would-be donors) who possess the resources to make more substantial donations, but do not do so because they lack confidence that their funds will be put to good use."

KEY ELEMENTS OF MAJOR GIFT FUNDRAISING ONLINE

How should a nonprofit attract and engage major donors via its web site?

- Ask for large gifts. Clearly, if there is no ask or content targeted at major donors, there is little likelihood of securing major gifts online.
- Ask for large gifts on the front page of your web site.
- Ask for large gifts elsewhere on your web site (e.g., next to project reports and financial reports).
- Include major gift asks on online donation forms (e.g., as a prompted level of giving, or in a shopping list of examples of how much particular donations can buy).
- Don't just ask for major gifts but explain the need for them. Persuade high-net-worth individuals who might not have considered giving a large gift.
- Offer dedicated information or a page(s) for major donors, explaining the nonprofit's track record in partnering with major donors and meeting their needs, and the current needs for major gifts. Include contributions from satisfied major donors.
- List detailed information on different ways in which major gifts can be acknowledged and recognized, both online and offline.
- List, with permission, major gifts already received.
- Provide named contact details for major gift fundraisers and/or senior staff whom prospective major donors can talk to or meet with.
- Consider featuring relevant partner organizations such as New Philanthropy Capital and link to their content.

BIBLIOGRAPHY

"A Bit Rich?" What the Wealthy Think about Giving
    Institute of Philanthropy
    2002
Best Practice for Major Donor Fundraising: Draft Code of Fundraising Practice
    Institute of Fundraising
    2005
Cybergifts, Part 9: Major Gifts
    Adam Corson-Finnerty
    2000
Frictionless Fundraising: How the Internet Can Bring Fundraising Back into Balance
    Michael C. Gilbert
    January 2003
Managing Major Donors: How Charities Manage Their Relationships with Major Donors
    The Institute for Philanthropy and the Ansbacher Group
    May 2003
    www.instituteforphilanthropy.org.uk/Managing%20Major%20Donors%20report.pdf
Nonprofit Website Effectiveness: The Role of Donor Relationships
    Adrian Sargeant and Elaine Jay
    December 2003
Online Donor Cultivation: The Quest for Metrics
    Michael C. Gilbert
    April 2005
"Virtual Promise—From Rhetoric to Reality"—A Report on Charities' Use of the Internet
    between 2000–2004
    nfpSynergy.net
    October 2004

CHAPTER 8

An Internet Strategy for Major Donor Fundraising

Anthony Powell

INTRODUCTION

As a fundraiser, technologist, and consultant, I'm constantly searching for ways to use technology to enhance the process of identifying and building relationships with major donor prospects. While many development organizations are fully realizing the potential of technology to automate the more fundamental back-office applications of gift processing and data management, many shy away from using technology to truly drive the prospect management and relationship-building processes. This is an unfortunate waste of opportunity, as many readily available technologies can be used to accelerate the process of communicating and building relationships with constituents—everyone from the occasional volunteer to long-time annual fund supporters to the millionaires in your database.

What's the catch? The key to using the Internet for enhancing a major donor program—as with anything else—is making the paradigm shift from "it won't work" to "it will work."

The Rise of ePhilanthropy

As anyone who has lived in the industrialized world over the past few years already knows, the Internet is revolutionizing modern life and, along with it, philanthropy. Less than a decade ago, email and the World Wide Web were foreign concepts to everyone but the occasional computer whiz. Now they are a part of everyday life, as many of us spend hours a day online checking email, reading news, managing finances, conducting research, buying products and services, and, as many nonprofits have found, responding to solicitations (see Exhibit 8.1).[1]

---

[1]Pew Internet & American Life Project. More detailed information is available online at www.pewinternet.org/.

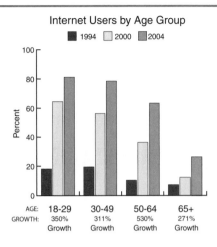

Internet Users by Age Group

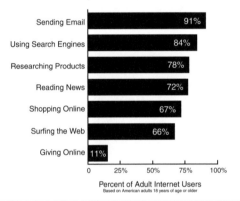

Most Popular Online Activities

EXHIBIT 8.1   Who's Online and What They Are Doing
Source: Pew Internet & American Life Project. All figures refer to U.S. Internet usage.
Available at www.pewinternet.org/trends/UsageOverTime.xls.

A Pew Internet & American Life Project study shows that Internet usage in the United States is increasing for all age groups. The surge in popularity of shopping online provides a strong indicator of the upcoming growth of online giving. While giving is less prevalent than other online activities, relationship-building activities over the web have been readily adopted by the American public.

It is important to note the exponential increase in online donations over the past five years—a compound annual growth rate (CAGR) of approximately 200 percent—as well as the projected increase over the coming years (see Exhibit 8.2). Some experts have estimated that online giving will approach $70B annually by 2008.

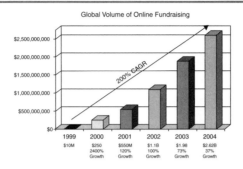

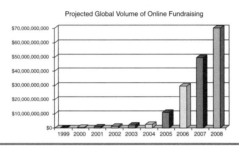

EXHIBIT 8.2 The Changing Dynamics of the Internet and ePhilanthropy
Source: ePhilanthropy Foundation.org

However, many organizations still struggle to understand how the Internet could possibly help to build meaningful, long-term relationships. The Internet is just a form of technology, right? How can you interact on a personal level through the web? Can you really build lasting relationships online?

The web will never completely replace the benefits of face-to-face interaction. However, it can enhance and change the deeply personal relationship being built between donor and organization. When used properly, the Internet is not a substitute for the proven activities major gift officers carry out, but rather a strategic tool that supports and supplements each step in the relationship-building process.

UNDERSTANDING THE FUNDAMENTALS OF MAJOR GIVING

People give to people, and face time with key prospects is critical to getting them to understand and support an organization's mission, which means that building relationships with major donors can be an expensive, labor-intensive process, with few guarantees for success. Many organizations with otherwise strong fundraising programs have little or no success with major giving. Often, these organizations give up completely, focusing solely on special events, membership drives, and their annual appeal. To me, abandoning a major giving program seems like a waste of opportunity.

What Is a Major Gift?

Major gifts—sometimes referred to as principal or leadership gifts—have the potential to play a critical role in an organization's overall fundraising strategy. They can set the tone for a campaign, raise awareness for an important cause, and encourage other donors to give—not to mention bring in much-needed funding. While the size of a major gift can vary widely among organizations—anywhere from several hundred dollars to over seven figures, depending on the size of the organization—they are generally a significant investment on the part of the donor, a transfer of wealth and assets rather than a distribution of discretionary income.

Needless to say, major gift fundraising is much more than just asking a prospect for a large amount of money—it comes as the result of a long-term, relationship-based process predicated on close collaboration, deep respect, and mutual benefit. Because of the financial implications, major gifts are generally the result of thoughtful and careful planning, with involvement from accountants, estate planners, researchers, family members, and, of course, the organizations themselves. Major donors care deeply about the organizations they support, want to make a significant impact on a cause, and many expect to see a return on their investment.

Whether it is with a donor, a close friend, or soul mate, the process of developing a relationship is the same: meeting, establishing common ground, building on shared interests, and, over time, cultivating trust. Success in this process requires detailed knowledge and effective communication, which is where the Internet can come into play: collecting the information solicitors need to carry out successful cultivation activities for major donors, and pushing highly personalized information out to prospects in order to initiate, build, and enhance relationships.

For more information see Chapters 1, 5, 9, and 10.

COLLECTING INFORMATION AND LEARNING MORE ABOUT PROSPECTS

One of my most interesting experiences as a major gift officer came when I was working for a large museum in a major metropolitan area.[2] I had

---

[2]While loosely based on actual events, the situation, events, and people depicted in this anecdote have been changed to protect the privacy of all parties involved.

been handed a dossier on a prospect and was assigned to explore his viability as a major donor. The numbers added up: he owned a highly successful business, was a longtime subscriber to the museum's magazine, and donated $10,000 a year to our annual membership campaign for the past decade. Amazingly enough, due to our decentralized organizational structure and somewhat antiquated information systems, he had gone virtually unnoticed by the major gift staff.

After several calls to his office, I was able to schedule an initial face-to-face meeting with him. After almost 40 years in the oil business, the gentleman was preparing to retire and was busy transitioning leadership of the company and tying up loose ends. The museum's research team had prepared an inch-thick dossier on the prospect, and I had spent the better part of several days beforehand reading through the materials and researching his company to prepare for the meeting. The timing, I thought, was impeccable. In addition to retiring and selling off a controlling share of his business, the museum had an upcoming exhibit related to the petroleum industry. Based on his life's work trekking the globe in search of new sources of oil, I was convinced he would jump at the chance to support the exhibit.

When I entered his office, I noticed something that wasn't mentioned in any of the newspaper clippings, financial reports, and public records of the team's research . . . the walls of his office were covered in glass shelves housing hundreds of exotic rocks and gems, each professionally labeled and illuminated with museum-quality lighting. I briefly hesitated—should I continue with my carefully researched talking points around the petroleum industry and our upcoming exhibit? Or, should I try to engage the prospect on what was obviously a personal interest? I scrapped my initial proposal and began a conversation around what I soon found was a lifelong avocation—geology.

Overflow of Information

With all the tools available to researchers today, finding information on prospects may seem relatively simple. Even the most sophisticated organizations, however, can find that identifying those people most likely to make gifts of significance can be exceedingly complex, a challenge exacerbated by the overflow of information available to researchers. Additionally, traditional research methods—peer review, public records searches, and even queries on online databases—are relatively passive in that they provide secondhand information that may or may not be helpful in the solicitation process.

When used as a strategic tool, however, the Internet offers a more proactive means of gaining information—that is, collecting detailed information directly from prospects. So, how can the web help with this? Just ask one of your friends who may have tried his hand at online dating. In these services, an online survey is used to collect information, build a member profile, and connect the user with other members with similar interests. While not perfect—what survey could account for the complexity of variables that go into a relationship—the online service provides some structure to the process of meeting people, as well as dramatically increases the odds that members will speak with someone with similar interests.

Aside from sheer novelty, the popularity of the service comes in three forms: quickly identifying a number of people with compatible interests, reducing energy spent building relationships likely to go nowhere, and briefly cultivating enough of a friendship to take the edge off a more traditional first date. If nothing else, the tens of millions of people who have used services such as Friendster, Match.com, eHarmony.com, and other dating sites speak to the viability of such a concept.

Just as online dating services can solicit information to identify potential dates, there are a number of online tools that can proactively collect the information necessary to help identify those most likely to give to your organization and can provide information to support cultivation and relationship-building activities. To facilitate this, a number of vendors offer prospect and wealth screening services, such as Blackbaud Analytics, WealthEngine/WealthID, P!N, TargetAmerica, BIG Online, and Grenzebach, Glier & Associates (for more information see Chapter 2, "Knowledge Management, Data Mining, and Prospect Screening"). These services mine stores of public records and other databases to find the financial, biographical, and demographic data necessary to identify and profile the wealthiest individuals in your database. They supplement the information on giving and relationship history in order to provide a more complete and accurate picture of your prospects.

Additionally, vendors such as Blackbaud Analytics and Grenzebach, Glier & Associates offer data modeling services that go beyond wealth identification to predict which individuals in your database are your best major giving prospects. Data modeling services analyze previous donor behavior, identify common traits and attributes, then develop models to predict which other individuals in your database are most likely to make a certain type of donation. (See Chapter 2, "Knowledge Management, Data Mining, and Prospect Screening" for more information on prospect screening and data modeling.)

Three Major Gift Indicators

While I can only speculate as to the methods online dating services use to match their members, generally there are three traditional indicators of a

Major Giving Indicator	Description and Criteria
Capacity	Capacity is generally considered the final qualifier for major gift prospects and is often used to help estimate gift range. ■ How much are they worth and how much can they give? ■ What is their income, investments, and personal holdings? ■ Current economic obligations—are they already committed to large gifts elsewhere or do they have major business debts?
Inclination	Inclination is a measure of an individual's general philanthropic nature and historical support of similar causes. ■ Do they give to charities and support similar causes? ■ Do their interests and hobbies align with your mission and programs? ■ Have they volunteered or served on the board of similar organizations?
Linkage	Strengthening existing relationships is easier and less expensive than building new ones, meaning your best prospects are probably already in your database. ■ Are they regular givers or do they have a high lifetime value? ■ Have their families been beneficiaries of your services or are they otherwise close to your organization? ■ Have they volunteered, attended events, or given other support?

EXHIBIT 8.3 Major Giving Indicators

prospect's ability and willingness to give a major gift to a particular organization: capacity, inclination, and linkage (see Exhibit 8.3).

The combination of these three indicators provides a rough estimate of an individual's viability as a major donor and, just as important, provides the information necessary to develop a successful cultivation and solicitation strategy. While only a rough composite of an individual's giving potential and likelihood, this helps to manage the vast amount of information available on a prospect and quantify the initial viability of a donor (see Exhibit 8.4).

Together, capacity, inclination, and linkage ratings of a prospect can help to quantify giving potential for your organization.

Prospects with a high rating in all three areas, obviously, should receive priority, while prospects severely lacking in any one area may be better suited for the annual fund—or left unsolicited. Bill Gates may have the world's highest capacity rating, but if he has no linkage to your

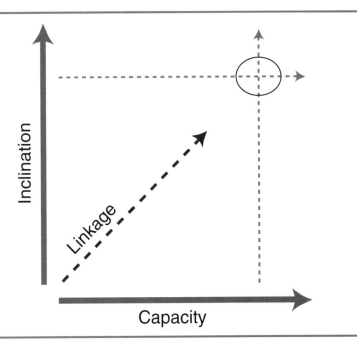

EXHIBIT 8.4   Combining Capacity, Inclination, and Linkage Ratings

organization and no inclination to give to your cause, is he really a viable prospect?

Following the Footprints in the Sand

Creating interest and drawing visitors to your organization is a critical function of any web site. A less obvious but perhaps just as important function is collecting information on the demographics, interests, preferences, and behavior of those same visitors. Once collected, this information can be used to supplement research efforts with specific details on pages visited, search terms, sticky content, and referring pages—in short, the exact information a visitor looked for on your site, the specific content viewed, how long they remained on each page, and what content moved them to action—much like following a set of footprints in the sand, left by someone who walked the beach before you.

In this regard, an effective web strategy can provide elusive, yet often critical, information on the interests of major giving prospects. For example, a visitor may be drawn to your site to view information related to your programs and mission, or news about a particular cause, event, or need. High-level information might pull visitors into a site, while detailed, high-value information may be available only after a brief log-in to an exclusive,

Determining Giving Interests Online

A Real-World Example

I was recently working with a higher education institution that had just implemented a new web site. Whereas the advancement office had previously solicited alumni based on their major and graduating class, the fundraising team was able to learn a lot more about the specific interests of their web visitors and alumni, and what they found was pretty revealing. One example that comes to mind was of a former economics major who was high on the capacity rating scale, and had been targeted by one of the business school's top solicitors without any significant results for several years.

When the school ran a standard web activity report, however, they found that the prospect was a regular visitor to the drama department's web site, not the business school's alumni site. Instead of sending a monthly eNewsletter on the latest projects of the business school faculty, they gradually started sending information from the drama department to see if a change in communications would move the alum to action.

Tracking the prospect's activity and responses to the theater department's email over a period of several weeks revealed a consistent interest in the school's year-long Shakespeare festival, and a fundraiser from the school of fine arts began to fine-tune her fundraising strategy accordingly. She immediately contacted the alum to extend a personal invitation to a sold-out Shakespeare event. Afterward, the fundraiser sent an email to follow up on the event, as well as a link to a Shakespeare professor's classroom blog.

A few weeks later, the fundraiser was taking the prospect to lunch with the faculty's expert on Shakespearean comedies and Renaissance theater. By the end of my consulting engagement, the prospect was in discussions to make a major donation to renovate the drama department's performance space. Over the period of a few months, the fundraising team was able to use the web to convert a nondonor into a viable major giving prospect.

members-only area. Once logged in, a visitor's preferences, interests, search terms, pages viewed, and other information could be tracked in elaborate detail and saved to a relationship management database.

A staff researcher can then combine the user's profile information and site activity with historical relationship information and data available through online research tools—public records, online research databases,

Google searches, or any other resources currently in use—to provide a more complete picture of activities, affiliations, associations, and potential giving interests. In this way, researchers can gather information from a visitor's web activity to determine an appropriate plan for further engaging the donor.

SHARING INFORMATION AND BUILDING RELATIONSHIPS

While the meeting with the oil magnate went slightly differently from what I had anticipated, I still considered it a success. The upcoming sale of his business clearly indicated major giving capacity, while his long-standing donations to and interest in the museum showed linkage and inclination. The ball was now in my court to develop the right strategy to engage with him further and develop a proposal that would captivate his interest.

Considering the timing of his retirement and the sale of his business, I suspected solicitors for dozens of other organizations would be fighting for his attention and interest at the same time. I needed something to keep up the momentum of our first conversation and make us stand out. As a major gift officer, I had all of the standard cultivation tools—a budget for lunches with staff, behind the scenes passes for various exhibits, access to the key players in the organization, even one of the leading museum web sites at the time—but I wanted to do something different. We had done little to actively engage the prospect or appropriately thank him for his long-time loyalty and support. I wanted to show that we had really listened to his interests and had some compelling ideas about how his support could make an impact on both the museum and the community.

I asked the head curator of the geology department if he had any ideas. Interestingly enough, we were in the process of digitizing our museum's collection—a massive, multiyear effort that, considering it was the late-1990s, was well ahead of its time. The plan was to develop one of the first "virtual museums," an online complement to the brick-and-mortar museum. The site would provide additional information and resources to enhance the experience of a visit, as well as showcase previous exhibits and collections not on permanent display.

The head geologist agreed to invest some of his staff's time in mocking up a portion of the virtual museum as a prototype for showing the prospect some of their ideas. While our efforts would pale in comparison to some of the online exhibits in place, we added some high-quality photos of our existing collection, some notes from a planning committee meeting, a sneak-peek of a recently acquired gem collection, and—perhaps most important—contact information for the various curators in the department.

I knew that technology alone wouldn't convince anyone to sign a check, but I hoped it would be enough to pique his interest with some of our current programs, as well as give him an idea of how we could partner with him to develop our vision for the future.

How to Leverage Information to Drive Fundraising Results

We've discussed at a high level the potential of the Internet for capturing information—something online marketers and data miners have been doing in the for-profit world for years. The question then becomes how to leverage this wealth of information to target communications, build relationships, and support fundraising goals.

The majority of cultivation activities does, and probably should, take place face-to-face. That said, helping people to understand and believe in a cause doesn't necessarily have to take place in a boardroom, at a special event, or on a site visit. The power of the Internet derives largely from its ability to disseminate information quickly and easily, making it an ideal method to communicate with donors and prospects.

Thanks to Amazon, eBay, and other leaders in the online space, your constituents have come to want and expect fresh, engaging content based specifically on their interests and preferences. University alumni, for instance, want to see information about their favorite sports team, the department they majored in, the clubs they participated in, a directory of their other classmates, their class's reunion schedule, updates on a professor's latest projects, and other content specific to their experience. In the same way, prospects interested in supporting a museum are looking for information on upcoming exhibits, past shows in line with their interests, and a means of personal contact with artists, researchers, and other like-minded philanthropists. Targeted content increases the chances that visitors will return to a web site, as well as provides the feedback to the organization to refine a prospect's profile.

Personalized online content may seem like the result of a Herculean effort, but it doesn't have to be. In fact, nothing is further from the truth. Anyone familiar with Amazon's site has seen the power of technology to seamlessly automate the personalization process, as the site makes recommendations based on search terms and pages viewed, then pushes out targeted recommendations and content based on this historic information. Changes in the online behavior of the visitor are reflected in continuous adjustments to the personalized content. Over time, this feedback loop refines the user's preferences, increases the value of the content provided to the visitor, and provides a compelling reason for return visits and brand loyalty. When integrated closely with offline activities, the result is an integrated relationship-building strategy that continuously refines communications and improves results over time.

An Integrated Strategy

Exhibit 8.5 provides a theoretical model of an integrated relationship-building strategy that aligns online and offline relationship-building activities. This model is based on close integration between a Web Content Management System (CMS) and a Constituent Relationship Management (CRM) system that tracks and integrates both online and offline activity and data. Together, this solution platform can track all activities and communications between a constituent and your organization in a single record, providing a comprehensive picture of each prospect. Moreover, automating the transfer of information—between the web site, CRM system, prospect screening services, research staff, and solicitors—streamlines many labor-intensive processes and simplifies a complex flow of information.

Note that while this model is useful for building relationships with all constituents, for the purpose of this chapter I am going to focus primarily on how this model can be used to build relationships with major donor prospects.

Interactions and Web Activities

The first time a constituent visits the web site—whether to register for an event, read articles from an eNewsletter, bid in an online auction, respond

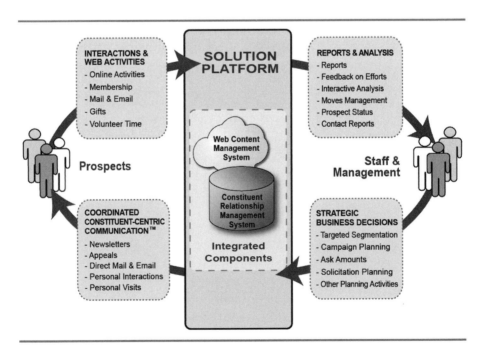

EXHIBIT 8.5   An Integrated Relationship-Building Strategy
Source: © 2005 Blackbaud, Inc. All rights reserved.

to a solicitation, or simply learn more about an organization and its cause—she is asked to complete a brief registration in order to log in to the site and access its content. This brief log-in enables:

- *Delivery of personalized content.* The Web Content Management System can immediately begin pushing personalized content to the visitor based on the preferences provided during registration.
- *Tracking detailed web activity.* The system can immediately begin activity tracking, including pages visited, referring pages, search terms, and sticky content to better understand and model interests and behavior.

Reports and Analysis

Because the web CMS and the CRM system are closely integrated, information is consolidated into a single database to enable:

- *A holistic view of prospect information.* Combining web activity with historical information related to interests, communications, and past behavior provides staff with a single, complete view of a prospect's interaction with an organization.
- *Leveraging prospect screening services.* If the visitor does not have a record in the CRM system, the database can create a new record, then automatically export the visitor's demographic information to a prospect screening service. The screening service would return an overlay of rich information from public records and other online databases.
- *Real-time solicitor updates.* When a major donor prospect logs in to the site—or when a screening service indicates a visitor has major donor potential—the information can be automatically routed to a major gift officer.

Strategic Business Decisions

Information is key to planning and executing effective cultivation activities. Researchers and gift officers can use interactive analytical tools to enable:

- *Targeting the best prospects.* With detailed information from screening and modeling services, web activity, and historical relationship information, researchers can identify the individuals best suited for annual campaigns, capital appeals, or major donor solicitation.

■ *Planning an approach.* Staff can drill into the wealth of information on prospects to identify approaches for engaging the prospect in a way that aligns with his unique interests, preferences, and giving capacity.

Coordinated Constituent-Centric Communication™

Solicitors can use the solution platform to carry out, manage, track, and report on their cultivation activities. This approach will enable:

■ *Increasingly personalized communications.* Whether it is an email, eNewsletter, personal phone call, or invitation to a special event, solicitors can track the results of and feedback on cultivation activities to ensure each future effort is more effective than the last.
■ *Automating communications.* The Web Content Management System continuously updates the personalized content on the site. This feedback loop helps to refine a prospect's profile and improve the effectiveness of communications over time.

Automating Manual Processes

Pushing targeted information on a web site and tracking the subsequent online activity and behavior can be augmented by automating many of the other traditional cultivation activities such as sending a handwritten note, mailing magazine articles of interest, arranging a personal visit with a beneficiary of the gift, or making an introduction to the chairman of the board. Each of these activities has an online component that not only can provide an additional channel for engaging the prospect, but can reduce administrative effort as well.

Let me provide an example. As a former major gift officer and avid reader, I used to spend an afternoon a week literally clipping articles out of magazines and sending them to prospects that may be interested. Though time consuming, the exercise provided an opportunity to keep in touch with prospects in between more formal cultivation activities, and sometimes it even helped me receive some feedback on interests and giving preferences.

Many solicitors do the same thing today, although by using the Internet it takes much less effort. Subscribing to email alerts on keywords and subjects of interest can automatically direct articles of interest to a solicitor's inbox, which can then quickly be rerouted to a donor along with a personalized note. Instead of combing the pages of the arts section of the *New York Times* every day, cutting out relevant articles, and then snail mailing them to a prospect, a solicitor can use a tool such as Google Alerts to receive the latest news items and articles in their inbox, which can be quickly and easily rerouted to a prospect with a few strokes of the keyboard.[3] Needless to say, these are also great tools for keeping up with the latest news regarding prospects, their businesses, and major philanthropic gifts.

In the same way, many organizations have found weblogs (blogs) and message boards can provide compelling information with a personal touch by updating major donors on the progress of a campaign or program. A blog written by the staff member overseeing the construction of a new hospital wing, a missionary in the field, or a scientist performing leading research can put prospects in direct contact with the people carrying out programs. Greenpeace.org has a great site with blogs from activists giving a first-person account of the work in the field. The activist blogs connect donors with the very people they are supporting, and help put a very personal face on the work of a global organization.

In the same way, message boards can be used to facilitate communication between members. The March of Dimes online community Share YourStory.org—winner of the 2005 International ePhilanthropy Award for community building—does a great job of connecting visitors through message boards, as members can post questions, respond with answers or advice, or just offer a word of confidence to each other. Reading the first-hand experience of another member can be just as interesting and meaningful as a face-to-face meeting, not to mention much more convenient for all parties involved.

Finally, while it goes without saying that an organization's web site should address the needs of all constituents, the specific needs of major giving prospects are often overlooked. Today's donors are more web-savvy than ever, and your web site should include detailed information on how your organization defines a major gift, the critical needs of your organization, examples of previous major gifts and their impact, and detailed information on your organization's privacy policies and record of accountability. A members-only community might contain a planned gift calculator, a live chat with a major gifts officer, or multimedia testimonial by previous major donors that articulates their reasons for giving and what they have received in return. The members-only community should both make a statement about the importance of major givers to your organization and connect prospects with each other, creating an online major donors community with exclusive benefits, privileges, and value. The features on your site should promote your organization as a strident supporter of a valuable cause, as well as an organization that values and appreciates its donors.

---

[3]Google Alerts is a free service available at www.google.com/alerts. Also note that many applications can route relevant content to prospects automatically, eliminating the need for solicitor involvement altogether.

Communities, message boards, blogs, and other technology-driven cultivation activities are relatively simple to implement but can have a significant impact on donors who have the opportunity to interact directly with people they supported. Moreover, the small gains in efficiency provided by technology add up over time, meaning solicitors have more time to build relationships face-to-face.

CONCLUSION

After sending the virtual museum link to our prospect, we sat back and waited. The next morning I had an email from the prospect. He found the idea of the virtual museum interesting, and had sent along a few of his ideas on how we could develop the site to extend the reach of the geology department beyond the four walls of the museum. "You guys have a great collection," he said. "But you need to get the community involved. School kids, especially. People need to understand that geology is more than just rocks and dirt."

I replied that I thought this was a great opportunity and that I would like to send his ideas to some other people involved with the project. I immediately forwarded his email to the head curator and a fundraiser from the geology department. The curator emphatically agreed and shared some of his ideas for educational programs and partnerships with local schools. Soon the two were not only brainstorming ideas on how to promote the collection and make the exhibits more educational, but swapping "war stories" about their time working in the field. The two had never met, but their connection was immediate and tangible.

While I knew we were still a long way from closing the gift, the web had helped us engage and connect with a key prospect by providing an example of what his support could do for our organization. The web had helped to bridge the gap between an interested prospect and an important need in our organization, a critical first step to any successful solicitation.

The aim of this chapter has been to demonstrate how the Internet offers nearly endless possibilities for engaging donors and prospects: publishing interactive content, providing direct access to solicitors, and almost anything else an organization can conceive. This chapter has only touched upon the potential uses of the Internet for building relationships with major donor prospects. Today's donors are more web-savvy than ever, and organizations interested in earning their support must increasingly cater to their needs—both online and off.

If you're ready to make the paradigm shift to start driving relationship building with major donor prospects online, try the following steps for getting started:

- *Assess peer organizations.* What organizations are getting the results you want? What are similar organizations doing to engage major donors online? Could you apply any of their ideas to your major giving program? Keep in mind that what is considered leading edge today will become an expected level of service in the future.

- *Evaluate current efforts.* What are you currently doing well in your major giving program—both online and offline—and how do you stack up against your peers? Are there offline functions that you could extend to the web or automate? What are your biggest challenges, and how could the web help address them?

- *Articulate your vision.* After an internal and external assessment, work with managers and executives to define your vision for a major giving program. What would you like to accomplish? How could you provide value to major donors? How will your Internet strategy complement and enhance your offline activities? At this point, think outside the box and involve key stakeholders throughout your organization to get buy-in and build momentum.

- *Set quantifiable goals and define information needs.* How will you define success and track your progress toward it? What information will you need to track in order to evaluate and improve your efforts? Is there information that you'd like to have—such as more detailed information on interests and behavior—that might be available exclusively through the web? Can your current systems readily track and leverage this information to provide a single, holistic view of your prospects and donors, both online and offline?

- *Build a strategic road map.* After your internal and external assessments, consider your ideas in light of the constraints of time, scope, and resources. What could be a quick win to build momentum for your program, and what will be long-term efforts? How will you get from your current state to realizing your vision? What staff members will be responsible for driving results and making sure the road map is followed? Building a technology solution is a process, not a single event. It will take the buy-in and ongoing commitment from all levels of your organization to achieve success.

Your specific uses of the Internet will be defined largely by the business requirements of your organization and needs of your donors. The concepts and guidelines presented in this chapter should be viewed as ideas to get you started; hopefully, many will help guide the alignment of your Internet strategy with your major giving programs.

CHAPTER 9

Using Gathered Information Effectively within Your Staff and Volunteer Teams

Nancy Johnson and Pamela Gignac[1]

INTRODUCTION

Communication is the foundation of what we are and it is just as important to communicate internally as with donors and the public at large. The key to this is the distribution of information among staff and volunteer teams. Using simple techniques and keeping abreast of advances in technology are the tools, but it's people who must manage and cooperate when it comes to success.

One process that has stood the test of time is the human element of peer screening and finding out who knows whom and what. An integral part of fundraising, this type of research is a forum that allows individuals to share detailed information about their contacts that may never be found in a document, hard copy, or on the Internet. The type of details shared by the stars of the sitcom *Desperate Housewives* can become the pot of gold that every nonprofit is trying to uncover. The process may be changing from sharing stories around a boardroom or in a living room on Wisteria Lane, to a virtual meeting with connections all around the world, but the backbone of the process is still *who knows whom* and *what do they know.*

The goal of this chapter is to help you put practices in place that will allow your organization to use the best information in the timeliest manner ultimately to help you raise more money for all your campaigns.

FUNDRAISING AND PROSPECT RESEARCH CYCLE

There is a strategic fundraising and prospect research cycle that donors and prospects are taken through as part of their commitment, growth, and

---

[1]Preparation of this chapter was aided by expert advice from James Greenfield (see Chapter 11 and his author bio for more information). His assistance is greatly appreciated.

our contact with them. All of this is to support our fundraising activities and pyramid of giving, taking donors from annual giving through major giving and planned giving; or alternatively, bringing in new prospects as donors for any one of these.

The Five I's	Example of Activities
Information	Gather information on selected key donors and new prospects. Segment donors based on criteria such as previous giving levels and history. Prepare confidential lists of those who might be appropriate prospects for major gifts and/or capital campaign support.
Identification	Begin to determine matching of their interest to your work and who might know whom. Research to learn how and where they might aid the organization in fulfilling its mission and vision. Research to find out about whom they are, their likely areas of interest and involvement, and their financial ability to help. If they have an inclination, prepare an approach strategy designed specifically for them, to bring them closer to you and a gift.
Involvement	Invite them to join in some capacity, such as attend a benefit event or public activity, tour the facilities, etc. Review lists with organization's donors and volunteers, board members, and professional staff can help to cultivate their interests and personal involvement.
Interest	Determine how strong their interest is and how closely the match with them might be. Fine-tune what might be appropriate to ask them for and when, including advice, time, door opening, as well as money.
Investment	Ask them to make an investment. Say thank you right away and often. Show them how it is used and keep them informed. Steward them and build an even closer relationship to continue their support.

Individuals also may be identified for the following:

- *Advice.* On financial goals and objectives, how the nonprofit is perceived, on specific prospects as well as their expertise and professional skills.
- *Time.* As champions and believers, including participation in meetings, feedback (often via email and telephone), participation in cultivation, and asks.
- *Door opening.* Tapping into their six degrees or circle of influence when appropriate to do so.
- *Gifts.* Financial support, gifts in kind.

The same strategy applies to individuals whose, by reason of their leadership positions in a corporation or business, foundation, or association, active affiliation in support of a nonprofit organization adds to its credibility with others. Relationships are all about linkages, and linkages are key advantages that nonprofit organizations must use wisely and well.

PERSONAL INTELLIGENCE GATHERING (PIG)

Circles of Influence and relationships can be tapped into to develop, network, and search out who might know whom and how well. Think of it as the six degrees of fundraising and use that when you are describing it to your volunteers and board members. That is the best way to describe how names in front of you can lead to someone more likely to support your work.

Whether you share lists of names that have been put together as a result of screening or other strategic searches through prospect research, the need for sharing the prospect results with others is a key way to bring them to life for you. It is a way to find the nuggets of gold that might have otherwise been missed. These nuggets can make the difference between your nonprofit and another seeking the same prospect's support. It can also increase your probabilities of success.

Two main types of prospect lists that are used are:

- Contacts needed list
- Circle of friends list

These tools and other techniques are also discussed in Chapter 1, "Prospecting for Major Gifts," as well as Chapter 10, "Moving from Prospect Identification to Making Friends for Life."

Taking the information you have gathered and sharing it within your closest group to bring it to life makes it unique to you and helps to expand upon the standard sources used in putting it together in the first place. Those that you should share your lists with include:

- Board members
- Key staff
- Close friends
- Volunteers
- Selected donors

These lists will assist in finding out:

- How up to date your information really is
- What other information lies beyond what is readily available in standard sources
- Perhaps most important, who knows whom and how well

People seem to appreciate being asked for their advice, so do so whenever you can. Seek out more than the obvious information on the prospects in your lists. Confirm what you have, find out what you have missed, such as company or foundation information, and determine if you need to find out more or take a new direction with each prospect.

Also, ask if those reviewing the lists for you have the type of relationship that will allow them to help your organization become more connected or a column that says "I can share more details and help solicit a gift."

Some people may be willing to share more information when talking to you personally than by putting it in a document. Know your team and always have multiple options of gathering information so everyone feels comfortable with the process. Be sure to communicate the fact that all information is handled with high levels of security and confidentiality.

Beware of gossip—as fun as it might seem, this can be extremely dangerous for many reasons. Be careful not only with regards to repeating it but storing it. Do not store anything that might be considered libelous or detrimental to the prospect or your nonprofit. Do not store it anywhere—electronically, on a desk, in a drawer, or a shoebox under your bed. Do not use special codes to disguise what is meant. Be ethical and responsible as you will often be privy to extremely sensitive and potentially damaging information. (See Chapter 4 for more information.)

PROSPECT SCREENING AND REVIEW

An effective method of confirming and gathering more information is sitting around a table and having a confidential discussion with board members, key volunteers, and staff regarding who knows whom and what they know about the prospects identified or even new ones that should be added. This type of format will generate lots of valuable information, but staying focused and getting through the list can be time consuming. It is also paramount that information shared is positive and should be captured as if the prospects themselves might see it someday.

This is also the time to request board members and volunteers to help introduce you to prospects that have been identified with wealth and other names of people they believe would have an interest in the organization's mission.

The main goal will be taking a large list of prospects and narrowing it to a list of best prospects capable of making a large gift. The most appropriate people to help with this process are those most dedicated to the mission and those who understand the importance of fundraising to help sustain the program. It is also important that they know many of the constituents, are community leaders, active volunteers, and/or are major donors themselves.

The process of peer screening typically is gathering people in a working social situation, often with food, and then a trusted member of the constituency explaining the process and the importance of its success. It is important to stress the confidentiality of information shared and anonymity. Besides the detailed information that individuals may be able to provide, they also are asked to rate a person on capacity to give and a connection to that person. Sometimes the biggest challenge can be keeping this from becoming a gossip session.

Prospect Session Agenda

According to Jim Greenfield (see Chapter 11, "Results Analysis and Performance Measurements" for further information), prepare an agenda for prospect review meetings to include evaluating the when, where, and how research information will be used. Participants will be asked to:

■ Review progress in current cultivation and solicitation strategies
■ Establish the series of next steps for each prospect; adjust contact teams if needed
■ Clarify donor recognition to be offered
■ Evaluate the use of communications materials

Allow time to review whether any added documents, financial details, invitations to social events, meetings with board and/or staff leaders, tours of facilities, and more will help keep the action moving forward. These meetings can decide on any added research needed, verify the estimated value of assets being discussed as gifts, match donor interests with specific major gift or capital campaign objectives, identify other volunteers, board members, and/or senior staff to join in the next series of cultivation and solicitation steps, and the like. Prospect meetings also study whether any future social or public events can be used to expand existing relationships. In each instance, new timetables and deadlines will be set for completion of all these activities.

Lastly, agenda time also will be scheduled to review the status of all donors who have made their gift decisions. The focus here will be to verify that all gift acknowledgments have been completed, to review the progress to complete required recognition details, to make plans for donor receptions and dedications, and more. Each agenda for prospect review meetings is significant to eventual success and can be guided by the following general parameters.

Prospect Lists

In order to facilitate prospecting sessions, it is invaluable to have a well-researched list to use as a reference and talking point to show the participants what you are seeking to do and the types of people and organizations you are trying to reach. There are two lists that support this: the circle of friends and the contacts needed lists.

Circle of Friends The circle of friends is used to discover ways through contacts and friends to encourage donors to give more. It involves a strategic program to build relationships with these donors to maintain their interest and raise their level of giving. You are looking for those who might become major donors. Expect to see larger numbers of names, around 10–20% of your database or more. In this case you have the contact and need the research to determine an approach strategy.

This list is usually in a database-generated report format, and shows current top donors who have given above a set level as a one-off gift or cumulatively over a period of time. *This is confidential, never leave it with anyone to take away or email.* Review the names with your staff and volunteers, including any high-profile individuals who know the community well. Aim for a review group of around six people.

Contacts Needed This list is based on high-quality prospect research and can consist of 100 to 250 prospect names from current and past donors as well as new prospects. It will be used to determine whom you will look at first to set up personal and face-to-face approaches. You're looking for the closest person known to you and the prospect. This list forms the basis of a focused part of your PIG (personal intelligence gathering). *This is confidential, never leave it with anyone to take or email.*

In this case, you have the research basics but you need the contact to determine an approach strategy. This might include donors with known interest but no known past with you.

Share this list with high-profile volunteer leaders and donors who are well networked to determine their personal six degrees of networking. It's about friends leading to friends and peer-to-peer contacts. Those who have given to you already are the best-placed candidates to assist you with your asks.

You will then use the information gathered together with the rest of your research to determine your approach strategy for each prospect. Each of these reviews will generate new names—prospects you had not thought of before. Take a look for matches between new prospects and names on your database.

Ensure that people see that you have done your homework and

remember that this list, like all your work, is highly confidential. This is an ongoing management tool that will take time to implement and develop. It will be pivotal for the information you need to develop a personalized approach strategy for each prospect—who is best placed to make the approach. Look for three main responses:

1. Knows well enough to approach
2. Knows enough but needs assistance in approach
3. Comments and other information such as other contacts, relationships, other prospects mentioned

There is more on moving from prospecting to solicitation in Chapter 10, "Moving from Prospect Identification to Making Friends for Life."

Contact Reports

According to Jim Greenfield (see Chapter 11, "Results Analysis and Performance Measurements"), a somewhat misunderstood and often-abused fundraising rule is that the results of each and every contact with a qualified prospect be recorded and reported to the fund development office. This information is vital for continuous review by staff and volunteer leaders and to be added to each prospect's main data file.

This rule also applies to all other employees after their cultivation and solicitation calls, be they chief executive officers and other senior and professional staff members, as well as board members, volunteers, and all fundraising staff. "After the visit, write a short note of thanks for the prospect's time and interest. As appropriate, draft a further note of thanks from the chief executive officer and perhaps from the board chair. Prepare a complete summary report on the visit, with particular attention to new information on the potential donor's special interests, background, and idiosyncrasies."[2]

Among the several reasons this information is required is common courtesy—to thank people for their time and interest. Next, record brief comments on topics discussed and campaign objectives covered, questions asked and answers given, requests for additional information, others to be included in future meetings, follow-up actions and suggested next steps, and an overall impression or synopsis of the meeting.

Those who met with the prospect likely will remember some or all of these details but only for a limited time, after which they will not be able to recollect them accurately and completely. Unless recorded immediately

---

[2]Kent E. Dove, *Conducting a Successful Capital Campaign,* 2nd ed. San Francisco: Jossey Bass, 2000, p. 120.

after each visit, these crucial details will be lost and future contact and communications with the prospect will be handicapped. Failure to capture these details is discourteous to each individual prospect, harms any potential interest in the organization, fails to fulfill the best interests and wishes of the donor, and diminishes the good efforts of all those involved. Without a record of what was discussed, those who call on this prospect next will be poorly prepared to carry out their assignment with success.

Contact report forms should be designed as a one-page summary that also can be used after a telephone call to record the discussion details (see Appendix D). The amount of detail reported should concentrate on the purpose of the meeting, how the discussion progressed, how the prospect responded, their specific questions or objections, were they relaxed or tense, appeared open or closed-minded, friendly to the visitor(s), expressed a sincere interest in the project, was inclined to consider a gift toward it, and whatever else was relevant to the purpose of the visit. Each is a piece of the puzzle that leads to a successful decision for both the prospect and the organization.

THE IMPORTANCE OF INFORMATION RELEVANT TO CAMPAIGN GOALS

Defining what information is to be used for each campaign helps determine who should have access to it and overall strategies to manage and implement it. The simplest way is to segment individuals who have never given a large gift for an upscale direct marketing. The solicitation might be as simple as asking for a larger annual gift from those capable donors.

Initially, you will identify people with the interest and best potential for future major gift cultivation. The key is to identify those with wealth and interest and to communicate with personalized one-to-one messages from the start of the relationship.

Organizations that screen names on an ongoing basis are segmenting for upscale marketing at the beginning of their relationship with the nonprofit. Healthcare organizations have been successful in turning patients into donors. In the United States, in spite of recent HIPAA regulations, hospitals are becoming as successful as universities in building relationships with major donors.

Stop! Take out a pen or your Palm . . . who is connected to your organization in a way that an alum is connected to his school or a patient to her hospital?

- Did you list the people who attended an event?
- What about one-time attendees to a seminar or lecture? If I spend the evening with your organization, I'm pretty connected!

- How about your newsletter list?
- Surely you listed your web visitors! You do know how many hits a day you are getting?

These are just a few ideas of where one can focus to start uncovering more people interested in your mission and to build a foundation to better long-term relationships.

Overall Benefits of Research

The following outlines the benefits to make the case for research:

- Ensures appropriate resource allocation
- Allows an organization to focus its efforts on the prospects that can do the most good
- Helps you use your volunteer organization (number and types to build linkages to your group of best prospects)
- Establishes an ongoing research system to help you enlist top leaders (because volunteers will see the information that they require to succeed)
- Helps you target the leaders who will have the most influence on your selected group of major prospects
- Builds volunteers and staff confidence for the cultivation and solicitation process
- Allows those involved in prospecting to experience the joy of discovery (prospect research can be like being a detective and solving a good mystery)
- Gives you power, leverage, and confidence
- Matches the right program with the right prospect

Tools That Can Do the Trick

Being aware of the wealth information early allows for the best relationship formula.

Tools that can support your work include:

- Well-designed software and preferably a database
- Using email to capture info and share it with volunteers and staff
- Using forms to be completed
- Data entry—shared responsibility between fundraisers and support staff on behalf of volunteers
- Unique web site pages
- Internet

- Online databases
- Other information sources
- Intranet
- Your own data
- Your circles of influence (staff, board members, volunteers, donors, supporters)

A Word about the Internet

The tools that are designed for instant access to data are used to proactively push data to the appropriate person. Staff members can schedule continual Internet searches on their most important prospects, businesses, and organizations on a regular basis. Those scheduled searches normally occur weekly, but some may be appropriately scheduled for daily or even hourly updates. One will receive an email and link to new articles found on the scheduled name.

This proactive research will allow the nonprofit to be the first to congratulate a donor on an advancement or honor they have just received. This method has eliminated the need for an individual to physically scan multiple news sources for the latest information. A good system should allow additional publications and sites to be searched that are specific to the nonprofit's constituency. The links to the information can be stored in the media section of the donor's file. They also can be forwarded via email to people outside the organization who are associated with the cultivation process for that prospect.

Can Using an Intranet Be an Effective and Efficient Tool?

An intranet is a web site or a portion of a web site that is designed for internal use. Intranets support internal communication and information storage with easy retrieval of information. They are also commonly used to provide training to staff in multiple locations. An intranet can be used as a means of sharing detailed prospect information with the internal staff. Organizations may schedule regular chat discussions through their intranet on their prospect list.

With a focus on major gift fundraising, intranets can have an important role in nonprofits today. Ideas and techniques are being taken from the corporate sector and then applied by ePhilanthropy specialists and others with vision and resources. Any intranet strategy needs to include in its design a format that not only (passively) shares information but also actively pushes knowledge toward key decision makers.

More and more organizations are using intranets to implement training for fundraising teams, and use them to enable their geographically scattered major gift fundraisers and researchers to work effectively together. At the end of the day, information allows fundraisers to be prepared to ask the right person for the best gift at the appropriate time. It is a tool for success in a world based on relationships.

CAPTURING INFORMATION

So how do you get people to update and share what has just happened between them and a prospect or donor? Some will do so willingly; others will do so after some hesitations and there will likely be one or two who might never quite get it. One way is to have it included directly in job descriptions, no matter what the position or role, so that everyone is responsible to ensure that information is shared quickly and effectively. For those who are not as comfortable with technology, enlist the support of assistants. Put together special contact form pads (see Appendix J). These forms can be as simple as you need them to be depending on the audience and people who will be using them. The examples are the Rolls Royce version that can be more easily entered onto a database or other software program.

Keep it simple, clean, and easy, and more people will do as asked and produce results!

OTHER WAYS TO KEEP TEAM MEMBERS UPDATED

Reports, reports, and more reports. Who hasn't spent countless hours designing specific reports to provide information to board members and volunteers? Reports and proper feedback are important tools even if they are sometimes cumbersome and challenging. Then there are the meetings, meetings, and more meetings. These need to be set up, diaries coordinated, agendas prepared, and yes, reports to be shared! With proper planning and management, the optimum use of everyone's time (yours and theirs) can be made each time you are together with champions of the cause. Reports and meetings are the main tools for ensuring that strategies are being implemented effectively, actions are taking place, information is being shared appropriately, and goals are being reached.

It is important to verify where information originated and to confirm its accuracy before sharing the details. Organizations use multiple methods of gathering information, and the challenge is communicating any differences to the end users of the data. Other chapters in this book include suggestions for various report formats, including progress reports, call reports, and contact reports. Also, see the appendices for examples of some actual forms used.

LESSONS LEARNED USING SCREENING COMPANIES IN THE UNITED STATES

As discussed in more detail in Chapter 2, "Knowledge Management, Data Mining, and Prospect Screening," many organizations are turning to data mining and prospect screening to sift through their databases to identify key donors and prospects. Some organizations are doing it themselves, and others use specialized vendors who provide a variety of screening services. However, countries outside the United States have limited access to personal and financial information. As a result, other countries like Canada and the United Kingdom are taking the lessons learned in the United States and using them as a guide to develop a more holistic approach to screening. This is done by using more specific criteria and benchmarks relevant to the nonprofit world and fundraising needs and strategies.

Straightforward data mining doesn't always produce the desired or even expected results. Screening services are typically used by organizations that have a prospect research staff to disseminate the details delivered by the companies. Those services tend to be expensive and often used just for a capital campaign. A common statement is, "We can't afford to do a screening, but we also can't afford not to."

A dedicated researcher can definitely deliver more detailed information or expedite the implementation of a screening, but many organizations do not have the luxury of funding that position. Most fundraisers can take screening results and prepare for meetings with major prospects. The challenge is in understanding the data sources and how that data can be used effectively.

There are standard reliable data sources, and most vendors access basically the same pool of information. The difference in the companies is in the delivery tool and the expertise in how to use the data to raise more money. Training and strategy sessions are an important aspect in using the information from a screening service.

Information from a screening will typically be matched in an exact, or hard, format or at a geographic, or soft, level (e.g., the exact match confirms information on a person at his home address, as information matched to a home address is the most reliable). It is important to be realistic and know that data can never be considered 100 percent accurate. Data is only as good as it has been reported. After some of the recent corporate scandals, it becomes apparent that even government-required filings can't be considered completely reliable. It is also important to note that a screening will not uncover every wealthy person in a database. A goal should be to identify individuals who have not made large donations but have the capacity to in the future with appropriate cultivation.

Geographic Matches

The geographic, or soft, matches will require additional research to verify if the match is to the same person on the nonprofit data file. This is when a prospect research professional becomes a real time saver. She knows how to be a detective and uncover the missing pieces to confirm that your person is the person that the screening has matched geographically.

What's in a Name?

The often-called million-dollar middle initial can definitely help with the confirmation of search results when matching with your database records. This might be the time to talk to the data entry person and restate the importance of getting every piece of data from an envelope or check. Typically a middle initial is used in business filings such as Security Exchange Commission insider filing and tax returns. Middle initials and names on joint accounts are also often used.

Many confirmations of names are easy because fundraisers, researchers, and others will know the individuals and can quickly confirm the apparent wealthy individuals on the file that are well known in the community. This is particularly true for those with more unusual names versus a more common one such as Smith or Lee.

Share Your Findings with Others

As previously discussed, the goal of a screening is to uncover wealthy individuals that you do not know. The next step in the confirming process goes outside the development team to board members and volunteers. This is to help confirm your prospect lists and to identify connections and routes to them.

This is highly confidential and private information. Wealth facts should not be shared outside your inner circle, so keep the information to confirming a name to a business without sharing wealth details.

You paid for it and you don't want others to share your findings with nonprofits that might compete with you for gifts from the same prospects. In the United States, lists are sometimes carefully shared using email, but this method is probably not appropriate elsewhere due to privacy laws and regulations (see Chapter 4 for more information on privacy and regulations). Advances in technology and security (or lack thereof) impact the vehicles we can use, such as email.

If you decide to follow this route, present the exercise as an appeal to help us know our constituents better. Aside from verifying that the person works for a certain company, sits on a board, and so on, always leave room for "tell us more about this person."

What to Watch Out For

Common roadblocks to the successful use of a screening are delays until everything is confirmed and putting it in a drawer and not using it at all! Nonprofits that address newly identified wealthy prospects with an upscale communication will see results quickly as they start the confirmation process.

The goal of a screening is to identify wealthy individuals in one's database and adjust communications with those top prospects. It is not an exact science, but technology has truly made it more reliable and a tool to be considered when trying to find the most capable prospects for large gifts.

Information is only as accurate as it has been reported. Internet searches allow for easier research with more publications at your fingertips to verify information, but use your findings as a guide and not the gospel. The biggest challenge is connecting back to the donor database. It is important that the prospecting process does not start generating standalone data depositories that are not integrated or accessible by everyone.

OVERALL PITFALLS OF RESEARCH

The following outlines what to watch out for based on recommendations from the AFP in the *CFRE Study Resources Guide:*

- Putting off research until you have the time (you never will)!
- Spending too much time doing the paperwork, being tied to a computer and not going out to meet with donors and prospects and ultimately secure support!
- Becoming overwhelmed; start on manageable chunks of research.
- Letting the research guide you while not becoming its slave.
- Recognizing that unfortunately you often will not have the opportunity to do it as intensively or extensively as you might like, as you will need to simply make the ask.

- Setting weekly goals and blocking out time for research.
  - Even one-person shops should devote at least a half-day per week to each of the following:
    - Research
    - Producing reports and capturing information electronically
    - Sharing information through two-way communication
- Showing others such as volunteers what to look for but not expecting them to analyze what they find, as this needs to be done by a trained professional—you.
- Sending out a prospect profile, report, or other document containing incorrect, sensitive, or outdated information.
- Double-checking all information from at least two or three sources.
- Remembering that accuracy and sensitivity build trust.
- Getting carried away and trying to remember everything about everyone.
- Gathering enough information, but only enough research to facilitate thoughtful matches and interactions.

CONCLUSION

Even as we become more comfortable and proficient with technology and its increasing sophistication, it will still be a challenge to capture all the relevant information from colleagues, board members, volunteers, and others. This communication of detail needs to truly be a two-way relationship to keep everyone as up to date as possible.

That means *everyone* involved in searching for the necessary funds to support our work—you the fundraiser and also the researcher, management, operational staff, program and project staff, and anyone who works for your nonprofit—has a vested interest in providing information, feedback, and ideas to increase the probabilities of fundraising success.

All of this needs to be done with sensitivity and confidentiality, following definite and clear guidelines and policies. Everyone's reputation is at stake—your organization, your askers and door openers, your board, colleagues, volunteers, and yes even your own. Information is power and confidence, but it is about building trust.

Moving from Prospect Identification to Making Friends for Life

Andrew Thomas and Ken Burnett

Apply to all those whom you know will give something; next to those whom you are uncertain whether they give anything or not; and show them the list of those who have given; and lastly, do not neglect those you are sure will give nothing; for in some of them you may be mistaken.

—Benjamin Franklin

PANNING FOR GOLD

So you have researched and identified prospective donors. A few will be red hot. You know who they are. Hopefully they are already inspired and motivated by the work you do and you have in place the perfect person, identified and prepared, ready to ask them for the biggest gift of their life. Good. But most likely, most of your prospects will be a little cooler and you'll be somewhat further away from actually asking them for the money. However, there's still a lot to be done. Others will be a lot cooler, perhaps even cold. All need warming up in the appropriate way so that you can get them ready for the ask and as welcoming and receptive to it as possible. (It has to be accepted, the verb *to ask* has now, irrevocably, also become a noun, thanks mainly, if not solely, to fundraisers.)

This chapter focuses on moving prospects already identified by research to becoming donors who will stay with you for life.

There are many ways of defining and ranking prospects. As we want to keep things simple, we define *prospects* as people meeting three criteria (see Exhibit 10.1).

Individuals qualifying as prospects are those you believe can make a large gift. By definition they will be sufficiently wealthy to donate substantially from either income or assets. Big donations call for a big interest in your organization or compelling personal reasons to want to help.

143

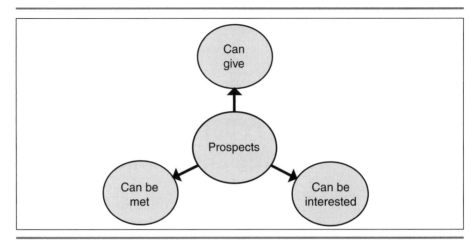

EXHIBIT 10.1   Prospect Criteria

Finally there must be a realistic chance of setting up a face-to-face meeting with the prospect.

It makes sense to rank prospects so that you can allocate effort and resources to those with the most potential. While many models exist, again we recommend keeping your prospect ranking system as simple as possible, as shown in Exhibit 10.2.

Prospect Category	Description	Typical Fundraising Comment
Cold Prospects	They can afford to give but we don't yet know whether or not they are interested in giving	We're not yet on their radar
Cool Prospects	They can afford it and have given to our kind of cause in the past	They ought to give to us
Lukewarm Prospects	They have the ability to give and are on our database	Alumni, members, mail donors, other audiences
Warm Prospects	We think they will give, given the right treatment	Screened and we have a plan to get to them
Hot Prospects	We have met them, they are interested, and can make a big gift	Further meeting with a peer is imminent
Red Hot Prospects	Potential donors whose behavior indicates a major gift is likely	Our top 20 prospects

EXHIBIT 10.2   Prospect Ranking

The six categories in Exhibit 10.2 are as complex as you're likely to need, and it's often possible to settle for just three—cold, warm, and hot (these terminologies are universally recognized but are not, perhaps, very donor friendly, so use them with care). Your aim now is to get closer to your prospects using friends, family, and any other contacts at your disposal to help the prospect become warmer.

See Chapters 1, 5, and 9 for more information. For the purpose of this chapter, it is assumed that you have:

- Produced a fundraising case and fundraising plan that identifies the pool of prospective donors
- Agreed on the table of gifts required to achieve the campaign target
- The leadership structure (e.g., appeal committee, financial development board, campaign board) in place
- Screened your supporter database to identify wealthy and affluent supporters (warm prospects) who might be involved
- Identified new cold prospects not previously known to you
- Profiled those prospects who you are likely to approach in the next six months

This chapter concentrates on moving from the desk research described earlier, through prospecting to donor cultivation and solicitation: moving prospects from cold to red hot. Along the way it makes sense to prioritize and reprioritize prospects so that you always have a manageable number of warm to red-hot prospects.

It's important that your prospect list is manageable. This means that at all times you will be able to recall your potential donors' names, faces, and relationships should they ever contact the office. As a guide, most development staff find it hard to keep more than 60 to 90 current prospects in mind at any one time.

With this in mind, the rest of this chapter will cover the following:

- Moving from desk research to solicitation
- Prospecting
- Enlistment
- Making new friends
- Donor development
- Cultivation
- Getting ready for the ask
- Stewardship

Before starting, it is worth pausing a moment to review the much larger number of other supporters that you will have as members, alumni, local group supporters, and other audiences who are not considered major donors but nevertheless have been loyal to your organization over the years. If we screen these donors carefully, we can identify those with the potential to give larger gifts now or perhaps make a major donation as a bequest. Too many fundraisers spend their time looking for new donors when their best prospects are already sitting on one of their databases. Screening these databases for wealth, philanthropic interest, location, age, and networks is simple, cost effective, and often a revelation.

For example, one of the United Kingdom's leading donor research agencies, Prospecting for Gold, reckons that 4 percent of most U.K. donor lists have donors capable of giving anywhere between £5,000 and £1,000,000. One nonprofit found that of three donors each giving £10 annually for the last 10 years, all three could have made £1,000,000 gifts. Examples of this screening process can be found at www.prospectingforgold.co.uk. Similar agencies exist in Europe, Australia, and North America and are developing in other countries.

MOVING FROM DESK RESEARCH TO SOLICITATION

Donors can be identified via myriad routes. A long and broad institutional fundraising history creates diverse prospects of many levels and types. Traditional methods of cold donor acquisition such as direct mail are now much more layered, with individual donors ranked into one-time or renewal donors, committed givers, mid- and high-level donors, and so on. Many organizations now have experienced success in soliciting quite high ($1,000+) donations via direct mail. The new trend for face-to-face street fundraising has introduced younger audiences (often, but not always, less affluent) who are predominantly recruited to regular, committed giving. Service users, event attendees, and even clients are all potential major donors, provided they meet the criteria of wealth, interest, and availability.

The process in which fundraising is the apparent end result is rarely just about asking for money. The final gift is only the outward sign of a donor playing a part in addressing something in which both you and the donor believe passionately—a problem, issue, or opportunity that urgently needs resolving and which you have brought to the donor's attention. You are giving that donor a chance to make a difference, in a small way, to change the world.

The relationship between donor and fundraiser, therefore, is crucial. People are much more likely to want to do business with those they know, like, and trust, and who are nice to them.

Extracting prospect names and data from computer files or paper-based lists can be costly and challenging, but in theory at least is fairly straightforward. Transforming them into real people we can talk to, involve, and inspire so they share our passion, vision, and commitment is what fundraising is all about. Only at that point, with all groundwork done, should the right person (ideally a peer who knows the prospect very well) ask the prospect for a large donation.

Many fundraisers and development staff are disheartened when prospects fail to give at the anticipated level. Yet obviously even the wealthiest person cannot give to every nonprofit that knocks on the door. Making a large contribution means understanding the work, believing in the vision and the fundraising cause, and trusting an individual or an organization personally to deliver on promises made. A major gift is an act of faith that the money will achieve the goals set. With public skepticism about philanthropy always high, fundraisers have to earn their donors' trust.

Success rates vary from cause to cause, but a useful rule of thumb for face-to-face major donor campaigns is to aim for one successful donation from every three warm prospects approached. Brilliant high-profile campaigns may do better and difficult causes may do less well, but if you are achieving a success rate below one in six, something is probably wrong. Perhaps too many people are being qualified as warm prospects who either are not sufficiently interested, don't have the money to give this year, or are being asked by the wrong person.

It is hard sometimes to accept that most prospects will say no. We should see each "no" as a step closer to the next "yes." In fact, if we are not getting a sufficient amount of "no" responses we are probably not asking enough people. Even failed solicitations may open up new prospect leads. Remember to celebrate all successes.

PROSPECTING

You have drawn up a list of cold to lukewarm prospects. Now, somehow, you have to get to talk to them.

If the prospects live far away, or for other reasons you cannot get to see them, you may have to develop their interest by telephone. For a particular campaign a colleague once telephoned an international philanthropist in Hong Kong to ask for introductions to other prospects who could help. Only later did we realize that the 45-minute interview had been conducted while the supporter was in the bath!

However well you might know the person you hope will do the actual asking for you, putting anyone on the spot to identify wealthy friends who might become donors can generate a slight panic and a denial that any friends or contacts have serious money. This natural reaction happens because:

- Individuals have different ideas of what it means to be rich. To one it's having at least £15 million of free assets, while another might consider an annual income of £100,000 sufficient to make a £50,000 gift, if spread over 10 years.
- Most people have little idea how much wealth their friends possess. In some cultures (e.g., in Britain), conversations about cash are still just not "the done thing."
- People often forget important connections, perhaps because they feel on the spot. Not everyone will give you his personal Christmas card list (though it might be worth asking).
- Most people hate asking their friends for money, not only because they may find it embarrassing, but also because they may have to return the favor at a future date.

A good way around such obstacles is to provide a current supporter, friend, or board member with a prompt or contacts needed list of individuals you want to reach, then persuade her to open the door for you. We are all familiar with the concept that everyone in the world is connected to everyone else by no more than six other people, so that, in theory, ultimately we could all get to talk to Bill Gates or Bob Geldof. While this concept may be unreliable, it is true that very often your cold prospects will be only two or three steps away from existing friends and supporters. So you need to persuade your existing friends and supporters to help you, as cultivators.

A good starting point is to give them your carefully researched list of cold to lukewarm prospects. This is often called a prompt list because it is designed to jog their memory. Instead of being asked to name people they know who might be able to give, they can just pick familiar names from your list. An example of the more detailed contacts needed list is given in Exhibit 10.3 (for more information see Chapter 9).

Your cultivators can use the A, B, and C columns to identify how well they know candidates and can be encouraged to make as many comments as they like. The better you know your cultivators the more easily you can encourage their fulsome sharing of knowledge, even gossip, to enhance the personal information you hold.

It is amazing how forthcoming, even indiscreet, some solid pillars of the community will become during prospecting group meetings. At a recent village meeting for a small school building project we were told who in the area has money, who lives well but on credit, and which

First Name	Last Name	Organization	A	B	C	Comments
Jim	Smith	Bird Airlines	A			Best friend of Mr. and Mrs. Jones
Ron	Jones	African Safari Fdn.			C	Known to the Foulks-Lanningham family
Billy	Black	Fishy Foods Inc.	A			Close friends of the Smiths and the Blacks
Bertie	Brown	Infestations R Us		B		Known to Mrs. Small. Difficult board member
Sally	Small	Slippery Fashions Ltd			C	Known to Mr. Jones but she is very shy and avoids publicity
Zoe	Foulks-Lanningham	Southern Mining Corporation	A			Gives to Mrs. Brown's favorite charity

EXHIBIT 10.3   Sample Contacts Needed List

people enjoy lavish lifestyles yet have no assets, all from a few local cultivators who know the community well and enjoy gossip. It all helps build useful data on how a community functions, which can boost your fundraising more than a little.

All campaigns will have critical or skeptical supporters among their cultivators, who can nevertheless be an invaluable source of prospects. It pays to try to interview these people on their own. Stress that the meeting is confidential and that you will not approach anyone without checking first with them.

In practical terms it's impossible to interview everyone individually, so bringing people together in a prospecting group often works better. The main features of a prospecting group meeting are:

- A fixed time for the meeting—two hours maximum.
- An effective meeting chair.
- A prompts or contacts needed list of 150 to 200 prospects.
- Eight to 10 participants and at least two home team members to take notes, spot body language, and generally keep the meeting on track.
- Some, but not all, of the participants should either know each other or have overlapping business or social networks.
- A mix of genders and ages.
- Preferably a boardroom or dining room table to work around.
- Some refreshments to ease any nervousness. Breaking bread together or sharing a glass of wine often eases an unfamiliar process.

The meeting then works its way through the contacts needed list discussing:

- Who knows whom? If more than one person knows someone, who knows her best and could they work together to plan an approach?
- How much might a prospect give? To overcome reticence, try to get invitees to be a little competitive here. This will also establish that you are after larger than average gifts.
- What would motivate them to give? Look for angles and personal motivations that might be helpful later.
- Who have you missed? Participants love to spot omissions but, of course, you missed them because there was only room for 150 to 200 names. At least you now know that someone around the table knows them.

After this, it's important to:

- Write up your notes that day.
- Try to prioritize prospects on the scale of cold to red hot and also rank them by size of potential gift, concentrating on bigger prospects in the opening stages of any campaign. This should be done the next day at the latest.

As we've said, people can be very indiscreet in prospecting groups. You may well come to love gossip and inside-track information but you must always treat it confidentially. Before relying on any information gathered in this way you should make sure it is accurate, and before you record it in a database you must ensure that storing and using information in this way is permitted under the terms of any data protection legislation that operates in your country. In light of this, it is wise to be cautious about sharing information. Finally, never leave lists with interviewees and prospecting group members or share with a third party information you have picked up in the course of your work.

Your now refined and detailed lists are the fundraising equivalent of gold dust. They have cost you precious time and scarce budget resources. Take care to ensure that your cultivators don't casually pass on your valuable lists to other nonprofits. If they do, you'll have only yourself to blame if they get to the prospect first.

ENLISTMENT

A few prospects may be warm enough and know you well enough that it becomes a simple step to organize a meeting to discuss a new project.

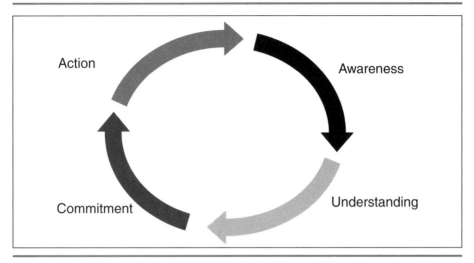

EXHIBIT 10.4 The Cycle of Understanding

However, younger, wealthy donors new to philanthropy or prospects a little removed from the cause will have to be recruited into support. They have to learn about your work and decide whether they want to be involved. Exhibit 10.4 describes this process.

- Awareness is the first step. Potential donors must know of and understand the cause and its desired outcome. For example, this may come through attendance at a special event, through a third-party introduction, or it might be that one of your cultivators creates an opportunity for you or a colleague to make an inspirational presentation.
- Understanding is when potential donors see the work you do and begin to appreciate the issues, problems, and challenges. At this stage they may be intrigued and interested but not necessarily ready to sign up.
- Commitment is the third stage, when prospects decide to support your cause, perhaps because they've been inspired by the mission and its proposed outcomes. Emotional buy-in to your program has begun and your prospect is ready to be cultivated as a donor.
- Action comes only when they are clearly ready and in a position to give.

Once a link has been made to cool prospects there are lots of ways to enlist them. The most obvious is an introduction from a friend who, believing the prospect might be interested in your cause, sets up a preliminary informal meeting perhaps over a meal or a drink. The friend effectively makes the introduction and endorses you and your cause in a relaxed and convivial setting.

It often makes sense to invite a group of people to an event, especially as the number of prospects increases. Enlistment events are often small, targeted at just 10 to 50 people. Some examples might include:

- A meal or reception added on to a special occasion—an opening, reunion, annual award day, etc.
- A reception or dinner at a prestigious location.
- A dinner hosted by a celebrity or VIP committed to your cause.
- A briefing for supporters about the new directions a nonprofit is planning.
- Open days.
- An annual lecture.
- A religious service of celebration.

Make sure you plan such events well in advance; diaries can get very busy so a useful idea is to send invitations in two, three, or even four waves so you can monitor acceptances, and if they are slow, can increase invitations to ensure a good attendance. If possible, invite people by telephone first and then mail the invitation, but if you have to send the invitations first, follow up by telephone a week later to make sure it has arrived and been read.

Plan the program for your event carefully. Avoid dull speeches and include only one or two speakers who can provide the right levels of charisma and inspiration. Be respectful of your prospects' time and make your event short and interesting. At the event, be very clear that you are not asking for money there and then, but you do want your guests' advice and to know their views and general interest in the appeal. Immediately after the event, sit down with your team of staff and volunteers, before their memories fade, and review the list of guests and how they behaved. Agree who was interested and what follow-up is appropriate. Ensure that chosen guests are contacted within a day or two of the event.

MAKING NEW FRIENDS

Most fundraising organizations deal with dramatic, real-life issues, often matters of life or death, or at least of great local or community importance and significance. Fundraisers usually have exciting, moving, uplifting stories to tell, stories that will involve and motivate donors if told with power and passion to inspire action.

Effective storytelling is at the heart of fundraising. At its most basic, it is one person telling another about a cause or issue that they both care about and between them agreeing on the best way that they both can do something worthwhile to help.

To be effective, fundraisers really need to understand their donors as individuals and to develop the ability to see the cause and issues through their donors' eyes. Fundraising is a long-term activity rather than a series of one-time hits. At its foundation is a relationship of mutual trust, respect, and consideration between donor and fundraiser. To inspire a donor, the fundraiser must fully believe in and commit to the cause personally. You can't fake sincerity.

Trust, confidence, and loyalty from donors, built up over years of considerate development, will be the fundraiser's greatest assets. All donors have a choice, encapsulated in the three little words that should be engraved on each fundraiser's heart—may change mind. Every donor is a volunteer, supporting your cause only because she chooses to. At any time she can go elsewhere. There are always lots of other good things to do with money. So the fundraiser must provide regular, appropriate, and motivational feedback to show donors why of all the choices they have, not continuing to give should be one of the last options. The fundraiser's job is to steward each donor's interest and commitment, to ensure the relationship is mutually rewarding and fully developed so that it will grow and mature to everyone's benefit, most of all the donor's.

Most donors are already committed in their giving to other charities and nonprofit causes. Much as we might wish it, they are not ATM machines where if you type in the correct code words they will spit out money. Instead they are as varied as only humanity can be. Some will be exemplary donors; some extraordinarily difficult. Some will intuitively understand your needs and interests; others will not, and will read nothing you send them. When embarking on a new relationship, ponder on what the prospect is looking for and attempt not to be too judgmental about the motives for giving. Most give for complex, often irrational reasons. While there are undeniably cultural and national differences, the striking thing about fundraising is how similar most societies around the world are, whatever the religion, background, or ethnic makeup. Take a look at Exhibit 10.5, which is based on research in the United Kingdom by the British author Lady Theresa Lloyd, and ask yourself how well prepared you are to enlist prospects with these motivations and aspirations.

We have identified sufficient warm prospects. Desk research has told us that they have wealth and interest in our cause. They have moved from being cool prospects to warm; we now have a real contact with them, either from a personal introduction or an enlistment event. The next step is cultivating them to the point that they become red-hot prospects.

Motivations	Belief in cause
	Being a catalyst for change
	Duty and responsibility
	Personal relationships
Relationships with recipients	Effective and appropriate communications
	Simple appreciation and recognition
	Being consulted and offered a chance to influence
	Good governance
Major gifts	Real commitment
	Allocating resources to different causes
	Relationships with recipients
Asking for money	Few people enjoy asking for money
	Poor staff support or backup
	Importance of giving yourself before asking
	Getting the timing right
	Enthusing people
	Public recognition

Adapted from Why Rich People Give *by Theresa Lloyd, published by Philanthropy UK.*

EXHIBIT 10.5   Some Thoughts about Giving

CULTIVATION

Turning a warm prospect into a red-hot prospect is a little like gardening. Warm prospects like to be in a friendly, warm, greenhouse environment. They prefer to mix with similar plants and often need a little fertilizer to encourage their interests to bloom. Sometimes a little more sunlight, in the form of appropriate recognition, can be an incentive. Above all they respond to being talked to before blooming into full flower.

The first cultivation step is preparing an approach strategy, where you decide how to take the prospect from enlistment to solicitation, or making the ask.

1. Start by reviewing the original desk research profile. Look at the information you now have from the personal contacts made during enlistment and see what other desk research is needed. For example, you may need to refine the donation target, personal networks, or previous giving history.
2. Decide who will be the lead staff and volunteer contact to coordinate approaches.
3. Go back to the circle of understanding (Exhibit 10.4) and decide where the prospect currently is on it. He will certainly be aware of you

but may not fully understand the challenge. If so, you need to put in place some cultivation to enhance his understanding if you are to have any hope of gaining commitment. Alternatively, your prospect may understand the organization but is not yet ready to commit. He may need more information, project proposals, and so on, or need reassurance about the staff leadership. Often prospects are sympathetic to the issue but not prepared to donate at the level required by the schedule of gifts.

4. Completing the circle of understanding may call for activities and interventions specific to the donor. Writing these down will clarify your thinking and show other staff or volunteers that this is a step-by-step approach. If you ask too early you will achieve only a fraction of the larger contribution sought. A few headings and examples are given in Exhibit 10.6 to develop an approach strategy. (For more information, see Chapter 5.)

Background	A short paragraph about why the person is a warm prospect
Lead contacts	Lead staff person Lead volunteer
Links to your organization	The history of their involvement with the cause
Research	Current research Additional desk research Personal intelligence required—talk to x, y, and z
Potential	Personal giving Corporate giving Foundation giving Access to public sector funds Access to other donors Total potential target gift(s)
Next immediate steps	Plan and fix next follow-up meeting Decide who else should be involved
Possible lines of approach	Known strong motivations No go areas of difficulty Best people to involve
Specific activities before asking for a gift	E.g., need to see the project Must involve family members
Cultivation timetable	E.g., must meet CEO Should be invited to anniversary dinner Her partner needs to visit the project
Making the ask	Target date

EXHIBIT 10.6 Common Approach Strategy Headings

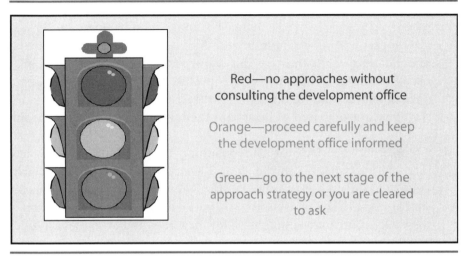

Red—no approaches without consulting the development office

Orange—proceed carefully and keep the development office informed

Green—go to the next stage of the approach strategy or you are cleared to ask

EXHIBIT 10.7   Approaching the Traffic Light

5. The approach strategy is a dynamic tool. The top 50 donors should be reviewed monthly and cooler prospects at least every quarter. With modern fundraising databases it can often be integrated into the prospect management database, but for smaller campaigns handling less than 400 prospects, a simple spreadsheet or contact management software is sufficient.
6. Build the approach strategy into the fundraising timetable to enable you to bring prospects together at cultivation activities.

If a lot of their friends are asking at the same time, especially for different things, many donors can easily get upset. Equally, few donors want to be entirely alone. The principle of peer group–led fundraising rests on the assumption that prospects prefer to be asked by their peers—people they know, like, and respect. As in football, teamwork is essential but only one person can score the goal. As part of the approach strategy, marshalling and coordinating the team approach is an art that all fundraisers must learn.

It sometimes helps to think of this in terms of a traffic light, as in Exhibit 10.7.

ARE YOU READY TO ASK?

Hopefully everything is in place and you are ready to ask someone for the largest gift of their life. Just one list of checks before you fly solo:

Is the fundraising case clear, agreed, and robust?

Do we have enough warm and red-hot prospects?

Do we know enough about them?

How much will we ask them for?

Why do we expect them to give that much to us?

Have they been cultivated properly?

Who will do the asking and have they given themselves?

Have they been briefed and trained properly?

After the successful ask there is still a need for a final step, which we refer to as closure. Closure is part of formal gift acknowledgment and completes the solicitation process with confirmation of details such as the amount given or pledged, how it will be paid, asset(s) used, use to which the gift will be put, any tax details, media release (if appropriate), donor recognition options, and any other details, however small, that might be important to the donor and the organization.

STEWARDSHIP: TURNING DONORS INTO FRIENDS FOR LIFE

It's amazing how many organizations fail to thank donors properly, if at all. Even after all the time and effort involved in acquiring a new donor, the idea of stewardship and caring for these donors seems completely alien to many development staff. Many ignore the old fundraising adage: thanking people today is the first step toward tomorrow's gift.

It often helps to think of a donation as a present from a friend or neighbor. With friends we make small reciprocal gifts, we invite them to low-key family occasions, and encourage them to share in and celebrate our family triumphs. When we hit hard times, friends and family rally around precisely because we have that feeling of shared values and community.

So it is with donors. They want to be seen as partners helping us achieve our goals. They trust us to invest their money wisely because they believe in our dreams, understand our plans, and like and trust us as individuals.

As part of any major donor program you will probably have considered a formal recognition structure. Fundraisers often get very excited about various levels of recognition. There are seemingly endless permutations on the theme of platinum, gold, silver, and bronze donors. Such layers can be helpful for civic pride or prestige but most donors want to be treated as individuals, so it pays to build a stewardship program accordingly. Special events and regular written communication play vital parts, but asking for little things can help, too. If a donor has loaned you her prestigious boardroom for a meeting each year, remember to congratulate her when you have a success. If appropriate, remember your donors' birthdays, take an interest in their families or business, and show an interest in any big events in their lives. Above all, make a point of seeking your donors' advice and involving them in your operational work. Such genuine rather than contrived involvement will encourage donors to give again and to reach out to other prospects, too.

As you finish this chapter, grab your calendar and write down five ways you could thank and involve your leading donors this month. Then create a different list for the next month, and every month.

The process described in this chapter is an efficient and very effective way of developing major donors through the three heat levels, from cold through warm to red hot. Yet too often, people who have been through it feel as if they've been sucked into a highly systematized sausage machine. So you always need to temper your professional techniques with your understanding of and sensitivity to the comfort and well-being of your donors. That way you and they will get much more out of the relationship, and you'll both enjoy it, too. And that's what fundraising is all about.

Happy prospecting.

CHAPTER 11

Results Analysis and Performance Measurements

James M. Greenfield[1]

"Without solid research, fundraising is reduced to hucksterism and panhandling—hit-and-miss activities without direction and with little respect. Research provides knowledge, formulates strategy, inspires confidence, and ensures that practitioners achieved desired results."[2]

FUNDRAISING IS AN INVESTMENT STRATEGY

Fundraising is an investment strategy with expectations of a profitable return, now and in the future. Evaluating performance of the variety of fundraising activities in nonprofit organizations today is guided best by using uniform tools with some frequency. Consistent analysis will illustrate:

■ Where problems may lie
■ Effectiveness and efficiency
■ Options for increased performance
■ Proposed improvements, and more, all based on results

Without such analysis, results are too often measured with bottom-line summary figures, as misleading as they are inaccurate in revealing details of actual performance.

Counting the number of gifts and gross income received from each solicitation method is fairly simple if gift recording and accounting

[1]Preparation of this chapter was aided by expert advice from research professionals Margo Allen, Vanderbilt University; Christina Pulawski, Loyola University, Chicago; Deborah Miller, Virginia Tech; Pamela Gignac, JMG Solutions; and Des Gregory and Martin Kaufman, Brakeley, London. Their assistance is greatly appreciated.
[2]Kathleen S. Kelley, *Effective Fund-Raising Management*. Mahwah, NJ: Lawrence Erlbaum Associates, 1998, pp. 402–403.

systems are designed to capture these details. Evaluating the overall performance of each solicitation activity will take more work. By using a common measurement tool, analysis will reveal details of how productive and profitable each method is in its own performance. Further, effectiveness and efficiency analysis will reveal how each method has performed measured against its own past results and can serve as a reliable predictor in forecasting future returns.

Success in major gift and capital campaign work begins with accurate and comprehensive research to identify, qualify, and quantify each prospect, whether an individual, corporation, foundation, or association. Success in fundraising is "a carefully orchestrated, purposeful effort to raise substantial sums of money by identifying and cultivating potential donors and by soliciting gifts from them when their goals and wishes are congruent with the [organization's] goals and priorities."[3] Given that mandate, prospect research is the vital partner and reliable predictor of likely success. How well these two functions perform, separately and together, is the focus of this chapter.

Setting Objectives and Goals

The objective in all analysis is to appreciate how results, using consistent measurement tools, reveal facts for performance evaluation, aid future decisions and directions, and facilitate the best use of budget, staff, technique, timing, volunteers, and more. Spending the time and effort to evaluate and analyze fundraising and research activities needs to be weighed against getting the job done. Find a formula that works and keep it simple, but regularly review it for updating and adding more in-depth criteria. Smaller nonprofits can do some form of evaluation, too. What is important is to meet the needs of information gathering and statistics to serve management planning, fundraising evaluation, accountability, and feedback to donors in a way that is meaningful and not too restrictive.

It is important to state early that the uses made of prospect research products differ widely across the range of nonprofit organizations in the United States, despite equal access by all to vast amounts of public information on the Internet and other sources. These same practices can differ greatly outside of the United States where most nongovernmental organizations (NGOs) have limited access to personal information, few data sources, cultural constraints, local privacy regulations, and more, depending on national customs and history.

---

[3]Victoria Steele and Stephen D. Elder, *Becoming a Fundraiser: The Principles and Practices of Library Development.* Chicago: American Library Association, 1992, p. 3 (emphasis added).

"However, while confidentiality of donor information may be at stake, generally we can compile prospect information to any extent that is practical and ethical, and we have relatively unlimited resources for doing so. Contrast that with the situation in the Baltic States, where the KGB is a vivid and frightening memory. Learning about potential donors may not even be allowed by governments in some countries. In fact, resources such as indexes or Who's Who directories do not exist in many nations. Donor research is highly restricted by cultural mores in some areas. As a result, rapid, effective donor research cannot take place as in the United States, and the donor base takes longer to broaden, or even define."[4]

To find out more about these similarities and differences, see Chapter 5 on U.S. and Canadian strategies as well as Chapter 6 on international strategies, specifically in Europe and Southeast Asia.

In this chapter, evaluating prospect research results and its management will be presented first, followed by measuring how research data is used in major gift and capital campaign activities. Continued communication with donors after their gift, to preserve their friendship and enhance their active involvement with the organization, will be the final area for results analysis in this chapter.

EVALUATING PROSPECT RESEARCH

Investing the time and effort to evaluate and analyze fundraising and prospect research activities needs to be weighed against the following criteria for each nonprofit:

- Size of operation
- Fundraising resources
- Number of fundraising staff
- Fundraising goals and objectives
- Fundraising income in the past
- Income targets

The key is to find, develop, and implement a formula that works and keep it simple while regularly reviewing it for updating and adding more in-depth analysis as well as new ideas. Smaller nonprofits can do some form of evaluation and analysis. What is important is to allow information

---

[4]Lilya Wagner, "U.S. Models and International Dimensions of Philanthropic Fund Raising" in *Critical Issues in Fund Raising*, Dwight F. Burlingame, editor. *The NSFRE/ Wiley Fund Development Series*. New York: John Wiley & Sons, 1997, p. 207.

and statistics to serve management planning, fundraising evaluation, accountability, and appropriate feedback to donors and the community.

The complete value of prospect research to a nonprofit organization is not often recognized outside of its applications to fundraising practice. Individuals, be they single persons or families, also are direct links to access with corporations, foundations, associations, and other potential gift sources. Each person is important beyond being a mere candidate for money. Each also is a potential advocate of the cause as well as a reliable supporter through a variety of volunteer roles, including leadership on the board of directors.

Willing advocates and supporters result from investments in time to build relationships between people who share beliefs in the mission, have confidence in its leaders, and support its current and future plans. Champions and believers are important roles that donors and supporters can play. These are the positive relationships that are so essential to major gift and capital campaign work in particular, as Kay Sprinkel Grace so wisely observed: "fundraising is about relationships more than it is about money."[5] These individuals are the best friends the organization can hope to have; treat them so. They also are generous and reliable patrons willing to continue to invest their personal time and energy along with their money to help the organization fulfill its mission and its future plans.

But, first, they have to be found. That's where research and prospecting comes in.

CRITERIA FOR RESULTS

How should one measure results and what criteria are appropriate in evaluation of the performance of everyone involved, whether a prospect researcher, major gifts officer, campaign manager, volunteer solicitor, or other? Is analysis only about money raised? Or is it also about how much time and effort was required for the eventual success? How effective was the use of cultivation strategies based on research in developing positive relationships? Relationships make all the difference.

Performance analysis needs to be sensitive to a host of variable circumstances involved, such as distinctive cultural factors among nations and societies around the globe, levels of maturity and sophistication in fundraising practice, and more. Each organization has a unique mission

---

[5]Kay Sprinkel Grace, "Can We Throw Away the Tin Cup?" in *Taking Fund Raising Seriously: Advancing the Profession and Practice of Raising Money,* Dwight F. Burlingame and Lamont J. Hulse, editors. San Francisco: Jossey-Bass, 1991, p. 185.

that is enhanced or limited by its geographic location, cultural practices, image and reputation, leadership and volunteer strengths, prior history of fund development operations, variable staff size and budget, volunteer leadership and participation, and much more, all of which will need to be considered in performance evaluation proceedings.

The best tool to capture these details is likely to be a design exclusive to each nonprofit organization. Organizations are not the same in how they structure and manage their prospect research activities, and prospect research programs do not perform the same for every organization.

Lastly, consideration must be given to the time required to do this work well. Fiscal years have an end date when the accounting of all contributions received is prepared. However, major gifts and capital campaigns are multiyear activities; it takes time to develop relationships to the point where a proper solicitation is in order. Major gift fundraising is a long-term process. Lasting 18 months on average, it takes at least three face-to-face meetings with a prospect: a discovery meeting, an ask meeting, and a negotiate-and-close meeting.

Obviously, this relationship-building process and long-term effort to obtain major gifts cannot be evaluated annually in the same way that other fundraising programs might be.[6] A bit of guidance based on tried-and-true aphorisms when asking for gifts is: *volunteers and staff can ask; donors decide.* Remember always that *giving is voluntary.* Time, lots of time, is going to be required to do this work with success.

Research Staff Qualifications and Skills Set

As introduced in Chapter 1, "Prospecting for Major Gifts," there are creative and innovative ways to find the right person to perform research for any shop, large or small. There are various skills and levels of experience needed to fulfill the tasks assigned to prospect research that include a range of activities from entry-level employment to management of a research department with multiple, full-time staff members.

Just as important is the necessity that the nonprofit organization's long-range plans and strategic objectives be completed. These decisions establish financial priorities and, based on this information, what level of fundraising capacity and expertise will be required to support them, including budget, space, staffing, systems, training, and more. "Without

---

[6]Ernest W. Wood, "Profiling Major Gifts Fundraisers: What Qualifies Them for Success," in *Developing Major Gifts*, Dwight F. Burlingame and James M. Hodge, editors. *New Directions for Philanthropic Fundraising.* San Francisco: Jossey-Bass, 16 (Summer 1997), pp. 13–14.

the link to institutional goals, fundraising goals are meaningless."[7] It is against these well-defined goals that staffing positions and expertise levels, along with consistent methods to quantify results as performance criteria, will be evaluated.

As a reference, the skills set recommended by the Association of Professional Researchers for Advancement (APRA) is an excellent starting point to design the right role, job description, and skills needed to fit within organizational goals, objectives, and budgets. In particular, APRA has developed *information proficiencies* that include awareness, understanding, and knowledge along with the *skill proficiencies* of ability, proficiency, and mastery.[8] These basic qualifications in a job description could also serve as the criteria for evaluation and analysis (visit www. aprahome.org for the complete four-part text of APRA's "Skills Set").

Qualifications and proficiency levels will, of course, need to be adjusted to fit each organization's size, current level of activity, and prior success in fundraising. Future fundraising goals will identify the level of demand for research products. Initiating even a part-time prospect research effort will require a level of maturity in the existing fundraising program, especially when it will be required to support major gift and capital campaign programs. By contrast, typical annual giving programs have only minimal needs for personal, corporate, or foundation research.

The capacity to investigate, analyze, and produce comprehensive research products is a function of investment, training, and budget. Another benefit enjoyed by larger shops is the generally larger budget for training, professional development, and resources.

A researcher with access to specialized fee-based resources, particularly ones online such as Lexis Nexis (www.lexisnexis.com), Dialog (www.dialog.com), iWave (www.iwave.com), BIG Online (www.bigdata base.com), Foundation Search (www.foundationsearch.com), Foundation Center (www.foundationcenter.org) and others (for more information please see Chapter 5 and visit www.ephilanthropy.org), and the training to use the tools properly, is going to be more productive than a researcher without these tools. Period. The web is not a substitute for all sources but is a good starting point. Unlike what most believe, everything is *not* available on the Internet and every prospect will not be found there. Nevertheless, there are free and fee-based online sources that can be utilized by small and large shops alike.

---

[7]Thomas E. Broce, *Fund Raising: The Guide to Raising Money from Private Sources,* 2nd ed. Norman, OK: University of Oklahoma Press, 1986, p. 186.
[8]"The APRA Skills Set," Association for Professional Researchers for Advancement: Naperville, IL, updated January 26, 2005. (earlier drafts had copied the four "skills set" text, now deleted from this edition).

A venture to a library can be extremely helpful to access some sources not available in the office, including some of the online sources, and it offers access to printed directories and press articles. This is particularly helpful for smaller shops. However, time away from the office can be less productive than for those who have access to these and similar tools (in either hard copy or electronic format) close at hand.[9]

Higher dollar goals and multiyear campaigns are the precursors calling for a commitment to invest more in research expertise and its professional practice, each having quantifiable and measurable components. At its core, research includes the following objectives:

- To identify people and their relationships with other people
- To determine people's interest in, associations with, and gifts to the institution
- To discover facts about the ownership, control, influence, and wealth of people, corporations, and foundations
- To reduce great quantities of information to readable, understandable, concise reports pertinent to the current campaign[10]

Some areas may be difficult to measure, while others may require a two-tier rating scale, such as (a) knowledge and use of available assets coupled with (b) expectations and proficiency levels as personal skills to be developed. Performance can be measured by following the more traditional "exceeds expectations; meets expectations, below expectations" style or by whatever rating method is currently in practice or required by the organization's human resources department (see Appendix G).

Areas of Responsibility in Data Management

The foundation for research and ultimately fundraising is data management, its use, and maintenance of all records and files. This includes the management and strategic input for the use of specialized fundraising software or designed systems to capture, disseminate, and share information. An important role for research is to ensure the integrity and quality of data in and data out.

It is also extremely important that fundraisers fully participate in the planning and management of information to make sure that their needs

[9]Susan Cronin Ruderman, *Woodchucks and Prospect Researchers,* Arlington, MA: Veritas Information Services, 2000.
[10]Kent E. Dove, *Conducting a Successful Capital Campaign,* 2nd ed. San Francisco: Jossey Bass, 2000, p. 96.

and expectations are met based on their insights and perspectives. Equally important are the serious responsibilities due to privacy regulations of personal information about donors and prospects, their gift histories, and more (see Chapter 4 for a complete presentation on ethics and privacy). All who have access to prospect information need to be assured that research work has been performed according to established guidelines and professional practice (visit www.aprahome.org for the "APRA Statement of Ethics").

To build confidence and trust by all those who utilize the information found through research, from staff to board members and key volunteers, it is crucial to supply effective and accurate information. Information is power and confidence. In order to help ensure this happens, a researcher needs to have ongoing training in the latest techniques and upcoming trends in technology and other tools, as well as to gain insights into fundraising that will greatly enhance a researcher's abilities and the outcome of positive results for everyone involved (ideally, insight into not only fundraising but also management and all aspects of what a fundraiser needs and uses to be successful in the field). An adequate budget for this, as well as to purchase new and updated tools and resources, can have a huge impact on the quality of research and the accuracy of information.

Creating and Utilizing Research Data

Chapters 9 and 10 addressed how research information is used in major gift and capital campaign work. How shall these applications be evaluated? The first level of analysis must address success in completing cultivation and solicitation strategies, not just counting gifts and pledges received. Was the strategy effective? Was volunteer and staff time used efficiently? How accurate was the personal information? How accurate was the gift range proposed in the rating and evaluation process?

If it is true, as Fisher Howe has declared, that "It is proverbial that the success of (major gifts) fundraising is 90 percent in prospect identification, research, cultivation, and preparation, and 10 percent in the asking," how shall each of these features be measured along with their outcomes?[11]

As introduced in Chapter 1, "Prospecting for Major Gifts," a sensitive area for research is how to use public financial data to establish gift ranges and giving capacity. In addition to Internet and standard sources, it also is recommended that rating and evaluation sessions be conducted to establish

---

[11]Fisher Howe, *The Board Member's Guide to Fund Raising: What Every Trustee Needs to Know About Raising Money.* San Francisco: Jossey-Bass, 1991, p. 83.

a realistic figure of the prospect's potential giving capacity. Participants in these sessions may include board members, senior management staff, volunteers, donors, and other friends of the organization along with fundraising staff. *The objective of rating and evaluation analysis is to arrive at an estimated gift range, not an exact figure.*

A sample data grid to help sort out giving capacity is located in Appendix H. Without this degree of preparation, there is great risk involved when meeting with a prospect to answer his question: "How much do you have in mind?" This is not the time for wild guesses but a time to present a qualified idea as to how they can make an investment for positive impact. This will build confidence and trust in the soliciting team, the project, and the organization—in fact all nonprofits who might approach them for support. Due process is advisable each and every time.

Research Management

Another area of prospect research suitable for evaluation is to measure research productivity including:

- Time required to complete a prospect profile
- Number of profiles needed to meet major gift and campaign goals
- Number of profiles used in cultivation and solicitation
- How many profiles were unused or incomplete
- What collateral duties (and how many) were assigned research staff

There also may be other duties unique to each organization for its use of research staff and the information they prepare. Analysis of the research office may be of one or two styles, for a well-trained staff and well-equipped operation or for a less experienced and less well equipped office, as illustrated in the following.

A full-time researcher with at least one year of experience in a well-equipped office with Dialog/Nexis and with at least one other research colleague and no other significant nonresearch responsibilities might be expected to approximately produce in a year:

- 130 full profiles
- 650 briefs
- 50 new prospects
- 20 funder identification projects

A full-time researcher with at least six months of experience in a less well equipped office (no access to Dialog/Nexis, slower computer, etc.), with no other research colleagues and some other nonresearch activities might be expected to approximately produce in a year:

- 50 full profiles
- 200 briefs
- 25 new prospects
- 5 funder identification projects[12]

However, the actual outcomes will be based upon the variety of criteria that can impact the production of this information, including:

- Experience and skills of the researcher
- Number of people involved (staff, volunteers, etc.) in producing research results
- How much "research" the fundraiser does and wants to do
- Financial goals, objectives, and budgets available
- Maturity of the fundraising program and what other fundraising is taking place
- Access to tools and resources for short cuts and powerful searching
- Time available before results are needed (sometimes it's needed by tomorrow!)
- Ongoing research responsibilities, workload, and activities
- Matching of interests and public appeal
- The quality and number of prospects

A major fact that impacts all of this is that some prospects are higher profile, and as such, more information can be found quickly and easily. The downside is that there is a great deal to sift through, analyze, and report on. Other prospects will have little or sometimes no information readily available on them and take longer to dig up results, sometimes to no avail. This can be extremely frustrating for everyone, as the Internet has created expectations that anyone and anything can be found out.

Therefore, it can take one day or weeks to put together one profile. Also, the number of details to be entered into a database or word document to physically prepare a profile, briefing, or report can greatly impact the amount of time required to produce the desired outcomes.

Another guideline for determining the number of qualified major gift prospects and their role in an analysis of overall performance, according to Debbie Miller, director of development research for Virginia Tech, is that the top 10 percent of your major gift prospects will

---

[12]Susan Cronin Ruderman, *Woodchucks and Prospect Researchers*, op. cit.

contribute 60 percent of the campaign goal.[13] Given that outcome, quality research is imperative.

EVALUATING RESEARCH USED IN MAJOR GIFTS AND CAMPAIGNS

Activity reports are a straightforward method to display both progress and completed actions (see Appendix I). These reports reflect the actual work being carried out by staff and volunteers and can include contact or call reports, contacts needed lists, campaign or major gifts progress reports, financial reports, and prospect research reports. These are not areas where the researcher can be measured directly other than in evaluating the accuracy of the information prepared. If the data is reliable, both staff and volunteers will have greater confidence in such information and will use it to best advantage.

As discussed in Chapters 1, 5, and 9, before these data can be put to use, however, additional information is required to estimate each donor's likely interest and giving potential including what project might be of interest, who should be involved in the approach, the capacity to make a gift, and how close is the prospect to use now?

Some answers will come from research. The rest will come from prospect review meetings followed by a rating and evaluation session, each a critical step to calculate each prospect's interest and giving potential as accurately as possible.

Prospect Review Meetings

Once prospects are identified and full profiles have been completed, a period of intelligence analysis begins. These are working sessions organized as prospect review meetings. Participants required to attend include major gift officers, campaign directors, and prospect researchers along with fundraising staff and possibly volunteer leadership. These sessions examine all the research findings on individual, corporate, foundation, and association prospects. It is also when a plan is sketched out for the approach strategy:

■ How, when, and where each prospect's interest may fit best with current funding priorities

---

[13]Mary Lawrence, "Lights . . . Camera . . . Action! Screening Prospects for a Capital Campaign," in *NEDRA News*. New England Development Research Association (Summer 2003).

- A target gift amount and matching of interest
- Who needs to be involved, including staff, volunteers, and partners to manage and execute the approach strategy
- Further research to be done
- Initial plans for cultivation and solicitation strategies

The collective meetings over a period of time should follow a rule of thirds:

- One-third of the time is spent in the review and rating of new prospects.
- One-third of the time is required for strategy development.
- One-third of the time is for assigning prospects and reporting results.[14]

The variety of agenda topics also provides several criteria to use in capturing, refining and updating information, which can be done by the researcher and/or major gifts fundraiser. Specifically designed forms can be used to document these activities, to review progress, and to compile results (Appendix I is an example). Management skills are required to capture information, keep key team members informed and moving along with their commitments, and coach the approach strategy into action. Tracking these operations requires careful planning and supervision along with continued attention to detail. This level of sophistication is not likely to be maximally successful if assigned to a new or part-time research employee. Supervision from senior fundraising staff will be required at all times.

Rating and Evaluation Sessions

To prepare for each rating and evaluation session, research staff now must organize data to focus on two areas: potential gift range and inclination to give. Fundraising staff will organize several rating and evaluation sessions with small groups or hold individual sessions with well-informed and influential insiders committed to the organization's mission and vision.

Each participant's awareness and knowledge of these gift candidates will be helpful in this assessment. The participants can be selected from among current and former board members and other volunteer leaders familiar with the organization's fundraising programs. Prior donors with a long history of support at higher levels also can assist. Their task, after

---

[14]Bobbi J. Strand, "Prospect Development: An Art," in *The Nonprofit Handbook: Fund Raising,* 3rd ed. James M. Greenfield, editor. *The AFP/Wiley Fund Development Series.* New York: John Wiley & Sons, 2001, p. 720.

being briefed on the confidentiality of the material and privacy regulations regarding its content, is to provide suggested answers to these two key areas of assessment—gift range and inclination to give.

Additional information needed for these sessions will come from major gift and capital campaign staff that have prepared estimates on the number of donors needed and the size of gifts required to be successful. This traditional gift range chart is the usual method to calculate and display how many gifts at various sizes are necessary. Once the chart is in place, rating and evaluation sessions will attempt to match as many prospects as possible to each of the proposed gift levels.

Between three to five qualified prospects usually will be required for each gift that is secured, which is why research is an early task to complete and is a heavy workload for research staff. It also is true that many prospects, once qualified and rated, will be rated higher than they can give. If they are unable to make a gift of the size requested, they are equally qualified for a lesser gift amount, which will help fill the required quota of donors in that range.

Among the various methods used to capture and record gift ranges is a rating guide designed to allow session participants to match a series of giving potential levels alongside a giving inclination scale, such as in the following example:

Giving Potential	Giving Inclination
Rating 1 = $10,000 to $25,000	Rating A = Unknown interest
Rating 2 = $25,000 to $50,000	Rating B = Minimal interest
Rating 3 = $50,000 to $100,000	Rating C = Lukewarm interest
Rating 4 = $100,000 to $250,000	Rating D = Good interest
Rating 5 = $250,000 and above	Rating E = High interest

An essential part of these meetings is to be sure to instruct those present to provide their best estimates, prospect by prospect, of a likely gift range matched to the amounts on the gift range chart, and to add their personal perceptions of each prospect's inclination to support the project at this level, with the following results:

	Giving Potential					Giving Inclination				
	Low				High	Low				High
	1	2	3	4	5	A	B	C	D	E
Mr. & Mrs. Brown		X				X				
Mr. Black				X			X			
Mrs. Green					X					X

After each meeting, these ratings are summarized and identified as a reasonable projection of potential gift size and inclination to give for each prospect, which also is aligned with the gift range chart. This information can be shared with cultivation and solicitation teams in the following way: Mrs. Green should be seen first, then Mr. Black, and finally Mr. and Mrs. Brown in order to capture the largest gift first and to invite the others to join next at their best level of ability.

After several prospects have been rated with both giving potential and giving inclination, the next step is to proceed according to the recommended cultivation and solicitation strategy. Fundraising staff can prepare one or all of the following reports to aid volunteer solicitors and to monitor use of this information to track progress for the entire roster of qualified and assigned prospects, as follows:

1. Alphabetic order, by prospect name
2. Alphabetic order, by cultivation and solicitation team
3. Giving potential, by rating levels (lowest to highest)
4. Giving inclination, by rating levels (lowest to highest)

Tracking

In addition to contact reports on cultivation and solicitation activity, a variety of monitoring systems are needed to maintain current records on the volume of prospects and their progress in cultivation and solicitation activities. Tracking needs to record all contact with each prospect, and to monitor the next steps planned, important data to capture, and other tasks assigned to the prospect research staff.

Extensive work has been involved to identify and qualify each prospect, complete detailed research profiles, evaluate gift range and inclination, and plan cultivation and solicitation strategies. It is essential to be able to monitor continuously how these data and strategies are being applied in the field and are to be used in reviews and updates at prospect review meetings.

Another area for tracking is to measure the productivity levels for fundraising staff members assigned to major gift and capital campaign work—those with direct responsibility for carrying out the approved cultivation and solicitation plans. This responsibility is the final exam for all the work to prepare for a favorable gift decision.

Professional major gift fundraisers impose on themselves the most important evaluation and expectation. "All the successful major gift fundraisers I know have higher expectations of themselves than does anyone else. They never seem to be satisfied with their own performance and continue to function in an unfinished business mode. The mind-set they possess and the values and characteristics that drive them are their ultimate benchmark over time. They know that they, along with their major gift fundraising colleagues, are engaged in causes that are going to make the world a better place. They believe the adage that what you do for yourself dies with you, but what you do for others lives on. This motivates them at the highest level."[15]

Each nonprofit organization will need to establish its own criteria for these staff evaluations. Performance criteria and measurement methods used by one organization should not necessarily be the same as for other organizations any more than major gift and capital campaign objectives are the same nor are volunteers and staff teams identical. Appendix K offers one guideline to measure activity levels and the productivity of major gift and capital campaign staff.

Another guideline is linked to moves management theory and practice. What level of activity (i.e., amount of personal contact) is appropriate for a major gifts officer assigned to 100 prospects? Whatever the number of prospects assigned to each volunteer and staff team, the business of major gift and capital campaign cultivation and solicitation is all about direct contact with qualified prospects.

A final analysis is to review gift results themselves. Gift reports are useful in many ways beyond counting the money; they also reveal effectiveness and efficiency, productivity and profitability. Appendix L illustrates the results of a new major gift effort after three years. What this report shows is the growing number of major gift donors, an increase in average gift size, and a success rate in asking that has grown from 33 percent to 53 percent. Net income also is growing fast while the cost–benefit ratio is commendable given the size of this effort. Now that these gifts have come in, how well is the organization prepared to respond in its stewardship duty to the donor and use of her money?

EVALUATING DONOR STEWARDSHIP AND RECOGNITION

After the donor has made a decision and a new major gift commitment is received, how accurately and completely does the organization understand what the donor believes will happen next? Several answers are needed now, including:

- What is the amount of the gift and when will it be paid?
- What are the purposes or uses (restrictions) the donor has specified? If any, is it agreed to accept the gift with restrictions?
- Was the method and level of recognition discussed?

---

[15]Ernest W. Wood, op. cit., p. 15.

■ Was the donor asked about disclosure of identity, gift amount, and purpose in public reports?

Answers to these questions should be discussed and resolved with the donor as part of the solicitation discussion. Are decisions guided by a board-approved policy and procedure? Does the policy also include guidelines for gift acknowledgment, management of the funds, disclosure of donor gift details, and recognition to follow? A checklist of these details is useful to be sure each donor is considered (see Appendix M). However, first things first. Thank the donor.

"Once a donor has made a significant gift, cultivation can move to a new and higher level. A sincere expression of gratitude can show the human quality of an institution. It goes without saying that every gift should be acknowledged when it is received; the donor is expecting acknowledgment. If in fact the gift has played a part in strengthening the institution, then the real opportunity to give thanks will come in six months or a year, when the effect of the gift is more fully known. In the interim period, keep in close contact with the donor, and never fail to follow up and provide the information that will tell the donor what the full positive effect of the gift has been."[16]

Acknowledgment details must be added to the donor's records and files, including any follow-up obligations, recognition fulfillment, schedules for continuing contacts, progress reports, and more. What has now begun is a new cultivation strategy for the next gift.

Stewardship of Donor Funds

Accepting a gift in any form is to agree to use the funds given exactly as the donor has directed. Separate from the importance of keeping faith with the bond of trust between donors and their favored organizations, there are ethical and legal obligations to do so. Included in "A Donor Bill of Rights" are two provisions that promise each donor the following expectations (visit www.afpnet.org and the Institute of Fundraising in the UK for further information at www.institute-of-fundraising.org.uk).

■ To be assured their gifts will be used for the purposes for which they were given.
■ To receive appropriate acknowledgment and recognition.

Regular gift reports and campaign accounting summaries will disclose the number and value of all gifts and pledges received. This information

---

[16]Kent E. Dove, op. cit., p. 122.

aids board members and staff along with volunteers and donors in their appreciation of financial results achieved and progress toward major gift objectives and campaign goals. However, the identity of each donor and details of the gift decisions are not public knowledge until and unless the donor has given permission for their disclosure.

It is not unusual that some donors will deny any public disclosure of major gift decisions. Most donors will agree and can appreciate how their decision is encouraging to others to make gifts. For those who prefer to be anonymous, their decision must be kept faithfully.

A final step is to report to donors how their funds were used, in particular how the use of their money by the organization, through its programs and services rendered, were directly beneficial to others. This was the intent in the gift, and these results are the contents in a continuing communication with donors. The bond of confidence and trust between donors and the organizations they favor with gifts is enlarged and rewarded by the faithful stewardship of the relationship.

CONCLUSION

This book is about the role and importance of the prospect research function in major gifts work, whether for capital campaigns or planned giving purposes. Whatever you decide to implement and develop, make sure you keep it simple and manageable by setting levels that are realistic for meeting organizational objectives and resources. There is a danger that if evaluation and analysis is too complex it won't be used properly or at all, and could lead to inaccurate assessments. It is also important to ensure that staff is comfortable in how performances are measured and feel their work is having a positive impact, as this will be reflected in overall results as well as relationships with donors.

ADDITIONAL RESOURCES

Broce, Thomas E. *Fund Raising: The Guide to Raising Money from Private Sources,* 2nd ed. Norman, OK: University of Oklahoma Press, 1986.

Ciconte, Barbara Kushner and Jeanne G. Jacob. "Fund Raising Basics: A Complete Guide," *Aspen's Fund Raising Series for the 21st Century.* James P. Gelatt, editor. Gaithersburg, MD: An Aspen Publication, 1997.

Dove, Kent E. *Conducting a Successful Capital Campaign,* 2nd ed. San Francisco: Jossey-Bass, 2000.

Dunlop, David R. "Strategic Management of a Major Gift Program," *Developing an Effective Major Gift Program: From Managing Staff to Soliciting Gifts,* R. Muir and J. May, eds. Washington, D.C.: Council for Advancement and Support of Education, 1993.

Grace, Kay Sprinkel. "Can We Throw Away the Tin Cup?" *Taking Fund Raising Seriously: Advancing the Profession and Practice of Raising Money,* Dwight F. Burlingame and Lamont J. Hulse, eds. San Francisco: Jossey-Bass, 1991.

Greenfield, James M. *Fund Raising Cost Effectiveness: A Self-Assessment Workbook.* New York: John Wiley & Sons, 1996.

Hart, Ted, James M. Greenfield, and Michael Johnston. *Nonprofit Internet Strategies: Best Practices for Marketing, Communications and Fund Raising.* New York: John Wiley & Sons, 2005.

Howe, Fisher. *The Board Member's Guide to Fundraising: What Every Trustee Needs to Know about Raising Money.* San Francisco: Jossey-Bass, 1991.

Johnston, Michael. *The Fund Raiser's Guide to the Internet.* New York: John Wiley & Sons, 1999.

Joyaux, Simone P. Strategic Fund Development: Building Profitable Relationships that Last. *Aspen's Fund Raising Series for the 21st Century.* James P. Gelatt, ed. Gaithersburg, MD: An Aspen Publication, 1997.

Kelly, Kathleen S. *Effective Fund-Raising Management.* Mahwah, NJ: Lawrence Erlbaum Associates, 1998.

May, Jerry A. "Meshing Development Efforts with Major Gift Fundraising," in *Developing Major Gifts.* Dwight F. Burlingame and James M. Hodge, eds, San Francisco: Jossey-Bass, 1997.

Ruderman, Susan Cronin. *Woodchucks and Prospect Researchers.* Arlington, MA: Veritas Information Services, 2000.

Smith, Paul B. "Managing a Successful Major Gifts Program," *Developing Major Gifts,* Dwight F. Burlingame and James M. Hodge, eds. San Francisco: Jossey-Bass, 16 (Summer 1997).

Steele, Virginia and Stephen D. Elder. *Becoming a Fundraiser: The Principles and Practices of Library Development.* Chicago: American Library Association, 1992.

Strand, Bobbi J. "Prospect Development: An Art," *The Nonprofit Handbook: Fund Raising,* 3rd ed. James M. Greenfield, ed. New York: John Wiley & Sons, 2001.

Wagner, Lilya. "U.S. Models and International Dimensions of Philanthropic Fund Raising," *Critical Issues in Fund Raising.* Dwight F. Burlingame, ed. New York: John Wiley & Sons, 1997.

Warwick, Mal, Ted Hart, and Nick Allen, eds. *Fundraising on the Internet: The ePhilanthropyFoundation.Org's Guide to Success Online.* San Francisco: Jossey-Bass, 2002.

Wood, Ernest W. "Profiling Major Gifts Fundraisers: What Qualifies Them for Success," *Developing Major Gifts,* Dwight F. Burlingame and James M. Hodge, eds. San Francisco: Jossey-Bass, 16 (Summer 1997).

CHAPTER 12

Challenges for Tomorrow

Chris Carnie

INTRODUCTION

It's all change. While major donors are changing and fundraising techniques are evolving, prospect research is going through its first major revolution. This chapter tracks each of these changes and extends them into the future.

My intention is to do that dangerous thing: to risk my career and my friendships by telling you how research and fundraising will look 10 years from now. So if you have just selected this book from the remainders pile at your local library, circa spring 2016, please don't laugh out loud. It disturbs the off-planet visitors.

Anyone involved in creating strategies for major gifts or any other area of fundraising must look ahead. Thanks to the hard work of some real experts, there are plenty of texts to guide us. These range from the global resource arguments of *Limits to Growth* to the nonprofit scenarios of *Looking Out for the Future* written by Katherine Fulton and Andrew Blau of the Monitor Group. The latter combines thoughtful analysis of current philanthropy with a range of more-or-less plausible scenarios.

MAJOR DONORS: MAJOR CHANGE

Major donors are not who they were, and as they change, so fundraising changes. These changes are leading to developments in prospect research.

Money, and More of It

First, the number of people with substantial wealth is increasing. Each year's World Wealth Report, a standard analysis of wealth, shows a growth in both the number and value of the wealth held by high-net-worth individuals (HNWIs, defined as people who have US$1 million or more in financial assets).[1]

The report in 2005, citing 2004 figures, showed a global total of 8.3 million HNWIs, of whom 2.7 million lived in North America. The number of North Americans with US$1 million or more in financial assets increased by a staggering 500,000, or 23 percent over the period 2002 to 2004. Wealth held by this group of fortunate individuals amounted to US$30.8 trillion worldwide, of which US$9.3 trillion was held in North America—an increase in percentage terms of 8.5 percent over the previous year.

Other older sources confirm that this is part of a long-term trend. Compare the personal wealth tables of the IRS for 1989 and 1998 and you will note a growth in the number of people with US$1 million or more in personal wealth from 1.2 to 2.7 million—an increase in nine years of 125 percent.[2]

These trends are now global—with the number of HNWIs growing by almost 14 percent in Africa over the period 2003 to 2004, by 9 percent in the Middle East, by 8 percent in Asia-Pacific, and by 4 percent in Europe. These percentages look small—but consider them in whole numbers; during 2003 to 2004 there were 1,643 new U.S. millionaires created every single day, 547 of them in North America.

So the motor driving major donor fundraising—the creation of personal wealth—continues to increase the market size. This is reflected in the importance now attached to major donor fundraising in North America. There is a widespread view that middle-of-the-road fundraising techniques have had their day and that it is time for fundraisers to go back to their roots and start asking for gifts face-to-face. The rapidly increasing numbers of people with wealth means an increase in the workload of our already hard-pressed researchers. We, the researchers, can only respond by getting faster—and that means *automation,* a process we will explore further.

This is not to say that the progression toward more HNWIs necessarily means more major gifts. Relatively short-term shifts in stock values seem to have an effect. Contrast these two statements, the first from July 2002. Will Baker, president of the Chesapeake Bay Foundation, said, "People feel poor, in terms of making major gifts. They are also

---

[1]World Wealth Report, 2005 and annual, New York, Cap Gemini and Merrill Lynch, 2005.
[2]Personal Wealth, 1998: Type of Property by Size of Net Worth, IRS, 1998. Note that these numbers are not directly comparable with the World Wealth Report statistics because they use different recording methods. See www.irs.gov/taxstats.

very worried about the uncertainty of the future. I think it's a difficult time to be asking for that big gift, that five-figure or six-figure gift."[3] Less than two years later the *Chronicle of Philanthropy* was able to start an article headed "Big Giving Makes a Comeback" with, "Big donations to charity rose along with the nation's economy and stock market last year, as many of the largest donors increased their foundation endowments or supported big projects at universities, arts groups, and the Salvation Army."[4]

In the time between these two quotes the Dow Jones Aggregate Index rose from 193 to 253, a rise, in terms of market capitalization, of just under 35 percent.[5]

The globalization of wealth means that researchers are getting more international in their approach (this morning I completed a profile on a Mexican educated in California, living in Spain, with a directorship in New York, all on behalf of a British nonprofit's major gifts officer who wants to ask her for a million). The 300,000 HNWIs living in the Middle East or Latin America and the 2.6 million HNWIs in Europe are all becoming targets for prospecting researchers. We can expect this trend toward *research without frontiers* to continue.

New Causes

Wealth and the growth or decline of assets is one of the key motors for change in major gift philanthropy. But there are others. In "Wealth with Responsibility," Paul Schervish and John Havens surveyed factors that would increase charitable giving among a group of 112 people, all with wealth at or above US$5 million and almost all (97 percent) of whom had contributed to charitable causes in the previous year.[6] It's worth noting that the results of a U.K. survey ("Why Rich People Give," Theresa Lloyd, 2004) show a very similar pattern.[7] For comparison, both sets of figures are shown here.

---

[3]*Baltimore Sun,* July 28, 2002.
[4]Nicole Lewis and Matt Murray, "Big Living Makes a Comeback," *Chronicle of Philanthropy,* February 19, 2004.
[5]Calculated from indices published by Dow Jones Indices at http://averages.dowjones.com.
[6]P. Schervish and J. Havens, *The Mind of the Millionaire,* Social Welfare Research Institute, Boston College, 2002.
[7]Theresa Lloyd, *Why Rich People Give,* London: Association of Charitable Foundations, 2004, p. 298.

Factors that would increase giving	Percent of respondents US	Percent of respondents UK
New cause about which to care passionately	90	55
Better information that donations are making a difference	65	10
Increased net worth	65	75
Increased tax incentives	65	35
More time to think about philanthropy	45	25
Better information about tax benefits	20	5

Increased net worth is only part of the story. In the United States, new causes are more important in changing behaviors of major donors. Over the lifetime of modern major gift fundraising we have seen a series of new causes starting with universities (still the largest group by number of major gifts according to *Chronicle of Philanthropy*) and hospitals and going on to museums, libraries, human service organizations, health, and environment.[8] Had you suggested in 1990 that Greenpeace should run a major gift campaign, you would have been laughed out of the room. Nowadays Greenpeace, Amnesty International, and other campaigning environmental and rights groups are running professional major gift fundraising programs. The new causes that are joining the major donor fray are crying out for good researchers (we researchers have never had it so good.) Organizations that have rarely or never employed researchers to assist major gift drives are now recruiting—for fields such as sports, animal welfare, public affairs, and humanitarian aid.

Some of these new causes in the major gift field are coming up without us being aware of it. Armed only with a credit card, donors can give to causes that they had not heard of just a few years ago. Fundraisers in faraway places are taking advantage of this fact and attracting donors directly.

Think about the implications of this for a moment: you are, say, Save the Children Fund, founded in 1919 as a response to conditions in Europe immediately following the First World War. You have spent the last 80-plus years building a brand and recognition among loyal donors. Suddenly those same donors can give directly to projects in the countries in which you operate, because indigenous nonprofits have their own web sites with donation forms. Take a look at the Christian Worship Centre Orphanage in Ghana (www.cwcorphanage.com) to select one of many hundreds of

---

[8]Center for Women's Business Research, April 2005.

possible examples—just the kind of organization that you would expect to collaborate with big multinational NGO, and now accessible on the web to donors who want to give.

In 2016, with the inevitable expansion of the Internet, and the likely growth in air travel, there will be more of this direct giving. Some of it will be major giving—with multiple implications for the research profession. Gifts to these entities will be harder to trace, so we will be unable to research complete information on a donor's philanthropy. Humanitarian aid organizations like Save the Children will have to work harder to persuade donors that their role as an intermediary between northern donor and southern recipient is important. And researchers may find themselves just as much in demand in Accra, Laos, or Bombay as they currently are in Boston.

New Donor Concerns

In "Looking Out for the Future," Katherine Fulton and Andrew Blau describe the "new ecology of social benefit," the context in which people make decisions about their philanthropy. They describe the forces shaping that ecology, such as privatization, connection, and acceleration, and imagine a future (they are writing about 2025) in which the pressure for accountability, the demand for effectiveness, and the need for infrastructure create new types of philanthropy.

Their scenarios mix good news with bad, and some of them describe major giving futures. A recurring theme is that donors will demand more accountability from their nonprofit partners. How will this affect major giving and prospect research? It will certainly mean that the trend toward more and better stewardship will continue, and that will probably involve prospect researchers in tracking both the donor and her gift post-donation. It will mean that researchers will need more and better ways of measuring their added value in the organization—along with every other staff member. It is also likely to mean closer media scrutiny of all activities—with the inevitable concerns about donor and data privacy.

New Donor Societies

Researchers don't normally get the chance to meet the prospects they investigate. It's embarrassing, standing in front of someone whose business you have analyzed and, likely, whose sisters, cousins, first husband, and dog you can name. So my first meeting with a real, billionaire-family major donor was a trauma only relieved by the fact that she was utterly delightful, easygoing and, well, lovely. That she was also a woman was, in the context of today's major giving, no big surprise.

Women are taking an increasing role in major gift philanthropy. We are moving from the slightly depressing era in which it was ". . . and his wife" toward truly substantial gifts. Here is a selection from the 2004 list:

- Susan T. Buffett, a director of Berkshire Hathaway, who left a bequest of $2.6 billion principally to family foundations
- Caroline Wiess Law, oil heiress, who left a bequest of $450 million to the arts, to education, and to medical work
- Oprah Winfrey, the television host, who donated $50 million to her own foundation

These outstanding examples from the United States are reflected abroad. A leading example is Mama Cash (www.mamacash.nl/english/), a Netherlands foundation created by women who had inherited wealth. The foundation has set up a "Women with Inherited Wealth" working group, reasoning that "it's often difficult for women to safely navigate their way through the mostly male-dominated, conservative financial world." A similar group, women who have inherited and who wish to use part of their wealth in philanthropy, has been established in Germany.

We can expect some changes as major giving by women increases in value. Bear in mind that the number of women-owned employer firms in the United States grew by 37 percent between 1997 and 2002, four times the growth rate of all employer firms, and that 31 percent of women business owners contribute US$5,000 or more to charity annually.[9] It is already known that women's organizations collaborate more than gender-neutral organizations, and we can speculate that major donor women will want to promote and develop these collaborations.[10] The growth of major gifts from women may shift the emphasis of major giving, or at least dilute the dominance of the health/education/culture triumvirate that has so long dominated this field.

At the same time, other social groups are becoming more active in major philanthropy. People from our ethnic minority communities are increasingly important philanthropists—as are many other social or geographic minorities. Researchers in North America and Europe face new challenges as they struggle to find sources of information on prospects whose minority status may make them near invisible in the mainstream.

New Techniques

Fundraising is entrepreneurial, and new fundraising and philanthropic products, or cleverly repackaged old ones, appear every day. Tired of

---

[9]M. K. Foster, A. G. Meinhard, "Women's Voluntary Organizations in Canada: Bridgers, Bonders, or Both?" *Voluntas*, 16 (2).

[10]"America's Top Donors," *Chronicle of Philanthropy*, March 3, 2004.

traditional philanthropy? Prefer to try venture philanthropy? Want to invest in a social enterprise? How about a nonprofit Eurobond? The future means more of these products, and many of them are targeted at major donors.

These new techniques are the result of innovations in fundraising and in giving. The fact that a bunch of people in Greenpeace in Austria in 1995 decided to go out onto the streets of Vienna to recruit supporters face-to-face (they called it Direct Dialogue) has meant that there are teams of hopeful recruiters on the streets of most of our capital cities, worldwide.[11]

The same, broadly, has happened with venture philanthropy—the high-engagement philanthropic model first proposed in 1988 by Mario Morino and the Morino Institute. Venture philanthropy has spread around the world, creating networks and associations such as the European Venture Philanthropy Association.

Which new techniques will we have for major donor fundraising in 2016? What will be their impact on the prospect research community? Pass. The one certainty is that there will be change, and rapid change, as tens of thousands of young, bright fundraising minds face up to the challenges of organizations who want to do more than they can afford.

PROSPECT RESEARCH: THE NEXT REVOLUTION

The Old Days

It's a hand-built, craft-made world, the world of prospect research. Sitting in our darkened backrooms, craft workers use hand tools ranging from a well-eared copy of *Who's Who* to a finger-shiny keyboard to produce, one-by-one, the tailor made products of our age: profiles, lists of prospects, news updates and memos to the fundraisers, invitation lists to the dean's cocktail evening, and a report on new businesses opening up in our home town.

These beautiful craft products deserve to be framed, held in the Oklahoma Museum of Fundraising History, and carefully preserved (no direct sunlight, please) so that future generations of fundraisers can gawk at their intellectual beauty.

However, they should no longer adorn the prospect researcher's desk. Because now is the moment for a revolution in research. Automation abounds, and the future will be full of it.

---

[11]Direct Dialogue was first tested in Austria in 1995, led by Greenpeace fundraiser Jasna Sonne and an agency called Dialogue Direct. The tests were funded by Greenpeace International as part of its commitment to new product development and innovation. It now runs in some 24 Greenpeace countries.

Profiling, Fast

There are now a number of web sites that will generate automatic profiles on prospects. For example, try www.zoominfo.com. The site has generated some controversy in prospect research circles because it does the job that a researcher used to spend around four hours doing in, check this out, around two seconds.

No, it's not the same as a handcrafted profile. It does not explain the link between Rich Prospect Jr.'s aunt and your dean of industrial studies' first cousin. Nor does it explain why Rich Prospect Jr. is likely to give to your cause. But we are at the Arkwright's cotton mill end of this particular revolution. By 2016 we can expect much more targeted, powerful search software and a wholly personalized service for your institution or charity.

The automation process really started a long time ago—with the advent of the personal computer and its application to alumni databases. These databases are enabling us to work with large volumes of prospect data, to carry out analyses of donor behaviors, and to record links between donors and prospects in ways that were unthinkable two decades ago. It would not be an exaggeration to say that the prospect research profession arose because of the existence of the PC. Thank you, IBM.

Profiling, Outsourced

Profiling, the bread-and-butter activity of prospect researchers, is increasingly being outsourced. The key is the facility, with the Internet, by which a person sitting at a desk in Durban, Delhi, or, in my case, rural Spain can carry out research. He has the same access to the same prospect data as the director of prospect research at Harvard University. In fact, he's hired by Harvard to produce the same profile, including the personal details Harvard knows about these prospects, such as gift history and personal involvement in the university. However, Harvard's expense for this service is not one-tenth the cost in Cambridge, Massachusetts. By 2016, outsourcing will be the norm for big-institution prospect research.

Modeling

We can expect more and better databases as we move toward 2016, but they are just the tools we use. What about the data we manipulate? Wouldn't it be great to understand donor motivations? To be able to say with *certainty* that a prospect will give? To move away from the era where we send our major gifts officer across the country on a visit that turns out, sadly, to have been a waste of time?

Consumer marketers believe they are close to this goal. By combining powerful new computers with a huge, but huge, array of data on consumption, marketers are able to say with increasing certainty that John X and the people in his cohort will all buy a new dishwasher, a car, or a financial product this year. One leading U.K. supplier in this field claims it can:

- Target the right customers through the right medium at the right time
- Increase return on investment by targeting the right type of potential customer
- Mirror your ideal customers across the United Kingdom
- Better retain and develop customer lifetime value

The technique is known as propensity modeling. Each individual is given a series of scores according to the likelihood of exhibiting desirable behaviors (such as repeatedly sending you large checks). It starts with the analysis of donors known to exhibit the chosen behavior and focuses on combinations of attributes that set them apart from those who do not. A scoring scheme is devised from this analysis that can be applied to any other population of donors or prospects. By using the scoring scheme we can predict behavior.

By 2016 this type of modeling will be commonplace, cheap, and accurate. Specialist teams of outsourced prospect researchers, called prospect analysts, will use wildly complex formulae and a huge range of data from inside and outside your organization to select the four prospects who will give between US$1,345,894 and US$1,345,900 during the second semester. And they'll do it on machines the size of a packet of gum (gum having been banned in 2010, of course, because of the risks to public health).

Knowledge

We refer in Chapter 2 to the big, but big, new theme in prospect research—knowledge management. Combining some aspects of modeling, some aspects of automation, and a good deal of people management, knowledge management is already creating change in forward-looking nonprofits.

Knowledge management means repositioning the researcher. No longer the quiet obedient mouse in the corner, the prospect researcher circa 2016, now renamed senior knowledge director, will be at the heart of each institution's development office. She represents the institution's knowledge and thus its competitive advantage—and as a result she'll be the best-paid person in the room. Deans will tremble in her presence (she knows *all* about them). On her say, institutions will revise and rewrite their strategies, budgets, and structures, and hire and fire board members and staff. Beware, Mr. Development Director.

Prospect Luddites?

So will we really need prospect researchers in 10 years' time? Are we going to be able to automate the whole process from identification to ask? Will prospect researchers react to automation and outsourcing by becoming the new Luddites, smashing the computer machinery of this modern revolution?

No. Quite unequivocally, no. In fact, the trend is in the opposite direction. As society has become more automated (the worldwide number of PCs in use surpassed 820 million in 2004 and is projected to top 1 billion in 2007, according to figures quoted in www.usagewatch.org/), so fundraising has become more personalized. Face-to-face fundraising, whether with a major donor or on the streets of Paris, Rome, or Tokyo, has grown as quickly as new technology has spread. People in an increasingly automated age seek the personal contact and stimulation that philanthropy gives them.

> *"I meet new people. The social reward is considerable. It's fun."*
> Male philanthropist quoted in *Why Rich People Give,*
> Theresa Lloyd, 2004

People give to people, and it will take people to understand them, research them, and work with them. And long may it be thus.

The CSA Model Code
for the Protection of
Personal Information[1]

1. *Accountability.* An organization is responsible for personal information under its control and shall designate an individual or individuals who are accountable for the organization's compliance with the following principles.

2. *Identifying Purposes.* The purposes for which personal information is collected shall be identified by the organization at or before the time the information is collected.

3. *Consent.* The knowledge and consent of the individual are required for the collection, use, or disclosure of personal information, except where inappropriate.

4. *Limiting Collection.* The collection of personal information shall be limited to that which is necessary for the purposes identified by the organization. Information shall be collected by fair and lawful means.

5. *Limiting Use, Disclosure, and Retention.* Personal information shall not be used or disclosed for purposes other than those for which it was collected, except with the consent of the individual or as required by law. Personal information shall be retained only as long as necessary for the fulfillment of those purposes.

6. *Accuracy.* Personal information shall be as accurate, complete, and up-to-date as is necessary for the purposes for which it is to be used.

---

[1]Source: The Canadian Standards Association, www.csa.ca/standards/privacy/code/Default.asp?articleID=5286&language=English

7. *Safeguards.* Personal information shall be protected by security safeguards appropriate to the sensitivity of the information.

8. *Openness.* An organization shall make readily available to individuals specific information about its policies and practices relating to the management of personal information.

9. *Individual Access.* Upon request, an individual shall be informed of the existence, use, and disclosure of personal information and shall be given access to that information. An individual shall be able to challenge the accuracy and completeness of the information and have it amended as appropriate.

10. *Challenging Compliance.* An individual shall be able to address a challenge concerning compliance with the above principles to the designated individual or individuals accountable for the organization's compliance.

Data Mining and Prospect Screening Checklist[1]

Data Mining and Prospect Screening Checklist[1]

The purpose of this example checklist and not a comprehensive list but an example of what one might look like. This example is to illustrate the need for:

- Logical integration with other fundraising and research activities,
- The importance of relationships externally and internally,
- Data screening does not need to be so complicated that it scares people off,
- The case to do data screening at all,
- Screening in a holistic way that encapsulates all areas of fundraising activities.

It is important to note that no matter what the investment made in data screening, it is crucial to involve researchers and fundraisers as a coordinated team effort to make sure any results actually get used. This checklist is a good starting point and not a complete or thorough list but one that people can use as a foundation to develop their own process specifically tailored for their needs. For further information contact Carol McConaghy

---

[1]**Sources:**

Carol McConaghy Thorp, Senior Applications Consultant, SunGard BSR Inc (*carol.thorp@sungardbsr.com*) Implementing Electronic Database Screening Results: Part II, APRA Conference, San Diego, California August 2005 (*www.sungardbsr.com*).

Comments provided by Steven Hupp, Manager Development Research & Records, Chicago Botanic Garden (*shupp@chicagobotanic.org*) and founder of Prospect Research Blog, August 2005 (*http://stevenhupp.typepad.com/prospectresearch/2005/04/electronic_scre.html*)

Visit *www.ephilanthropy.org*

Thorp, Senior Applications Consultant, SunGard BSR Inc (*carol.thorp@ sungardbsr.com*) and (*www.sungardbsr.com*).

Area	Comments
What's best?	*Best* is defined as what's best for your organization. Don't define it as what Harvard or Yale or University of Toronto or Oxford University or other larger campaigns are doing. Always seek ways to improve your relationship with your donors. Test the water to see what truly works for you.
Be specific	When determining how many prospects you need, use an actual number. Looking for a specific number of prospects focuses your work more efficiently. It's best if that number comes from an analysis of your campaign; for example, looking at your gift table to see where you fall short.
Plan, plan, and plan again	A successful implementation plan should have three parts: ■ Short-term impact (quick start) ■ Longer-term goals ■ Ongoing review to revise it according to your successes The plan should be specific about goals, persons responsible, deadlines, end users, and the strategy that will be used. (Try to include some room in your plan for experimentation and even with thorough planning always remember to be flexible based on results.)
Policies and procedures	Don't create procedures that are brand-new. Make your procedures fit in smoothly with existing ones. Don't change the workflow too much, and your procedures will have a greater chance of being accepted and followed. Ensure that you follow your organization's privacy and accountability guidelines.
Use existing tools	Excel and Access can be used to analyze, sort, and filter results. So can the tools your vendor provides.
The teachable moment	It's important that end users (including development officers, fundraisers and researchers) understand what the ratings and match levels actually mean. It's a chance for you to teach them.
The long-range plan is to integrate data	Start with putting your results in the donor database in a way that lets you connect screening data with your organization's data. But don't stop there. Make that data easy for everyone to use. Use the data to meet strategic fundraising goals beyond the short-term need. Open that data up for annual fund and planned giving. Go beyond the first few obvious prospects. Work for the fullest utilization of the data possible.

continued

Area	Comments
Integration tasks	Migrate the data to the donor database. Train people so they can use the data. Track the activity that results from the data. Quantify and measure your return on investment and how effectively you're using the data.
Migration	Work on migrating discrete or quantifiable data elements rather than text. Input the codes rather than the descriptions. Capture data in a way that can be queried and reported on easily not hidden in general notes and comments. Always make sure it is set up in a way so that users can understand the information now and in the future.
Training	Don't sit on data. Empower people to use it. Create queries for users that are easy for end users. Make it easy for people to get reports and lists that use screening data.
Tracking	Whatever method you devise, make sure it works within your prospect management current procedures.
Evaluation	Test your assumptions about the screening and the expectations of your results. Keep hard numbers on how well the screening was utilized.

Checklist for a Development Strategy[1]

Aims
- To develop an ongoing plan covering a longer-term view of three to five years.
- Increase awareness of the charitable work and mission statement.
- A goal of ($5m) is to be reached over the next (5) years.

Case for Support
- The why, what, where, and how much with regards to your funding needs.

Focus
- For current donors and new prospects, what sources will be and how they will be approached:

  Corporate   Trusts and foundations
  Individuals
  Membership   Direct mail
  Special events   Planned giving
- What source has the highest probability for success? The least?
- Coordination with other fundraisers and volunteers within your charity as a whole.

Research
- What level of research is required to support your fundraising?
- Who should do the research?
- Develop and implement approach strategies.
- Talk to people; carry out personal intelligence gathering as part of your information feedback.

---

[1]Pamela Gignac, JMG Solutions Inc.

- Learn about their needs and beliefs in order to ensure you are building the right relationships.
- Know their potential for their unique support for you.

Resources

- Match the sources with the highest probability of success with concentration of effort and resources.
- Requests for additional resources such as:
Staff
Computers
Databases
Software
Prospect research
- Commitment to expenditure

Communications

- Aim to achieve donor loyalty.
- You can turn negatives into positives by asking some simple questions and listening to the answers.

IT'S ALL FUNDRAISING

- Remember, you are building relationships with your donors and supporters to secure their ongoing loyalty.
- Any time people are getting together on your behalf, it should be viewed as a fundraising event for all of the previous reasons.

Ethics

- Always use high-quality and accurate information research.
- Get your facts right before you talk to someone.

Sample Contact Forms[1]

CONTACT FORM EXAMPLES

- Corporate
- Foundation
- Individual

---

[1]Created by Pamela Gignac, JMG Solutions Inc.

Contact Form Example—Corporate

Company Name:	**Web site:** www.

Address:
Tel:　　　　　　　　　**Fax:**　　　　　　　　　**Email:**

Head Office Location: (if not above address)

Initial Contact Name:	**Position:**	**Address:** (if different from above)
Tel:	**Fax:**	**Email:**

Secondary Contacts: (name, position)	**Address:** (if different from above)
Tel:　　　　　　　　　**Fax:**	**Email:**

Giving History:　　　　　**Total amount to date $:**　　**Last gift $:**　　**Date:**
Comments: (e.g., sponsorship only; donation; matching; employee fund; no of yrs as a donor; lapsed, etc.)

Contact Date(s):　　　　　**Method (tel/mtg/event/other):**

Giving policies: (please see attached for further details)
Interests:
Preferences:
Application procedures: yes/no　　　　　　　　**Deadlines:**
Other: (e.g., sponsorship; donations; matching; employee fund; employee fundraising; etc.)

Approach Strategy: yes/no　　**Target Amount $:**　　　**Project:**
Donation Request:　　　　　**Sponsorship:** yes/no
Other Contact Links: (who else in the company; who else might know them and/or might they know)
Known Key Relationships: (to us; us to them; to others)
Comments: (sponsorship request only; donation request only; both; matching gift; employee program, etc.)

Meeting Arrangements:　　　**Who to Attend:**

Purpose of meeting: (e.g., advice, exploratory, connection, cultivation, ask, stewardship, etc.)

Actions Required:	**Who:**	**Date:**　　　　**Completed:**

Research:　　　　　　　　**Completed/Required:**　　　　**Sources:**
Profile: (location of profile document if available or to request one)

Proposal/application:	**Draft:**	**Final:**　　　　**Date Sent:**

Comments:

Please return this form to: (insert name/address/tel/fax/email)

Contact Form Example—Foundation

Foundation Name:	**Web site:** www.
Address: **Tel:** **Fax:** **Email:**	
Is this foundation connected to **a company:** yes/no If yes, who:	**Is this a family foundation:** yes/no
Initial Contact Name: **Position:** **Address:** (if different from the above)	
Secondary Contacts: (name, position, address if different from the above) **Tel:** **Fax:** **Email:**	
Giving History: **Total amount to date $:** **Last gift $:** **Date:** **Comments:** (e.g., donations; matching grants; memorial; employee fund; no of yrs as a donor; lapsed, etc.)	
Contact Date(s): **Method:** (tel/mtg/event/other):	
Giving policies: (please see attached for further details) **Interests:** **Preferences:** **Grants given:** (other not-for-profits who have received grants) **Application procedures:** yes/no **Deadlines:** **Other:** (e.g., matching grants, etc.)	
Approach Strategy: yes/no **Target Amount $:** **Project:** **Board of Directors/family members:** to be contacted—yes/no Who is to contact: Names to be placed on contacts needed list: yes/no Which names: **Other Contact Links:** (who else might know them and/or might they know) **Other Known Key Relationships:** (to us; us to them; to others) **Comments:**	
Meeting Arrangements: **Who to Attend:**	
Purpose of meeting: (e.g., advice, exploratory, connection, cultivation, ask, stewardship, etc.)	
Actions Required: **Who:** **Date:** **Completed:**	
Research: **Completed/Required:** **Sources:** **Profile:** (location of profile document or to request one)	
Proposal/application: **Draft:** **Final:** **Date Sent:**	
Comments:	

Please return this form to: (insert name/address/tel/fax/email)

Contact Form Example—Individual

Name: **Position:** (if applicable)		**Date of Birth:**
Primary Address: (indicate if business or home) **Tel:** **Fax:**		**Email:**
Secondary Address: (indicate if business or home) **Tel:** **Fax:**		**Email:**
Family Details: **Spouse Name:**	**Date of Birth:**	**Other:**
Giving History: **Total amount to date $:** **Last gift $:** **Date:** **Comments:** (e.g., donation; memorial; special event; planned gift; bequest; employee fund; no of yrs as a donor; lapsed, etc.)		
Contact Date(s): **Method:** (tel/mtg/event/other)		
Giving Preferences: **Special Interests:** **General Background:** (e.g., education; past employment; links to other organizations; donations to other organizations, etc.) **Contact Links:** (who else might know them and/or might they know) **Known Key Relationships:** (to us; us to them; to others)		
Approach Strategy: yes/no **Target Amount $:** **Project:** **Donation Request:** **Planned Gift:** **Comments:** (e.g., donation; memorial; special event; planned gift; bequest; employee fund; no of yrs as a donor; lapsed, etc.)		
Meeting Arrangements: **Who to Attend:**		
Purpose of meeting: (e.g., advice, exploratory, connection, cultivation, ask, stewardship, etc.)		
Actions Required: **Who:** **Date:** **Completed:**		
Research: **Completed/Required:** **Sources:** **Profile:** (location of profile document or to request one)		
Proposal: yes/no **Draft:** **Final:** **Date Sent:**		
Comments: 		

Please return this form to: (insert name/address/tel/fax/email)

ePhilanthropy Code of Ethical Online Philanthropic Practices

The ePhilanthropy Foundation exists to foster the effective and safe use of the Internet for philanthropic purposes. In its effort to promote high ethical standards in online fundraising and to build trust among contributors in making online transactions and contributions with the charity of their choice, this code is being offered as a guide to all who share this goal. Contributors are encouraged to be aware of non-Internet-related fundraising practices that fall outside the scope of this code.

Ethical Online Practices and Practitioners will:

SECTION A: PHILANTHROPIC EXPERIENCE

1. Clearly and specifically display and describe the organization's identity on the organization's web site;
2. Employ practices on the web site that exhibit integrity, honesty, and truthfulness, and seek to safeguard the public trust.

SECTION B: PRIVACY AND SECURITY

1. Seek to inspire trust in every online transaction;
2. Prominently display the opportunity for supporters to have their names removed from lists that are sold to, rented to, or exchanged with other organizations;
3. Conduct online transactions through a system that employs high-level security technology to protect the donor's personal information for both internal and external authorized use;
4. Provide an opt-in and opt-out mechanism to prevent unsolicited communications or solicitations by organizations that obtain email

addresses directly from the donor. Should lists be rented or exchanged, only those verified as having been obtained through donors or prospects opting in will be used by a charity;

5. Protect the interests and privacy of individuals interacting with their web site;

6. Provide a clear, prominent, and easily accessible privacy policy on its web site telling visitors, at a minimum, what information is being collected, how this information will be used, and who has access to the data.

SECTION C: DISCLOSURES

1. Disclose the identity of the organization or provider processing an online transaction;

2. Guarantee that the name, logo, and likeness of all parties to an online transaction belong to the party and will not be used without express permission;

3. Maintain all appropriate governmental and regulatory designations or certifications;

4. Provide both online and offline contact information.

SECTION D: COMPLAINTS

1. Provide protection to hold the donor harmless of any problem arising from a transaction conducted through the organization's web site;

2. Promptly respond to all customer complaints and to employ best efforts to fairly resolve all legitimate complaints in a timely fashion.

SECTION E: TRANSACTIONS

1. Ensure contributions are used to support the activities of the organization to which they were donated;

2. Ensure that legal control of contributions or proceeds from online transactions are transferred directly to the charity or expedited in the fastest possible way;

3. Companies providing online services to charities will provide clear and full communication with the charity on all aspects of donor transactions, including the accurate and timely transmission of data related to online transactions;

4. Stay informed regarding the best methods to ensure the ethical, secure, and private nature of online ePhilanthropy transactions;

5. Adhere to the spirit as well as the letter of all applicable laws and regulations, including, but not limited to, charity solicitation and tax laws;

6. Ensure that all services, recognition, and other transactions promised on a web site, in consideration of gift or transaction, will be fulfilled on a timely basis;

7. Disclose to the donor the nature of the relationship between the organization processing the gift or transaction and the charity intended to benefit from the gift.

Potential Planning Measurements for Results

It is important to stress that these criteria, although they are statistics, are to be used as a rule of thumb and a guide rather than for specific and true statistical analysis. At best, they can be considered an educated tool for analysis and at worst a rough methodology for tracking purposes. No one's job description or position should be solely judged using these numbers. It is also crucial to stress that it should be about quality not quantity as well as meeting the nonprofit's financial goals to serve people, so do not endanger the relationship experience and needs of donors.

The resources, time, and effort used to achieve success is not always reflected in the numbers that can be considered helpful statistics to guide planning and analysis. As professionals and nonprofits, in the nature of who and what we are, it really is about people. However, there is a need to be more efficient and effective, so statistics are necessary to plan and evaluate our efforts. The time spent on putting together the statistical benchmarks as well as preparing the corresponding reports is time taken away from actually doing fundraising and research that will lead to success—securing income and building long-term relationships. It is extremely important to ensure that there is a balance between the two as well as "cold" versus "real" and numbers of substance rather than wishful thinking.

Outlined here is a list of what criteria could be used for tracking and evaluation. This is to give ideas for further thought, but do not copy them directly to be applied at your nonprofit. Take those that are the most relevant and meaningful for your organization and needs. Remember that if implemented into a nonprofit's evaluation analysis to determine progress and balance of efforts, these criteria can be strongly impacted by a number of factors including:

- Legislation
- Public opinion
- Market and competition of $$
- Disasters

- Trends
- $$ goal (is it realistic or ambitious—a feasibility study can help determine this, but often it is based on need more than anything else)
- History of giving to the nonprofit
- Potential numbers of prospects needed to secure financial goals
- Community need
- Matching of interests

Statistics from gift chart or table of gifts:

- number of gifts required to meet $$ goal.
- number of gifts for each level.
- number of prospects for each level—the methodology used to be for every 6 suspects 1 becomes a prospect, for every 6 prospects 1 becomes a donor (36:1 ratio), which now appears to be more around 12 to 1. It depends on certain criteria such as the level of gift, the previous gifts received by the nonprofit, and how close it matches its work to prospects' interests. In reality, there are usually fewer prospects found for the upper level gifts than the middle and lower levels, which tend to have the larger numbers of prospects realistically available.
- number of donors for each level (yes, this could be different from number of gifts as donors can make multiple gifts, but at the middle to higher levels this is likely to be the same number).

Other elements to track:

- Potential prospects (suspects) identified
- Prospects from donor base identified
- New potential prospects identified
- Prospects qualified
- Hot prospects (As) identified
- Warm prospects (Bs) identified
- Cold prospects (Cs not sure) identified
- Potential links found (circle of influence, six degrees, etc.)
- Prospects being researched
- Prospects that were researched
- Prospects being monitored for research
- Full profiles prepared
- Briefings prepared
- Basic details prepared (name, address, phone, email)
- New records added to database
- Records updated

- Approach strategies planned
- Proposals prepared
- Proposals sent
- Stewardship reports prepared
- Stewardship reports presented
- Phone calls made for research
- Internet searches
- Web sites visited
- Calls, letters, meetings, newsletters, information feedback to donors, cultivation and stewardship activities

Sample Job Description Text

Director
Primary Job Functions   *Evaluation*

	Low				High
Works with development staff to identify potential donors and develop cultivation and solicitation strategies.	1	2	3	4	5
Compiles detailed research reports for development staff assigned to prospective donors.	1	2	3	4	5
Designs and maintains internal controls for safeguarding personal and financial information in compliance with all applicable laws, regulations, and professional practices.	1	2	3	4	5
Provides the agenda and support materials for prospect review meetings and maintains meeting minutes.	1	2	3	4	5
Provides status reports to track each prospect's cultivation and solicitation steps for all prospective donors.	1	2	3	4	5
Maintains files and records of all gifts and pledges.	1	2	3	4	5
Maintains status reports on fulfillment of donor benefits and recognition activities.	1	2	3	4	5

Manager
Primary Job Functions   *Evaluation*

	Low				High
Supervises research assistants including delegation of work assignments, overseeing research profile completions, training, and performance reviews.	1	2	3	4	5
Participates with fundraising staff in campaign planning, preparation, and decisions.	1	2	3	4	5
Coordinates cultivation and solicitation plans with major gift and campaign staff.	1	2	3	4	5
Manages continued contact and communications with all major gift donors and prospects.	1	2	3	4	5

Manager
Primary Job Functions   *Evaluation*

	Low				High
Manages stewardship of donor funds including researching and preparing reports on use of gifts.	1	2	3	4	5
Reviews all mail lists and timing of communications prepared for all major gift and campaign donors.	1	2	3	4	5
Maintains research systems and staff proficiencies as new software and Internet sources become available.	1	2	3	4	5

Data Grid for Estimating Giving Capacity

Basic Information Age (husband/wife) Marital status Home address Business position Business affiliations Education	*Associations/Linkages* Family members Social/business links Key colleagues/peers Major interest areas Major hobbies Lifestyle factors	*Background* Family history Origins of wealth Inherited wealth Donor gift history Other giving history Volunteer roles
Financial Details Salary/fees/bonus Stockholdings Stock options Other investments Property holdings Business ownerships	*Key Advisors* Family member Close friend(s) Attorney Accountant Physician Partners	*Encumbrances* Children in school Elderly relatives Living dependents Mortgages Alimony/child support Inventory
Other Income Sources Consulting fees Family business links Royalties Trusts Inheritances Partnerships	*Likely Contacts* Board member Professional staff Donor/volunteer Fundraising staff	*References/Sources* Internet references Print references Friends/colleagues Rating committee

Activity Reports

Activity Report on Prospect Research Status	2005	2006
Number of major gift/campaign prospects being researched	135	155
Number of prospect profiles completed	89	122
Number of prospects qualified for major gift cultivation and solicitation in prospect research meetings	77	108
Number of trained/experienced volunteers available for personal solicitation assignments	24	46
Number of prospects assigned to volunteers and volunteer/staff teams with cultivation plans	18	32
Number of prospects assigned to volunteers and volunteer/staff teams in active solicitation	36	58

Activity Report on Major Gift Results	2005	2006
Number of prospects assigned to volunteers and volunteer/staff teams with cultivation plans	18	32
Number of prospects assigned to volunteers and volunteer/staff teams in active solicitation	36	58
Number of major gift/campaign decisions made	14	32
Number of major gift/campaign gift rejections	10	22
Value of major gifts made and funds received	$225K	$665K
Value of major gift pledges made and received	$125K	$350K
Number of gift acknowledgments in process	14	32
Number of donor recognition plans approved by donors	12	27
Number of donor reception plans approved by donors	10	21
Number of donor recognition plans completed	8	19

Sample Contact Report

Cultivation/Solicitation Team: (1) _____

(2) _____ (3) _____

Prospect(s) name: _____

Mail address: _____

Telephone: (_____) _____ _____ Email address: _____

Contact person to secure appointment: _____

Place of meeting: _____ Time: _____

Meeting objectives: (1) _____

(2) _____ (3) _____

Proposed funding priorities: (1) _____

(2) _____ (3) _____

Proposed gift range(s): (1) _____

(2) _____ (3) _____

Comments on meeting: _____

—Use other side for additional comments—

Additional information requested: _____

Specific questions needing answers: _____

Follow up; next steps: (1) _____ due by: _____

(2) _____ due by: _____ (3) _____ due by: _____

Submit This Report Promptly to Office of Fund Development by

Email to: _____ or fax to: (_____) _____ _____

Thank You

Performance Criteria for Major Gift Staff

How many prospects can a major gifts officer supervise?

150:   65 in cultivation (43%)
          35 in solicitation (24%)
          50 in stewardship (33%)

How many meaningful cultivation calls can a major gifts officer make per year?

180:   Face-to-face personal calls

How many major gift solicitations can a major gifts officer make per year?

30:   A minimum of 30 solicitations should produce 15 to 20 gifts

How many new major gift prospects need to be qualified to replace the 15 to 20 new donors now removed from the prospect pool?

50:   A minimum of 50 new prospects will be needed to replace the 15 to 20 new donors

Nine-Point Performance Index
Analysis of Major Gift Solicitation

	Two Years Ago	Last Year	This Year	Totals
Participation	12	18	23	53
Income	$172,500	$215,000	$358,000	$745,500
Expenses	$16,850	$18,200	$18,900	$53,950
Percent participation	33%	46%	53%	45%
Average gift size	$14,375	$11,944	$15,565	$14,066
Net income	$155,650	$196,800	$339,100	$691,550
Average cost per gift	$1,404	$1,011	$822	$1,018
Cost of fundraising	10%	8%	5%	7%
Return	924%	1081%	1794%	1282%

Checklist for Major Gift Acknowledgment

Gift Acceptance
    ☐ Gift accepted by: _____ Date: _____/_____/_____
Amount of the gift: $_____ Pledge period: _____ yrs
    ☐ Purpose of the gift: _____
    ☐ Any special restrictions? _____
                 _____
    ☐ Form of the gift: [ ] Cash/check [ ] Credit card [ ] Securities
                       [ ] Real estate [ ] Personal property
                       [ ] Other: _____
    ☐ Other details: _____

Gift Acknowledgment
    ☐ Gift receipt:
Date mailed: _____/_____/_____ *or* emailed: _____/_____/_____
    ☐ Formal acknowledgment letter with gift substantiation text:
Prepared by: _____
To be signed by: _____
Date mailed: _____/_____/_____
    ☐ Additional "thank you" letters, calls, cards, notes, emails:
        Author: _____ Date sent: _____/_____/_____
        Author: _____ Date sent: _____/_____/_____
        Author: _____ Date sent: _____/_____/_____

Gift Processing
    ☐ Data entered on: _____/_____/_____
    ☐ Gift deposited on: _____/_____/_____

Donor Recognition Details (See donor file for full details and schedules)
    ☐ Package A: Routine benefits   Date confirmed: _____/_____/_____
    ☐ Package B: Added benefits   Date confirmed: _____/_____/_____
    ☐ Package C: Plaques, etc.   Date confirmed: _____/_____/_____

Continuous Contact Schedule
    ☐ Three month follow-up: Due by: _____/_____/_____
    ☐ Six month follow-up: Due by: _____/_____/_____
    ☐ Annual follow-up: Due by: _____/_____/_____

Prospect Research Online[1]

Web Sites for the United States, Canada, United Kingdom, Europe, Australia, and Latin America[1]

Outlined here are just some of the vast number of web sites that a prospect researcher could visit to find out various bits of information on a number of topics and prospects. This is by no means a complete list but is a good starting point and reference for new sites and contains some of the more common sites visited. Even though a site might be listed under "free" or "fee" for access, many have free elements to their sites and then ask for a fee to access or obtain certain parts of their site or information. For the most up to date listing go to http://ephilanthropy.org/global.

Even though you might be based in the United States or Canada or Europe, by looking for information at sites that are based in other countries you will often be able to find useful details on your prospects. This is particularly true for large international companies as well as high-profile individuals. In addition, you can find out how other countries are dealing with legal issues such as privacy and protection of information.

Please note that web site addresses frequently change and become invalid for a number of reasons. Those listed here are for your information only. The contents and accuracy of the information listed here or in these sites is not endorsed or supported by JMG Solutions Inc. and are not responsible for any use or adverse effects of visiting or utilizing any information that they provide.

---

[1]Compiled by Pamela Gignac JMG Solutions Inc.

NONPROFIT WEB SITES:

Professional Organizations

- Association of Fundraising Professionals (AFP), www.afpnet.org/
- Association of Professional Researchers for Advancement, www.aprahome.org/advancement/privacy.htm
- Institute of Fundraising (in the UK), www.institute-of-fundraising.org.uk
- Association of Healthcare Professionals, www.ahpcanada.com/govtissues.htm
- Canadian Association of Gift Planners (CAGP), www.cagp-acpdp.org/
- Canadian Council for the Advancement of Education (CCAE), www.ccaecanada.org/
- Council for the Advancement and Support of Education (CASE), www.case.org/

Useful Sites

- About Nonprofit, http://nonprofit.about.com
- Internet Nonprofit Center, www.nonprofits.org
- Charity Village, www.charityvillage.com
- Fundraising UK, www.fundraising.co.uk
- Canadian Center for Philanthropy, www.ccp.ca
- Nonprofitscan.ca an initiative of Canadian Center for Philanthropy, www.nonprofitscan.ca

Canadian Privacy—Useful Information and Resource Sites

- Association of Fundraising Professionals, www.afpnet.org/
- Greater Toronto Chapter, Association of Fundraising Professionals, www.afptoronto.org
- "Privacy 101: A Guide to Privacy Legislation for Fundraising Professionals and Not-for-Profit Organizations in Canada" (provided by AFP Toronto), www.afptoronto.org/new_on_site/Privacy101.pdf www.afpnet.org/public_policy/canadian_public_policy_issues further info from AFP (U.S. site)
- Information and Privacy Commissioner—Ontario, "Privacy and Boards of Directors: What You Don't Know Can Hurt You," www.ipc.on.ca/ (Go to Hot Topics)
- "Privacy Commissioner of Canada," www.privcom.gc.ca/index_e.asp

- Canadian Standards Association,
  www.csa.ca/standards/privacy/Default.asp?language=English
- Association of Healthcare Professionals, www.ahpcanada.com/
  govtissues.htm
- Association of Professional Researchers for Advancement,
  www.aprahome.org/advancement/privacy.htm
- Canadian Center for Philanthropy, www.ccp.ca/
- Ontario Hospital Association: "Guidelines for Managing Privacy,
  Data Protection and Security for Ontario Hospitals,"
  www.oha.com/ (Go to Publications/Other)
- Chartered Accountants of Canada, Privacy Resources,
  www.cica.ca/index.cfm/ci_id/1008/la_id/1.htm
- Michael Geist, columnist for *Toronto Star* specializing in privacy
  issues, Canada Research Chair of Internet and E-commerce Law at
  the University of Ottawa and serves as Technology Counsel to
  Osler, Hoskin & Harcourt LLP, www.michaelgeist.ca/
- Charity and Not-for-profit Law—Carter & Associates, www
  .charitylaw.ca/

Sample Online Privacy Statements

- World Wildlife Fund, www.wwf.ca/en/privacy.asp
- London Health Sciences Center Foundation, www.lhsf.ca/
- United Way of Greater Toronto, www.unitedwaytoronto.com/
- Ontario Lung Association, www.on.lung.ca/global/privacy.htm

US FREE AND FEE SITES:

Free Search Engines

- Yahoo!, www.yahoo.com
  - Or www.realestate.yahoo.com
  - Or www.finance.yahoo.com
- Google, www.google.com
- AltaVista, altavista.com
- Search Engine Watch, www.searchenginewatch.com

Newspapers and Magazines

- *New York Times,* www.newyorktimes.com
- *LA Times,* www.latimes.com
- *USA Today,* www.usatoday.com
- *Chicago Tribune,* www.chicagotribune.com
- Editor and Publisher Online, www.mediainfo.com

- Internet Public Library, www.ipl.org/col
- Financial Times, www.ft.com
- *Forbes* Magazine, www.forbes.com incl Forbes 500: layoffs, Celebrity 100, Private 500
- *Fortune* Magazine, www.fortune.com incl Fortune 500, 40 richest under 40
- Business Journals, www.bizjournals.com

Stock Web Sites

- EDGAR (proxy statements, annual reports, and other SEC documents), www.sec.gov/cgi-bin/srch-edgar
- FEC political donations over $200, www.tray.com/FECinfo/index.html-ssi
- 10K Wizard.com—fully searchable SEC documents. Reg. users can rerun searches, www.10kwizard.com
- CBS Marketwatch, http://insiders.marketwatch.com/tools/quotes/insiders.asp?siteid= mktw
- Insider trader information for last two years. Free monitoring of 50 companies, www.insidetrader.com
- CNBC, www.cnbc.com
- 500K Dun & Bradstreet's company database, www.companiesonline.com/asearch.asp?
- 350K business profiles and reports, www.corporateinformation.com

New Economy Web Sites

- IPO information, www.ipo.com
- Dot Com Directory, www.dotcomdirectory.net/nsi.com/index. htm?nl=1
- Merger and acquisition market information, www.thedailydeal.com
- Silicon Valley Community Foundation, www.siliconvalleygives.org/

U.S. Government Sites

- U.S. Government web pages, www.nttc.edu/gov_res.html
- Common Cause, www.commoncause.org/congress/
- Federal Gateway, http://fedgate.org
- Office of the Federal Register, www.access.gpo.gov/nara/index.html
- Access to the Federal Government via New York State web site, www.state.ny.us/federal_acc.html
- FedWorld, www.fedworld.gov

- Library of Congress, http://lcweb.loc.gov/homepage/lchp.html
- Nonprofit Gateway, www.nonprofit.gov
- OMB Watch, www.ombwatch.org
- U.S. Census Bureau, www.census.gov
- 50 States, www.50states.com/

Other Useful Sites (Including Women in Philanthropy)

- Ann Castle—Women's Philanthropy, www.women-philanthropy. umich.edu/
- Oprah's Angel Network, www.oprah.com/uyl/uyl_landing.html
- Remind it, www.netmind.com
- Copernic, www.copernic.com
- Worth.com, www.worth.com/cgi-bin/gx.cgi/AppLogic%2bFT ContentServer?pagename=Worth/root

Fee-Based Web Sites

- Lexis-Nexis, www.lexis-nexis.com
- *Wall Street Journal,* http://interactive.wsj.com/ushome.html
- Hoovers, www.hoovers.com
- Dun & Bradstreet, www.dnb.com
- Thomson Financial Wealth Identification, www.wealthid.com
- Dialog, www.dialog.com
- Chronicle of Philanthropy, http://philanthropy.com

CANADIAN FREE AND FEE SITES:

Canadian Government Sites

- Canadian Federal Government, www.gc.ca
- Order of Canada, www.gg.ca/honours/ordersrch_e.html
- Canada Customs and Revenue Agency, www.ccra-adrc.gc.ca/ menu-e.html
- Voluntary Sector Initiative, www.vsi-isbc.ca
- Ontario Public Sector Salary Disclosure, www.gov.on.ca/fin/ hmpage.html

Search Engines

- Canada 411, www.canada411.com
- Canadian Yellow Pages, www.yellow.ca
- Infospace Canada, www.infospace.com/canada

- Yahoo! Canada, www.yahoo.ca
- Altavista Canada, www.altavista.ca

Newspapers and Magazines

- Globe and Mail, www.globeandmail.com
- National Post, www.nationalpost.com
- Canada Newswire, www.newswire.ca
- Canadian Jewish News, www.cjnews.com
- Canadian Business, www.canadianbusiness.com
- Maclean's, www.macleans.ca
- Profit, www.profitguide.com
- Canadian Business, www.canadianbusiness.com
- Toronto Life, www.torontolife.com
- Chatelaine, www.chatelaine.com/read/work/entrlist.html

Stock, Disclosure, and Insider Information

- System for Electronic Document Analysis and Retrieval (SEDAR), www.sedar.com
- Factiva (Dow Jones and Reuters Company), www.factiva.com
- Carlson Online, www.fin-info.com
- Stockwatch, www.stockwatch.com
- Strategis, www.strategic.ic.gc.ca/engdoc.main.html
- CanCorp Canadian Financials (DIALOG File 491), www.dialog.com

Researching Canadian Individuals

- Canada's Who's Who, http://utpress.utoronto.ca/cww/cw2w3.cgi
- Directory of Directors, www.financialpost.com/product/directory.htm
- Who's Who in Canadian Business, www.canadianbusiness.com/ whoswho/wwbusiness.htm or www.canadianbusiness.com/whoswho/women.htm
- Who's Who of Canadian Women, www.canadianbusiness.com/ whoswho/wwbusiness.htm
- Canadian Medical Directory, www.southam.com/Magazines/ dental.html

Researching Companies (in addition to various U.S. sites)

- Blue Book on Canadian Business, www.bluebook.ca
- Scott's Directory, www.scottsinfo.com

- Canadian Key Business Directory, www.dnb.com
- Dialog File 520

New Economy Web Sites

- Silicon Valley North, www.siliconvalleynorth.com
- Ottawa Citizen High Tech Who's Who, www.ottawacitizen.com/hightech/whoswho/index.html
- Canadian Business Tech 100, www.canadianbusiness.com/index.shtml
- Corporate Affiliations of Technology Personalities, www.evert.com/persons/corporat/corp_ab.htm
- Technology Fast 50, www.deloitte.ca/en/Industries/HiTech/Fast50/h.home.html
- Branham 250, www.nationalpostbusiness.com/datamining/branham/branham.htm

Fee-Based Sites

- Big Database, www.bigdatabase.com
- Prospect Research Online—Pro, www.iwave.com
- Directory of Foundations and Grants, www.ccp.ca
- NewsCan, www.newscan.com
- InforGlobe–DowJones Interactive, www.djinteractive.com
- NewsCan, www.newscan.com
- CBCA: Canadian Business and Current Affairs Fulltext (DIALOG File 262), www.dialog.com

Other Useful Sites

- Canada Newswire, http://newswire.ca
- JournalismNet, www.journalismnet.com/canada.htm
- College of Physicians and Surgeons of Ontario, www.cpso.on.ca
- Martindale-Hubbell lawyer locator, www.martindalehubbell.com/locator/home.html
- Bay-Street.com, www.bay-street.com

UK AND EUROPEAN SITES:

- *Sunday Times* Newspaper, www.Sunday-times.co.uk
- *This is London,* www.thisislondon.co.uk/dynamic/news/business/top_direct.html
- *Times* Newspaper, www.thetimes.co.uk/
- *Independent* Newspaper, www.independent.co.uk/news/Business/

- *Guardian* Newspaper, www.guardian.co.uk/
- Companies House, www.companieshouse.co.uk
- Institute of Fundraising (UK), www.institute-of-fundraising.org.uk
- Fundraising UK, www.fundraising.co.uk
- Directory of Social Change, www.dsc.org.uk/
- Charities Aid Foundation, www.caf.org.uk/
- Association of Charitable Foundations, www.acf.org.uk/
- Association of Chief Executives of Voluntary Organizations (ACEVO), www.acevo.org.uk/main/index.php?content=main
- Association for Research in the Voluntary and Community Sector (arvac), www.charitynet.org/arvac/index.html
- Alliance of European Voluntary Service Organizations, www.alliance-network.org/
- Europa—Gateway to European Union, www.europa.eu.int/index_en.htm
- European Association for Gift Planning (EAPG), www.plannedgiving.co.uk/

AUSTRALIAN SITES:

- Philanthropy Australia, www.philanthropy.org.au/
- Council for the Encouragement of Philanthropy in Australia (CEPA), www.cepatrust.com
- Center for Philanthropy and Nonprofit Studies, http://cpns.bus.qut.edu.au/
- Givewell, www.givewell.com.au/
- Auscharity, www.auscharity.org

LATIN AMERICAN SITES:

Name	Web Site Address	Comments
IDC—Latin America	www.idc.com/idcla	Market research reports and other data on information technology in Latin America.
Internet Resources for Latin America	http://lib.nmsu.edu/subject/bord/laguia/	Contains these guide sections and the direct links to them: ■ Introduction & General Internet Guides ■ Current Events Links ■ Latin American Directories ■ Subscription Databases—Latin America

continued

Continued from the previous page

Name	Web Site Address	Comments
		■ Subscription Databases— General ■ Public Domain Databases— Latin America ■ Public Domain Databases— General ■ E-Books & Other Texts ■ Library Catalogs ■ Digital Library Projects ■ Organizations ■ News ■ List of Lists & Newsgroups ■ Latin American Networking ■ Miscellaneous Sites ■ Finding It on the Web ■ La Busqueda en Español
ISLA—Information Services Latin America	http://isla.igc.org/	Latin America on the Web. Including publication highlights and special reports.
LANIC Newsroom—Latin American Network Information Center	www.lanic.utexas.edu/ info/newsroom/	Includes current and recent news as well as archive information. This is considered the primary gateway for Latin American information on the Internet. For more information contact info@lanic.utexas.edu.
Latin Markets.com	www.latinmarkets. com/	Information on businesses. IPL trade directory. Commercial site for business information on 50,000 companies in Mexico and Central America. Contact Luc Delannoy at info@latinmarkets.com.
Internet de Mexico	www.internet.com.mx/	Commercial Internet provider in Mexico, provides service to businesses, individuals, and other organizations. The web provides access to *Notimex, La Jornada, Excelsior,* and other Mexican newspapers. Address questions to www@mail.internet.com.mx.

continued

Name	Web Site Address	Comments
Mexico Net Guide—Las Comunidades de Mexico	http://juarez.info/	Trade, business, tourism information in Mexico. Email contacts: info@mexguide.net; juarez@mexguide.net; monterrey@mexguide.net; morelia@mexguide.net
Arias Foundation	www.arias.or.cr/ceiba/ or try www.arias.or.cr/ceiba/ ceiba.htm	A database of Central American NGO's (nongovernmental organizations).
Spanish Language Search Engines (visit this web site or see below the short list of sources for search engines in Spanish)	http://lib.nmsu.edu/ subject/bord/laguia/ #find	This page includes links to other sites as well as Spanish language search engines.
Search LANIC, Latin America & the World	www.lanic.utexas.edu/ world/search/	Spanish search engine. Buscadores en distintos paises por medio de UT-LANIC
Motores de Busqueda en Español	http://lonestar.utsa.edu/ jbarnett/mainsearch. html	Spanish search engine.
Alta Vista en Español	www.altavista. magallanes.net/ jump.html	Spanish search engine.
Desde la Universidad de Texas en San Antonio; provee reseñas de los buscadores. Buscador Terra de España	http://buscador.terra.es/	Spanish search engine.

Please note this list is a guide to information sources only to give an idea of what *might* be available on the Internet. JMG Solutions is not responsible for the information provided by these sites or any of their links and does not guarantee that these sites will be up to date, accurate, accessible, or still valid.

APPENDIX O

Donor Development and Prospect Research Recommended Additional Readings

Burk, Penelope. *Thanks! A Guide to Donor-Centered Fundraising.* Burk & Associates Ltd, Burlington, Ontario, Canada, 2000, ISBN: 0968797806.

Burnett, Ken. *Relationship Fundraising: A Donor-Based Approach to the Business of Raising Money.* Revised edition. Jossey-Bass, San Francisco, June 2002, ISBN: 0787960896.

Carnie, Christopher. "How to Guide," *Find the Funds: A New Approach to Fundraising Research.* Directory of Social Change, London, England, 2000, www.dsc.org.uk, ISBN: 1900360543.

Carnie, Christopher. *Fundraising from Europe.* Directory of Social Change, London, England, 2003, www.dsc.org.uk, ISBN: 1903293081.

Greenfield, James M. *The Nonprofit Handbook of Fundraising,* 3rd ed. The AFP/Wiley Fund Development Series, John Wiley & Sons, Hoboken, 2001, ISBN: 041403040.

———. *The Nonprofit Handbook of Fundraising,* 3rd ed.—2002 Supplement with a chapter contribution by Jeff Gignac. The AFP/Wiley Fund Development Series, John Wiley & Sons, Hoboken, 2002, ISBN: 0471419397.

Hart, Ted, James Greenfield, and Michael Johnston. *Nonprofit Internet Strategies: Best Practices for Marketing, Communications, and Fundraising,* contributions by Pamela and Jeff Gignac. John Wiley & Sons, Hoboken, March 2005, ISBN: 0471691887.

Johnston, Michael, ed. *Direct Response Fundraising: Mastering New Trends for Results,* with a chapter contribution by Jeff Gignac. The AFP/Wiley Fund Development Series, John Wiley & Sons, Hoboken, 2000, ISBN: 0471380245.

Johnston, Michael. *The Non-Profit Guide to the Internet.* The NSFRE/Wiley Fund Development Series, John Wiley & Sons, Hoboken, 2000, ISBN: 047132857.

Joyaux, Simone P. *Strategic Fund Development: Building Profitable Relationships That Last.* James Gelatt, ed. Aspen's Fund Raising Series for the 21st Century, Aspen Publishers, Gaithersburg, Maryland, 1997, ISBN: 0834207966.

Lake, Howard. *Direct Connection's Guide to Fundraising on the Internet.* Aurelian Information, London, England, 1996, ISBN: 1899247068.

Nichols, Judith. *Pinpointing Affluence: Increasing Your Share of Major Donor Dollars.* Bonus Books, May 2002, ISBN: 1566251656.

Sloggie, Neil. *Tiny Essentials of Fund Raising.* The White Lion Press Limited, Kermarquer, 56310 Merland, France, 2002, ISBN: 0951897152.

Sprinkel Grace, Kay. *Beyond Fundraising: New Strategies for Nonprofit Innovation and Investment.* The NSFRE/Wiley Fund Development Series, John Wiley & Sons, Hoboken, 1997, ISBN: 0471162329.

———. *High Impact Philanthropy: How Donors, Boards, and Nonprofit Organizations Can Transform Communities.* John Wiley & Sons, Hoboken, December 2000, ISBN: 0471369187.

————. *Over Goal: What You Must Know to Excel at Fundraising Today,* Emerson & Church Publishers, April 2003, ISBN: 1889102148.

Warwick, Mel, Theordore Hart, and Nick Allen. *Fundraising on the Internet: The ePhilanthropy Foundation.Org Guide to Success Online,* 2nd ed., Jossey-Bass, San Francisco, ISBN 0787960454.

For Further Readings and Information Visit:

Association of Fundraising Professionals	www.aftnet.org
Association of Professional Researchers for Advancement	www.APRAhome.org
Canadian Center for Philanthropy	www.ccp.ca
Charity Village	www.charityvillage.ca
Council for Advancement and Support of Education (CASE)	www.case.org
UK Fundraising	www.fundraising.co.uk

GET IDEAS FROM:

- www.raisingmoremoney.com/stories/storyReader$497
- http://nonprofit.grizzard.com/articles.cfm?mode=single&article_id=68
- dept.kent.edu/advanceservices/InformationalPage/CASE%20Conference1.pdf
- www.thinkcs.co.uk/pdf/upgrading.pdf
- www.snpo.org/publications/articlesearch.php?category=fundraising
- www.malwarwick.com/handson-chap7g.html
- www.maydevelopment.com/resources/predicting.pdf
- http://lists.democracygroups.org/pipermail/odb-help/2003 September/000105.html
- www.charitychannel.com/article_2820.shtml
- www.stewardshipforum.org/pdfs/giving_08.pdf
- www.nycafp.org/handouts03/whelen.pdf
- www.nhi.org/online/issues/122/fundraising.html
- www.onphilanthropy.com/bestpract/bp2003-10-31.html
- www.fundraisingday.org/workshop2001.html
- www.bwf.com

A

Abell, A., 21n, 23n
Accountability. *See* Performance, measuring
Acknowledgment/recognition: checklist, 210
postdonation, 157–158, 173–174
thank-you notes, 134
Activity reports, 169, 206
Addresses, postal. *See* Postal addresses, international
Allen, Margo, 159n
Alumni, as donors: case study, 119
data mining example, 41–46
online giving, 104
targeting interests of, 121
web resources, 102
Amnesty International, 180
Analysis, results. *See* Performance, measuring
Annual gifts, 8–10
Annual reports, 13–14
Anonymity, donor, 174–175
Ansbacher Group, 107
APRA: ethics issues, 166
as industry advocate, 2, 65
recommended skills, 164
Archiving, privacy issues, 63
Asian fundraising: high-net-worth prospects, 178
research strategies, 85, 94–102
Association for Healthcare Philanthropy (AHP): and privacy legislation, 65
as resource, 69

Association of Fundraising Professionals (AFP): industry definitions, 3
and privacy legislation, 65
as resource, 69
Association of Professional Researchers for Advancement. *See* APRA
Auckland, Marc, 21n
Australian fundraising: Internet resources, 80
web sites, 218
Austrian foundations, 91
Autonomous trader, defined, 90

B

Baker, Will, 178
BBVA Foundation (Spain), 91
Becoming a Fundraiser (Steele and Elder), 160n
Benchmarking. *See* Performance, measuring
Berkshire Hathaway, 182
BIG Online, 116, 164
Biographic information. *See also* Strategies, profiling
in Asia, 99
in Europe, 92
Blackbaud Analytics: data modeling services, 116
relationship-building chart, 122
web site, 103n
Blanchard, Laura, 103–104
Blau, Andrew, 181
Blogs: defined, 30, 35
as solicitation tool, 125–126
Bmycharity (UK), 106

Board Member's Guide to Fundraising (Howe), 166n
Brabyn, Ben, 106
British Heart Foundation, 105
Broce, Thomas E., 164n
Browne-Wilkinson, Hilary, 107
Buffett, Susan T., 182
Burk, Penelope, 1n
Burlingame, Dwight F., 161n, 162n, 163n
Business forms, international, 89–91

C

Calling, one-on-one, 15–17
Campaign Against the Arms Trade, 90
Canadian fundraising:
   data protection laws, 65–69, 84
   Internet resources, 77–79
   research strategies, 79–71, 81–83
   web sites, 212–213
Canadian Standards Association (CSA), 67, 187
Cancer Research UK, 105–106
CFRE Study Resources Guide, 141
Chambers of commerce, 102
Charities Aid Foundation (CAF), 108
Charity21, 108
Charity Commission (UK), 92
Checklists:
   acknowledgments, 210
   activity reports, 206
   development strategy, 191–192
   giving capacity, 205
   job description, 203–204
   prospect screening, 189–190
Chesapeake Bay Foundation, 178
Christian Worship Center Orphanage (Ghana), 180
Chronicle of Philanthropy, 179, 180, 182n
Circle of friends list, 17, 130, 133
Codes of practice:
   CSA Model, 67–68
   ePhilanthropy, 64
   information resources, 68–69
   professional ethics, 53–56
Comic Relief (UK), 105
Communications. *See* Information sharing

Companies House (UK), 90, 93
Company identifiers (by country), 89–91
Competing with Knowledge (Abell and Oxbrow), 21n, 23n
Conducting a Successful Capital Campaign (Dove), 165n
Confidentiality. *See* Privacy issues
Consent issues, 58, 60–65
Constituent-Centric Communication, 124
Constituent Relationship Management (CRM), 122–123
Contacts, sample forms, 193–196, 207
Contacts list, 17, 130, 133–134
Content Management System (CMS), 122–124
Cookies, computer, 65
Corporations:
   Asian, 97–98
   contact forms, 194
   European, 89–91, 89–93
Corson-Finnerty, Adam, 103–104
Critical Issues in Fundraising (Burlingame), 161n
Cultural issues. *See* International fundraising
Cygnus Applied Research, 1n

D

Dalkir, K., 23n
Databases:
   integrating, 25
   management of, 165–167
   modeling, 184–185
   multinational, 87–93
Data mining, xxvii, 28–30, 139, 189–190. *See also* Information sources
Data protection. *See* Privacy issues
Data Protection Act (UK), 57, 59n, 61n, 84
Dellandrea, Jon S., 4–5
Developing Major Gifts (Burlingame and Hodge), 163n
Development strategy checklist, 191–192
Dialog (fee-based research), 92, 164
DirectDialog, 183

Disasters, philanthropy and, 85–87, 95–96
Discovery meetings, 7, 163
Documentation. *See* Checklists; Reports
Donations. *See* Donors; Gifts
Donors. *See also* Prospects
   "Bill of Rights," 174–175
   contact forms, 193–196
   net-worth factors, 177–179
   online, 103–110
   as prospects, 10, 146
   right to privacy, 51–56
Dove, Kent E., 134n, 165n, 174n
Dow Jones Index, 179
Dun & Bradstreet, 90, 92–93

E

Economist, The, 89
Effective Fund-Raising Management (Kelley), 159n
Elder, Stephen D., 160n
Employees. *See* Staff, fundraising
EPhilanthropy:
   ethics code, 197–199
   as resource, 69
   "spiders" policy, 64
   volume chart, 113
   web site, 77
Ethics. *See also* Privacy issues
   data storage, 131
   donors' rights, 174–175
   ePhilanthropy code, 197–199
   guidelines, 51–56, 166, 192
   importance of, xxvii
European Community:
   data protection rules, 57–65
   high-net-worth prospects, 178–179
   Internet resources, 80
   research strategies, 85–94, 102
   web sites, 217–218
European Foundation Centre (EFC), 91, 92, 94
European Venture Philanthropy Association, 183
Evaluation, performance. *See* Performance, measuring
Ex-pat, defined, 99

F

Feed reader, defined, 35
Financial factors:
   ability to donate, 37–40, 177–179
   impact on philanthropy, 95–96
Foster, M. K., 182n
Foundation Center, 164
Foundations:
   contact forms, 195
   European, 90–92
Foundation Search, 164
Friendships:
   cultivating, 152–158
   networking, 17, 130, 133
Fulton, Katherine, 181
Fundación Intermón Oxfam, 91
Fundación La Caixa, 91
Fundraising:
   evaluation of results, 161–175
   future of, 177–186
   as investment strategy, 159–161
   online, 103–110
   stages of, xxvi–xxvii, 6–7
Fundraising (Broce), 164n

G

Gates, Bill, 50, 117
Gifts:
   acknowledging, 134, 157–158, 173–174
   online, 103–110
   relative size of, 8–10, 171
Gignac, Pamela, 83, 159n
Gilbert, Michael, 104
Giving capacity grid, 205
Global issues. *See* International fundraising
Google:
   donor tracking, 32–36, 124
   web site, 124n
Government resources:
   privacy policy guidance, 70
   web sites, 214–215
Grace, Kay Sprinkel, 162
Greenfield, James, 128n, 132, 134, 170n
Greenpeace, 180, 183
Gregory, Des, 159n

Grenzebach, Glier & Associates, 116
Grimwood-Jones, D., 22

H

Hamilton Health Sciences Foundation, 1n
Havens, John, 179
Healthcare organizations, 135
Health Information Portability and Accountability Act. *See* HIPAA
Health issues. *See* Medical issues
High-net-worth individuals, 177–179
HIPAA, 66, 135
Hodge, James M., 163n
Hogan, C., 26
Hong Kong, fundraising in, 95–101
Hoovers, 90, 92
Howe, Fisher, 166
Hughes, Sarah, 108
Hulse, Lamont J., 162n
Humber College Institute of Technology & Advanced Learning (Toronto), 1n, 81
Hupp, Steven, 189–190

I

Information Management in the Voluntary Sector (Grimwood-Jones, Simmons), 22n
Information sharing:
   accuracy issues, 140
   caveats, 141–142
   confidentiality, 140, 187–188
   data selection, 135–137
   data vendors, 139
   personal intelligence gathering, 130–131
   purpose of, 128–130, 142
   screening lists, 131–135
   tools, 138–140
Information sources:
   Asia-related, 99–102
   Europe-related, 90–91
   general, 13–14
   Internet tracking, 114–126
In-group rules, defined, 97
Institute for Philanthropy (UK), 105, 107

Institute for Public Policy Research (UK), 107
Institute of Fundraising (IOF), 2, 8
   Code of Practice, 54–56
   legislative issues and, 84
   online-solicitation guidelines, 107
   as resource, 69
International Directory Inquiries Service, 100
International ePhilanthropy Award, 125
International fundraising:
   Asian strategies, 94–102
   European strategies, 85–94, 102
International Telephone Listings Directory, 100
Internet. *See also* Web sites
   impact on fundraising, xxviii, 77
   information collecting, 114–126
   key words searches, 11–12, 13
   online donations, 103–110
   privacy issues, 56, 63–65
   relationship building, 120–127
   as research tool, 136–137
   RSS donor tracking, 30–36
   as solicitation tool, 111–114
   user profiles, 44–46, 112, 184–185
Intranets, 137
IWave, 164

J

Jay, Elaine, 107
Job description forms, 203–204
Jonescu, Stephanie, 1n
Journal of Knowledge Management, 28n
Justgiving, 106

Kaufman, Martin, 159n
Kelley, Kathleen S., 159n
Key word lists, 11–12
Kharas, Zarine, 106
Kintera (online giving), 103
Knowledge management, 20–28, 185–186
Knowledge Management in Theory and Practice (Dalkir), 23n

L

Language barriers:
  in Asia, 101
  in Europe, 87–91, 93
Latin America:
  high-net-worth prospects, 179
  web sites, 218–220
Law, Caroline Wiess, 182
Lawrence, Mary, 169n
Legislation, data protection:
  consent issues, 60–65
  European, 57–65, 84
  influencing, 84
  IOF compliance guidelines,
    108
  North American, 65–69, 84
  privacy rights, 52, 56, 84
Lewis, Nicole, 179n
Lexis Nexis, 92, 164
Libraries, as resources, 165
Limited liability company, defined,
  90
Lists, prospecting:
  generating, 46–50
  prioritizing, 143–146
  sharing, 130–131
  types of, 17, 130, 133–134
Lloyd, Theresa, 153–154, 179, 186
"Looking Out for the Future" (Fulton
  and Blau), 181
Lottery winners, 39–40

M

Maclaughlin, Steve, 103n
Malhotra, Y., 28n
Mama Cash, 182
Managers. *See also* Staff, fundraising
  data, 165–167
  knowledge, 27–28, 185–186
March of Dimes, 125
Measurement, performance. *See*
  Performance, measuring
Medical issues:
  HIPAA, 66, 135
  impact on philanthropy, 85–87
  right to privacy and, 62
Meetings:
  discovery, 7, 163
  information-sharing, 138

  prospect review, 131–135, 169–170
  rating and evaluation, 170–172
Meinhard, A. G., 182n
Members-only communities, 125
Message boards, 125–126
Microsoft Corp., 28
Middle Eastern HNWIs, 178–179
Miller, Deborah, 159n, 168
Mind of the Millionaire (Schervish and
  Havens), 179n
Minorities, as philanthropists, 182
Modeling, predictive, 41–46, 184–185
Morino, Mario, 183
Morino Institute, 183
Motley Fool, 108–109
Multinational issues. *See* International
  fundraising
Murray, Matt, 179n

N

Names:
  accuracy issues, 140
  Asian-style, 97
  European-style, 87–88
National Health Service (UK), 87
National Trust (UK), 105
NEDRA News, 169n
Networking:
  circle of friends, 17, 130, 133
  peer-to-peer, 8–9
  research-driven, 4, 13
*New Directions for Philanthropic
  Fundraising,* 163n
New Philanthropy Capital, 109
News readers, 30–36
Nonprofit Handbook (Greenfield),
  170n
North American fundraising:
  data protection laws, 65–69,
    84
  high-net-worth prospects, 178
NSPCC (UK), 105

O

Opt-out laws, 57, 61–62, 64, 68
Out-group rules, defined, 97
Oxbrow, N., 21n, 23n
Oxfam GB (UK), 105

P

Partnership, defined, 90
Peer screening, 132
Peer-to-peer contacts, 8–9, 133
Performance, measuring:
   importance of, xxviii, 159–161
   measurable data, 200–202
   organization, 209
   prospect research, 161–169
   solicitation index, 209
   staff, 208
   stewardship, 173–175
   tracking results, 169–173
Permalink, defined, 35
Personal data, protection of. *See*
      Privacy issues
Personal Information Protection and
      Electronic Documents Act. *See*
      PIPEDA
Personal intelligence gathering (PIG),
      11, 18, 130–131, 133
Personalized web content, 121–126
Pew Research:
   Internet user profiles, 46, 112
   web site, 111n
Philanthropy:
   history of, 85–91
   online ethics, 197–199
   online solicitations, 103–110
Phone calls. *See* Telephone, use of
P!N, 116
Ping, defined, 35
PIPEDA, 66–69
Postal addresses, international,
      88–89
Predictive modeling, 41–46
Privacy issues, xxvii
   in Asia, 101
   best practices codes, 67–69
   CSA code, 187–188
   ePhilanthropy code, 197–199
   in Europe, 92, 93
   guidelines, 69–70
   international, 84
   legislation and, 56–67
   organizational, 131, 133, 140
   and professional ethics, 51–56
   in prospecting groups, 150
   web sites, 212–213
Productivity. *See* Performance,
      measuring

Professionals:
   as donors, 38–40
   online help for, 212
   research staff, 163–169
Profiling. *See* Strategies, profiling
Prompt list, defined, 148
Propensity modeling, 185
Prospecting. *See also* Prospect research;
      Prospects
   donor categories, 8–10
   importance of, 1–2, 18–19
   personal contact, 147–150
   resources, 13–18
   step-by-step, 10–11
   techniques for, 11–13
Prospecting for Gold, 146
Prospect pipeline, 26–27
Prospect research. *See also* Strategies,
      profiling
   benefits of, 136
   case study, 80–83
   data mining checklist, 189–190
   defined, 3
   future trends in, 183–186
   history of, 2–5
   Internet resources, 77–80
   online help, 211–220
   pitfalls of, 141–142
   practitioners, 6–8, 163–169
   purpose of, xxv–xxviii
   qualifications for, 163–169
   stages of, xxv–xxvii, 6–7
   strategies, 71–76
   techniques, 11–18
   tools for, 136
Prospect Research (Hogan), 26
Prospects. *See also* Strategies, profiling
   alumni as, 41–46, 102
   criteria for, 37–46, 143–144
   defined, 3, 10
   giving indicators, 116–118
   qualifying, 17–18
   ranking, 143–146, 170–172
   screening, 28–30, 123, 131–135,
      139–141, 189–190
   selecting, 46–50
   soliciting, 146–157, 209
   stewardship of, 152–158
   tracking, 30–36, 114–126, 172–173
Public company, defined, 90
Public domain information, 68–69
Pulawski, Christina, 159n

R

Rating systems, donor, 143–146,
  170–172
Really simple syndication. *See* RSS
Recognition. *See*
  Acknowledgment/recognition
Reed Information Services, 90
Relationship management cycle, 9
Religion, philanthropy and, 85–87
Reports:
  activity, 206
  contact, 134–135, 193–196
  information-sharing, 138
Research, prospect. *See* Prospect
  research
Researchers in Fundraising, 84
Results analysis. *See* Performance,
  measuring
RNLI (UK), 105
Rotteau, Amy, 1n
Royal Ontario Museum Foundation,
  1n
RSPCA (UK), 105
RSS (tracking tool), 30–36
Ruderman, Susan Cronin, 165n,
  168n

S

Safe harbor rules, data protection,
  65
SAIF, as resource, 69
Salary information, 13
Sample contact forms, 193–196
Sandoz Fondation de Famille, 91
Sarbanes-Oxley Act, 98
Sargeant, Adrian, 107
Save the Children, 106, 180–181
Schervish, Paul, 179
Screening:
  caveats, 141–142
  data mining checklist, 189–190
  professional vendors, 30, 32, 139
  prospect review meetings, 131–135,
    169–170
Simmons, S., 22n
Singapore, fundraising in, 95–101
Six degrees concept, 5, 14–15,
  129–130, 133, 148
SMART objectives, 72

Sole trader, defined, 90
Solicitation, donor:
  IOF guidelines, 107
  online, 103–110
  performance index, 209
  personal contact, 147–150
  success rates, 146–147
  tools for, 111–114, 125–126
Sonne, Jasna, 183n
Spanish foundations, 91
Spiders, defined, 64
Staff, fundraising:
  evaluation forms, 203–204, 208
  qualifications for, 163–169
Steele, Victoria, 160n
Stewardship, donor:
  enlistment stage, 150–152
  evaluating, 173–175
  friendship stage, 152–158
  ranking prospects, 143–146
  solicitation stage, xxvii, 146–150
Stock ownership:
  and philanthropy, 38–40
  web sites, 214, 216
Strand, Bobbi, 170n
Strategies, profiling:
  Asian prospects, 94–102
  case study, 80–83
  European prospects, 85–94, 102
  information sources, 77–80, 91–93,
    99–102, 184
  Internet tracking, 114–126
  legislative issues, 84
  North American prospects,
    71–76
Swiss foundations, 91

T

Taking Fundraising Seriously
  (Burlingame and Hulse),
  162n
TargetAmerica, 116
Telephone, use of, 16
Terrorism, impact on philanthropy,
  95–96
Thank-you notes. *See*
  Acknowledgment/recognition
Third-party information, 62–63
Thorp, Carol McConaghy, 35n
Trackback, defined, 35

U

U.K. fundraising:
  Internet resources, 79–80
  online giving, 105–107
  research strategies, 83
  web sites, 217–218
University alumni. *See* Alumni, as donors
University of Pennsylvania, 103–104
University of Toronto, 4–5
U.S. Department of Commerce, 65
U.S. fundraising:
  data protection laws, 65–66, 84
  Internet resources, 77–78
  research strategies, 70–71, 80–81
U.S. Treasury Department, 95

V

Venture philanthropy, 183
Volkswagen Stiftung, 91
Voluntas, 182n

W

Wagner, Lilya, 161n
Wars, philanthropy and, 85–87
Wealth:
  global trends, 177–179
  sources of, 38–40
WealthEngine, 116
"Wealth with Responsibility" (Schervish and Havens), 179
Web sites:
  APRA, 164
  Asian, 99–102
  Australian, 218
  Canadian, 212–213, 215–217
  CSA privacy code, 187
  donor screening, 30, 146
  Economist, The, 89
  European, 90–91, 217–218
  fee-based research, 164
  Google Alerts, 125
  Institute of Fundraising, 54
  international directories, 100
  IRS statistics, 178n
  Latin American, 218–220
  Mama Cash, 182
  news reader providers, 31
  professional organizations, 212
  prospect research, 77–80, 83, 184, 211–220
  U.S., 213–215
Who's Who, as information source, 89, 92
Why Rich People Give (Lloyd), 154, 179, 186
Wight, Scott, 81–83
Winfrey, Oprah, 182
Women, as philanthropists, 181–182, 215
Wood, Ernest W., 163n, 173n
Woodchucks and Prospect Researchers (Ruderman), 165n
World Health Report, 177–178
World Wide Web. *See* Internet
Wyman, Ken, 1n, 8, 14–15

X

XML, defined, 30, 35

Y

Yahoo!, 32–36, 90